RESEARCH HIGHLIGHTS IN SOCIAL WORK 20

Performance Review and Quality in Social Care

Editors: Anne Connor and Stewart Black

Jessica Kingsley Publishers
London and Bristol, Pennsylvania

Research Highlights In Social Work 20
Editors: Anne Connor and Stewart Black
Secretary: Anne Forbes
Editorial Advisory Committee:

Professor J. Lishman	Robert Gordon University, Aberdeen
Mr D. Cox	Robert Gordon University, Aberdeen
Mr K. Foster	Fife Region Social Work Department, representing Social Services Research Group – Scotland
Ms I. Freeman	Strathclyde Region Social Work Department
Mr M. King	Northern College, Aberdeen
Mr N. Munro	Robert Gordon University, Aberdeen
Dr F. Paterson	Social Work Services Group, Scottish Office
Dr A. Robertson	University of Edinburgh
Professor G. Rochford	Emeritus Professor, University of Aberdeen
Dr P. Seed	University of Dundee
Ms K. Stalker	University of Stirling
Ms J. Taylor	University of Stirling

Robert Gordon University
School of Applied Social Studies
Kepplestone Annexe, Queen's Road,
Aberdeen AB9 2PG.

First published in the United Kingdom in 1994 by
Jessica Kingsley Publishers Ltd
116 Pentonville Road
London N1 9JB, England
and
1900 Frost Road, Suite 101
Bristol, PA 19007, U S A

Copyright © 1994 Robert Gordon University, Research Highlights Advisory Group,
  School of Applied Social Studies

Library of Congress Cataloging in Publication Data
A CIP catalogue record for this book is available from the Library of Congress

British Library Cataloguing in Publication Data
A CIP catalogue record for this book is available from the British Library

ISBN 1-85302-017-6

Printed and Bound in Great Britain by
Cromwell Press, Melksham, Wiltshire

Contents

Part 3: Implementation

Part 4: Performance Revisited

Chapter 1

Introduction

*Anne Connor and Stewart Black**

Scope and significance of performance review and quality
Performance review currently enjoys unprecedented attention and, more impressively, appears to be the central concern not merely of social care or social welfare services but of public management itself.

This text takes 'performance review' as a generic term for systematised attempts to relate 'inputs' to 'outputs' and, less frequently, 'outcomes'. Performance review is something of a portmanteau term embracing at one extreme broad concepts such as 'quality' and 'accountability' and at the other techniques which offer some degree of measurement of performance such as performance indicators. Meanwhile, perhaps most significant of all, both commentators on strategic or general management and senior managers themselves within public sector organisations have become pre-occupied with 'performance management' – that is, with being able to demonstrate that managers are doing more than merely 'administering' the organisations in which they work and the services these provide.

The preoccupations and behaviour of social welfare organisations increasingly appear to relate to performance review – notably in terms of devising, introducing and refining measures of how resources are transformed into services; in the internal identification of standards and targets; and, gradually, in linking the two.

Social work and other social care services have not been immune from this. Indeed, the number and range of initiatives, developments and innovations which contain an element of performance review or have a

---

* The authors write in a personal capacity.

particular focus on this is remarkable. Moreover, this focus, while not new, has been given emphasis in the past decade, and particularly since 1989. The list of initiatives in social work and other social care services, and developments in other parts of the public sector which affect these services includes:

- new statutory, participative and public planning in relation to community care
- new ('arms-length') responsibilities for inspection and registration
- new statutory complaints procedures
- new financial control and accounting procedures (eg identification of cost centres; devolved budget-holding)
- introduction of separate 'purchaser' and 'provider roles'
- new and expanded contracting and grant-in-aid practices involving increasing specification of outputs
- the creation of central government social services/social work inspectorates
- expanded external scrutiny of local authorities by the Audit Commission and Accounts Commission
- development of national and local performance indicators
- initiatives to secure user views where these have previously been absent
- development of practitioner self-evaluation
- national reviews of the funding, structure and functions, and internal management of local authorities
- national reviews of the role, funding and accountability of voluntary organisations
- introduction and development of staff appraisal
- introduction of performance-related pay
- changes in the planning, purchasing and provision roles in the NHS (e.g. creation of self-governing hospital trusts; GP fundholding)
- 'national standards', for example, for offender services in Scotland.

It is not suggested that each development on the above (incomplete) list is concerned centrally with performance review, but this is an important feature of all.

Many of the initiatives on the list above relate to community care, and several chapters relate to the new provisions. We make no apologies for this concentration on one aspect of social work services. The process that was started by Caring for People (Secretaries of State 1989) represents a major sea-change in the organisation of personal social work services, which has been compared to the establishment of the welfare state or the creation of unitary social work authorities. The extent to which both policy and practice will be based on specific plans and reviews of performance is a fundamental part of that change. But we also recognise – and wish to emphasise here – that performance review and quality appraisal is an essential element of the delivery of effective social work services to all groups of users and in all situations.

Organisation of the book

This volume of Research Highlights contains an unusually large number of contributions. This approach has been adopted by the editors because, as suggested above, performance review and quality appraisal can take many forms and perspectives, and serve different purposes.

This has necessitated the need for appropriate organisation of the contributions. They have been grouped around four themes – management approaches, user perspectives, implementation, and performance reconsidered. In turn, each of these four parts into which the book has been divided itself contains four chapters.

Management approaches

The first set of papers attempts to delineate performance review and identify how it has been employed. Two chapters do so by considering organisations; two consider staff. A theme arising both here and in the other parts is that performance review has been noticeably government-initiated and management-oriented.

The opening paper by Mary Henkel provides an overview of performance review, tracing its origins in Government thought and how this has been put into effect since the early 1980s.

The chapter by Stephen Mitchell and Frank Tolan follows naturally from this, providing an account of the work of the Social Services Inspectorate (England and Wales), one of the agencies examined by Henkel.

Susan Willoughby's chapter explores both the theory and application of reviews of the work of individual staff, including the practical and professional issues which arise. This is the first of three chapters drawing on experience in health care settings. While the interface between social services/social work authorities and health authorities is important and close, practices in the two differ.

Balancing this, Malcolm Payne discusses supervision in social work. His review considers both managerial and professional elements of supervision, and how these are reconciled in practice. His analysis is interesting when compared to those provided by Willoughby and by Irvine in relation to health services.

User perspectives

As a balance to the managerial approaches discussed in Part One – and as a way of tackling the shortcomings inherent in this approach – the second set of papers focus on the currently burgeoning interest in user perspectives of performance both where these are seen as a corrective to management approaches and as being critical in their own right in ensuring responsiveness in services.

Assessment and care management is now the key process in delivering community care services to individual users. Sue Brace provides a comprehensive account of how this is intended to be developed by local authorities, and identifies the factors which are likely to contribute to a more satisfactory experience for users and carers.

Marion Barnes and Gerald Wistow then describe how one social services department sought to involve actual or potential users and their carers in service planning.

The chapter by Andrea Whittaker is an account of a rare process – people with disabilities undertaking a review on behalf of other disabled people.

In the second chapter which describes experiences in health services, Bridie Fitzpatrick and Rex Taylor describe initiatives intended to provide users with opportunities to assess their own services.

Implementation

These approaches are further developed in Part Three, where the focus moves to implementation techniques and experience, and the lessons this holds for practical development of performance review. The difficulties traditionally experienced in relation to implementation explain the need for the contributions in this part of the book.

Tom Leckie provides an account of how local authorities are attempting to identify and implement quality processes, in a brief review of initiatives which are found to be highly varied.

Donald Irvine, in the final chapter drawing on experiences in health, describes how performance is reviewed in the best known part of the NHS – general practice. A wide range of approaches is described and their impact discussed.

Another major development associated both with community care and children services is the introduction of complaints procedures which are statutorily based. Brian McClay reviews progress during the first two years.

Finally, the growing importance of voluntary organisations and the increasingly contractual context in which they provide their services provide the backdrop for the analysis by Anne Connor of how organisations' performance can be evaluated by funders and buyers and – no less important – by the organisations themselves.

Performance reconsidered

The concluding, fourth set of chapters returns to conceptual development of performance review by critically re-examining this in the light of recent developments and new perceptions of 'quality'.

Anna Coote provides a review of different concepts of quality; the implications of this for public services; and what the users of public services need from them.

Building on this, Ann James considers what quality has meant in social care; how organisations have attempted to put this into effect; and the resultant tensions this has created for users and providers.

Stewart Black considers a major performance and quality initiative, the Citizen's Charter. He examines its origins, aims, significance, and applicability to social welfare and social work services. He considers its achievements to date and its likely future significance.

The final chapter, by Connor and Black, focusses explicitly on research issues in performance review, and systematically considers the current central preoccupation of how to 'get the view of users', with material drawn from a range of settings such as social work, health care, housing and other services.

Conclusions

The book ends with a brief essay which provides an overview of performance review. This makes explicit the links between the themes explored in the different chapters, and acknowledges additional themes and issues which it was not possible to discuss previously.

The following chapters illustrate the potential contribution of performance review and quality appraisal to the efficient and effective delivery of social work services. However, in this introduction, we wish to mark the limitations of performance review. No matter how strong the commitment to, or technical integrity of, such review, performance review cannot of itself:

- solve management problems
- prevent serious malpractice such as the abuse of children or vulnerable adults in residential care, or form a safety net in situations carrying heavy risks
- substitute for other processes such as political accountability
- guarantee or improve access to services for individual users, although it can identify when the services that are delivered are not up to a specified standard
- compensate for inadequate resources.

If anything, performance review is more likely to highlight deficiencies such as poor management or potentially dangerous lapses in professional standards. It can also contribute to earlier identification of problems and to a culture of open debate where it is less likely that such events will occur.

Acknowledgements

As Editors, we wish to record our thanks to our contributors and also, in particular, to Anne Forbes, secretary to the Research Highlights series.

References

Secretaries of State for Health, Social Security, Wales and Scotland (1989) *Caring for People: Community Care in the Next Decade and Beyond.* Cm. 849. London: HMSO.

Part 1

Management Approaches

Chapter 2

Performance Review and the Managerial Revolution

Mary Henkel

The 1980s saw a new Conservative government embarking upon an agenda for fundamental political change. Evaluation and performance review of public services played and continued to play important roles in the clarification and implementation of that agenda.

In 1979 there was a perceived crisis in government and in the economy. The 'winter of discontent' had reinforced the argument that Britain was becoming ungovernable (see, e.g., King 1975; Brittan 1975). The new government's first objectives were the control of public expenditure, an assertion of strong government at the centre, and more precisely defined forms of accountability within public services, in which individual responsibility was emphasised.

Gradually, more radical purposes emerged: to transform the public sector, on the assumption that it was a burden and constraint upon individual freedom and the operation of the private market, and that its scope must be limited and its resources harnessed to maximum effect. In the longer term, the very boundaries and definition of 'public' and 'private' would be revised and the values and mechanisms of the market would be insinuated within the state.

At the heart of this programme for change was the belief that the public sector required a new culture of management and that this should supersede what was characterised as the more reactive and subsidiary tradition of administration.

> 'Efficient management is the key to the (national) revival... And the management ethos must run right through our national life – private

and public companies, nationalised industries, local government, the National Health Service.' (Heseltine 1980, quoted in Pollitt 1986)

The combination of generalist administration and professional leadership favoured in the public services of the 1960s and 1970s was thought to have led to uncontrolled demand for resources, a preoccupation with input and process and a lack of concern with outputs and outcomes. The new managerialism would install new disciplines in the form of well defined objectives, measurable targets and devolved and defined accountabilities. Evaluation and review of performance against objectives and targets would be key components of this new strategy, inspiration for which was to be found in the private sector.

The concept of performance was early evoked to symbolise what was wanted: 'action, dynamism, purposeful effort' (Pollitt 1986). More fundamentally, evaluation was moved to the centre of the political stage, a development conceptualised by one authority as 'the rise of the evaluative state' (Neave 1988; see also Henkel 1991b). In what follows, the changing influences in, and conceptions of, evaluation and performance review during the 1980s and early 1990s will be outlined. The prime focus will be the shifts from external to internal review and control, the changes in the knowledge base of evaluation, the broadening of performance criteria and the power of managerial as against professional perspectives.

Making it happen

The workings of central government were early targets for change. The reduction of public expenditure and financial control and accountability were the first objectives (see, e.g., Gray and Jenkins 1983). The Rayner scrutinies of departments' expenditure, the broader based Efficiency Strategy and the Financial Management Initiative (FMI) (Treasury and Cabinet Office 1982) were designed to produce efficiency savings and strict managerial control of resources. The means were to be delegation of financial accountability to cost centres and an improved financial information system for ministers (MINIS). At the same time, within these and other initiatives, the criterion of performance, individual and departmental, the requirement to measure output and the consequent need to develop performance indicators constituted a constant refrain.

Meanwhile ministers demonstrated a new and vigorous interest in machinery for the evaluation of lower levels of government, particularly local government. New evaluative institutions were created, old ones were reconstituted and the resources of private sector consultants were exploited on a far wider scale than in the previous decade (Henkel 1991a). Within all these developments a central theme was the need to embed the knowledge and culture of management in public services. The role allotted to evaluation is well exemplified in the reform of audit and inspection.

Audit, inspection and performance review

A milestone in the government's pursuit of its objectives was the incorporation of the District Audit Service into a new body, the Audit Commission for Local Authorities in England and Wales, under the Local Government Finance Act, 1982. The idea that public audit could be confined to matters of financial probity and *ultra vires* was finally buried with the creation of the Audit Commission and the National Audit Office. Auditors of local and central government were now required to assess public bodies against the criteria of economy, efficiency and effectiveness and to regard the achievement of good management as their concern.

At the same time, the predominantly professional culture of central government inspectorates (Hartley 1972, Rhodes 1981) and advisory services (Henkel *et al.* 1989) was under challenge. The conversion of the Social Work Service of the DHSS into the Social Services Inspectorate (SSI) in 1985 provides perhaps the clearest example. The SSI was to subsume its traditional role of identifying and disseminating good practice under a requirement 'to secure the most effective use of professional resources'. This was part of its new mandate to 'assist local authorities to obtain value for money in the efficient and economic use of resources' (Secretary of State for Health, 25 February 1985).

Both the Audit Commission and the SSI set up new national arrangements, in the form of the Audit Commission's special studies and SSI's annual programme of inspections, to implement more effective external scrutiny of local authority performance against nationally agreed priorities. At the same time they laid the foundations for more effective evaluation of their work by local authorities themselves.

The Audit Commission

It is suggested that the Audit Commission was the more successful of the two in these projects for a number of reasons: it was a new institution and able to establish structures and recruit staff to implement new philosophies of public management; its value base was more coherent than that of the SSI; it was formally independent of government but at the same time embodied government's key values and assumptions in its management and thus had more political influence; its central technical expertise was that of quantitative analysis and management consultancy and thus carried more authority; and it focused more systematically from the beginning on the dynamic between external and internal review: to ensure that audit, standards and measures were established not only as forms of external coercion or persuasion but as the means of generating internal processes of change. Local auditors were to play a key role in these objectives.

The Audit Commission established a central structure comprising four directorates in pursuit of its remit. Of these, two, Special Studies and Management Practice, were to spearhead the changes.

The programme of special studies was built round the selection of critical areas for evaluating, and enhancing the performance of, local authority services. The Management Practice Directorate was to improve general standards of local authority management. Both operated within an overriding purpose of embedding a managerial culture in local government.

But from the beginning the Commission's strategy faced in two directions: outwards to enhance the impact of external evaluation and inwards to encourage local authorities to install their own systems of performance review. It aimed to strengthen the external scrutiny of local government activity and ensure that it was more effectively accountable to the electorate. Special studies carried out from 1984 onwards pointed to the need for change in managerial infrastructure and practice, and in resource allocation methods and priorities in a whole raft of services. These national studies were carried out by specifically recruited teams, comprising Commission staff, local auditors seconded for individual studies and experts in the field under examination. They were converted into audit guides, on the basis of which local auditors would carry out 'value for money' audits in their own authorities, identify where greater economy, efficiency and (later (1988)) effectiveness could be achieved, demonstrate how the nationally generated models for improvement could be applied locally and monitor how far and to what effect that happened. Local auditors were encouraged to combine an external evaluative perspective with a collaborative approach to their work (Day and Klein 1990).

An equally important component of the Commission's strategy was to build up from the beginning a network of special studies advisers and consultants from within the fields under scrutiny, so that the selected focus of the audits was salient and the proposed solutions relevant, even if not universally acceptable, to the local authority departments concerned. This practice has been successfully extended to the Commission's work in the NHS. Audits have thus been internally as well as externally influenced.

At the same time, the Commission emphasised internal performance review as a key to the survival of local government in an increasingly competitive environment and its capacity to retain control of its own destiny (Audit Commission 1986).

The tools and measures developed by the Commission, such as local authority profiles and performance indicators, could be used not only externally to compare authorities' performance and to attempt to compel conformity with criteria of economy and efficiency, but also internally to raise questions about how and why authorities were spending their money and with what results. Although at first content to leave definitions of effectiveness to authorities themselves or to professionals, increasingly the Commission abandoned its reticence about policy goals and professional boundaries and responded to requests from local departments to help them in this complex area. It put forward explicitly normative models of service delivery in studies on mental handicap (*sic*) (1987; 1988a; 1989a). It promoted particular models of professional practice in its report of the Probation Service (1989b).

It also began to break down and, in effect, redefine what is meant by effectiveness, introducing the notion of 'service effectiveness'. Key questions for local authorities in the 1988 Action Guide on performance review were, 'Is the service getting to the right customers, in the right way, with the right services, in keeping with its stated policies?' (Audit Commission 1988c). Within this formulation, such measures of performance as amounts and levels of service delivered, response times and numbers and categories of service users could be used. Service effectiveness thus merged with efficiency in the measurement of performance and some recognition was given to the intricate relationship between, for example, process and output. It moved further towards 'qualitative performance and process measures' in its 1990 guide (Audit Commission 1990) but has tended to encourage continuing debate in these areas, in particular through its Quality Exchange initiative (Audit Commission 1991), rather than itself lay down a definitive approach (Pollitt 1992).

The Commission's Directorate of Management Practice produced its first guide on performance review in 1986, promulgating it as an essential tool of strategic and operational management. It

> 'should underpin a [continuous] management process in which needs and resources are assessed, vision and strategic objectives defined, service proposals and resource allocations translated into specific plans and budgets; outputs and achievements and resource use are monitored and the performance of one period is fed back into the process for the next.' (Audit Commission 1986)

It was presented as a top-down process that should be cascaded through the organisation. Members and then managers at each level should select critical areas and dimensions to review themselves and delegate the remaining review tasks.

As the Commission sought thus to encourage good management practice in local government, it also reinforced the government's view that the work of local authorities should increasingly be conceived within a managerial rather than a political paradigm, an approach strongly reflected in the sequence of management papers beginning with *The Competitive Council* (Audit Commission 1988b).

The Commission also contrasted the capacity of management to install coherence and effective accountability (Henkel 1992) with the expansionist and pluralist tendencies of professionalism (Audit Commission 1988a and 1989). A professional culture encouraged 'loose networks of independent practitioners' and produced services lacking shared and explicit standards or cogent evaluative systems.

To some extent the SSI could be seen as seeking to counteract such tendencies, while retaining a commitment to professional values and practice in the personal social services. At the same time, it gave priority to the improvement of the management of these services.

The Social Services Inspectorate

Unlike the Audit Commission, the SSI is part of government and provides a service for Ministers and the Department. At the time of its inception in 1985, social work and the personal social services were under attack, for failure to protect vulnerable people under their care or supervision or to harness scarce resources to effective use. It was important for the future of the SSI itself that it proved capable of helping government to identify the sources of problems and provide clear frameworks for putting them right. There were issues of authority at stake: that of the Inspectorate itself and that of government.

The SSI's main existing vehicle was that of external inspection: the use of the professional skills of the inspectors to evaluate service provision and practice against professional values and standards. These had now to be supplemented in two main ways: by the recruitment of inspectors with managerial skills and perspectives and by the application of conceptual and quantitative analysis. The tradition of the predecessor body, the Social Work Service, had been grounded in 'connoisseurial' knowledge (Rossi 1982) or practice wisdom and an evaluative model of professional peer review. Values had, in a wide range of work, remained implicit and little or no attempt made to set clear standards or measures.

Now the SSI brought in research advice to help it construct key indicators for service planning and analysis, performance indicators (e.g. SSI 1989a), outcome definitions and measures, and methods of relating inputs to service outputs. It began to establish systematic frameworks for inspection to replace the simple 'aides-memoires' of the past. *Homes are for Living In* (1989b) was an early example of an evaluative framework for the inspection of residential care built round a set of core values and intended to show how documentary information, observation and discussion with staff, residents and relatives could together be analysed and used as evidence of how far those values had been incorporated into a residential home. In 1990 the SSI published its method of inspection for a whole service, home care, centred on the use of surveys and interview schedules. At the same time, it was making more use of external help in the very difficult task of conceptualising the relationship between process and outcome in the long term care of children, as a basis for the review of performance in this area of work (Parker *et al.* 1991).

The SSI thus developed a range of tools that could be used for self-evaluation by authorities, in advance of the introduction of local inspectorates in the personal social services under the Children Act, 1989, and the NHS and Community Care Act, 1990. As a result, it began to persuade local authority managers that it could meet their needs for standards and norms against which to measure the performance of at least some of their services. At the same time, the injection of new blood into the SSI from the field enabled it to give stronger leads than previously on the management problems of the personal social services.

By 1990 it had undoubtedly increased its authority in both central and local government, although the ambiguities of its role were intensifying: to strengthen both managerial and professional values and identity, to provide policy advice and, if necessary, critique to central government, and to be a resource to local government, while also acting as an agent of central government policy implementation. An attempt to deal with this overload and ambiguity was made through the restructuring of the SSI in 1992 (SSI 1992). In the new structure, the inspection functions were separated from the policy functions.

The SSI's role in ensuring policy implementation gained more prominence under the NHS and Community Care Act, 1990. While significant responsibility for evaluation and review was delegated, under this Act and the Children Act, 1989, to the local authorities, the principle of arms length local inspection tended to reinforce the value of separateness and independence rather than of internal managerial performance review or the kind of professional or clinical audit being developed in the health service. The impetus of quasi-markets and the new contract culture towards this kind of development was perceived more gradually in social services departments. The influence of the SSI in this process has been implicit in its policy guidance on the detail of the reforms and in its training support policies in contrast to the explicit guidance from the Audit Commission on performance review.

Total Quality Management

Neither the SSI nor the Audit Commission has gone so far as to embrace Total Quality Management (TQM), an approach whose roots are in private manufacturing or private service organisations. However, with the advent of competition and markets has come the message that quality, and thus management for quality, is the key to survival. TQM can, in part, be seen as a set of ideas that transcends conceptions of quality control and quality assurance by embedding a corporate system of comprehensive and continuous performance review. In 1991, the Department of Health commissioned an evaluation of TQM projects in the NHS (Joss *et al.* 1994, forthcoming).

The key to the total quality management approach is obtaining the commitment of all staff to a philosophy of continuous improvement and individual responsibility for quality. Quality is defined by reference to customer or user requirements (again areas in which the Audit Commission and the SSI were relatively slow to take a lead in the 1980s) as distinct from professional or expert ideas of excellence. Continuous improvement is embedded through systematic analysis of work processes, particularly those requiring interdepartmental collaboration, and through internal monitoring against internal target setting shaped by analyses of customer or user requirements. There is thus organisational commitment to performance review at all levels and by all staff.

Total quality management as such may well not be the precise mode adopted for the quasi-market of the public services. But its espousal of radical cultural change, a key to which is the commitment to a continuous cycle of performance review framed by user definitions of need, is widely reflected in the rhetoric of these services. The role, and indeed the definition, of the professional in this change is uncertain, as indeed are the ultimate power and definition of the user. In contrast, the power of the manager and the language of targets, measurement and outcome are well embedded.

Conclusion

It has been suggested that the evaluation of performance was early established as a key component in the strategy of successive Conservative governments since 1979 to achieve revolutionary change in the public sector. Political power and authority were to be concentrated at the centre and the health of the public sector was to be secured through good management.

The concept of public audit was broadened and the authority of inspection strengthened, in the name of installing the culture of management at the heart of public organisations, at the expense of the traditions of public administration and professionalism. In England and Wales, the Audit Commission and the Social Services Inspectorate sought to establish clear criteria and, wherever possible, hard measures by which the performance of local authorities could be evaluated.

Gradually, more attention has been paid to the function of internal review of performance as against external evaluation. The Audit Commission adjured local authorities to see performance review as the key to effective management and to their survival and independence. The position of the SSI remains more equivocal. Despite the setting up of local inspection units, the SSI's role in overseeing the implementation of government policies by local authorities has been strengthened. The principle of arms length local inspection symbolises the continuing need to externalise evaluation. However, the SSI has helped to lay the foundations for more effective internal monitoring and review of performance in its development of evaluative methods and measures.

As management is increasingly the instrument of a more fundamental revolution, the subjection of the public sector to market forces and mechanisms, so the role of internal performance review of individuals and organisations is underlined. It is integrally linked to the espousal of quality as the key to survival in private sector management developments, such as Total Quality Management. It is, on the face of it, highly consistent with increasing reliance upon contracts rather than evaluative institutions as key external controls. Whether this form of control will be in the name of quality as against price in the public sector remains a matter for doubt, if not scepticism.

References

Audit Commission (1986) *Performance Review in Local Government: A Handbook for Auditors and Local Authorities.* London: HMSO.

Audit Commission (1987) *Community Care: Developing Services for People with a Mental Handicap. Occasional Paper no.4.* London: HMSO.

Audit Commission (1988a) *Community Care: Developing Services for People with a Mental Handicap: Audit Guide.* London: HMSO.

Audit Commission (1988b) *The Competitive Council. Management Paper no.1.* London: HMSO.

Audit Commission (1988c) *Performance Review in Local Government: A Handbook for Auditors and Local Authorities: Action Guide.* London: HMSO.

Audit Commission (1989a) *Developing Services for People with a Mental Handicap. Occasional Paper no.9.* London: HMSO.

Audit Commission (1989b) *The Probation Service: Promoting Value for Money.* London: HMSO.

Audit Commission (1990) Performance Review Supplement.

Audit Commission (1991) The Quality Exchange: Finance Services, Summary Report.

Brittan, S. (1975) 'The economic contradictions of democracy'. *British Journal of Political Science* 5 (2).

Day, P. and Klein, R. (1990) *Inspecting the Inspectorates.* York: Joseph Rowntree Memorial Trust.

Gray, A. and Jenkins, W. (1983) *Policy Analysis and Evaluation in British Government.* London: RIPA.

Hartley, O. (1972) 'Inspectorates in British central government'. *Public Administration* 50, 4 (winter).

Henkel, M., Kogan, M., Packwood, T., Whitaker, T. and Youll, P. (1989) *The Health Advisory Service: An Evaluation.* London: King Edward's Hospital Fund for London.

Henkel, M. (1991a) *Government, Evaluation and Change*. London: Jessica Kingsley Publishers.

Henkel, M. (1991b) 'The new "evaluative state"'. *Public Administration* 69, 1 (spring).

Henkel, M. (1992) 'The Audit Commission', in Pollitt, C. and Harrison, S. (ed.) *Handbook of Public Service Management*. Oxford: Blackwell.

Joss, R. et al (1994 forthcoming) *Total Quality Management in the National Health Service: Final Report of an Evaluation*. Centre for the Evaluation of Public Policy and Practice, Brunel University.

King, A. (1975) 'Overload: the problems of governing in the 1970s'. *Political Studies* XXVIII (2).

Neave, G. (1988) 'On the cultivation of quality, efficiency and enterprise: an overview of recent trends in higher education in Western Europe, 1986–1988'. *European Journal of Education* 23 (1–2).

Parker, R. et al. (1991) *Assessing Outcomes in Child Care*. London: HMSO.

Pollitt, C. (1986) 'Beyond the managerial model: the case for broadening performance assessment in government and the public services'. *Financial Accountability and Management* 2 (3).

Pollitt, C. (ed.) (1992) *Considering Quality: An Analytical Guide to the Literature on Quality and Standards in the Public Services*. Centre for the Evaluation of Public Policy and Practice, Brunel University.

Rhodes, G. (1981) *Inspectorates in British Government*. London: George Allen and Unwin.

Rossi, P. (1982) in House, E. (ed.) *Evaluation Studies Review Annual*, Vol. 7. London: Sage.

Secretary of State for Health. Hansard, Written Answer Col 74, 25 February 1985.

Social Services Inspectorate (1989a) *Health in Homes*. London: HMSO.

Social Services Inspectorate (1989b) *Homes are for Living In*. London: HMSO.

Social Services Inspectorate (1990) *Inspecting Home Care Services: A Guide to the SSI Method*. London: HMSO.

Social Services Inspectorate (1992) *Concern for Quality. The First Annual Report of the Chief Inspector. Social Services Inspectorate 1991/92*. London: HMSO.

Treasury and Cabinet Office (1982) *Efficiency and Effectiveness in the Civil Service*. Cmnd 8616. London: HMSO.

Chapter 3

Performance Review Through Inspection and Monitoring by Central Government

Stephen Mitchell and Frank Tolan

Introduction

In her article 'The New Evaluative State' Mary Henkel (1991) referred to Government promotion of 'a new managerial culture in the public sector' in which 'evaluation was presented as a pre-requisite of effective accountability and significant change'. As part of this, the Social Services Inspectorate (SSI) for England and Wales was created in 1985 out of the former Social Work Service, which had operated primarily as a professional advisory service of the then DHSS. This process of evolutionary change is described by Day and Klein (1990) in the report on their research 'Inspecting the Inspectorates'. They noted that the SSI's methods of inspection, particularly those developed for the programme of inspections of home care services in 20 per cent of English local authorities between 1986 and 1989, demonstrated convergence with the analytical approaches of the Audit Commission. This methodology was published in 1990 (SSI 1990). Day and Klein also found that the SSI 'has begun to put almost as much emphasis on the importance of clear policy objectives, appropriate managerial structures, and adequate information systems', as on practice and service delivery issues.

The SSI has a professional staff of approximately 100, the majority of whom are professionally qualified in social work, and have considerable experience of the management and delivery of social services. Approximately 10 per cent of this workforce was recruited primarily on the basis of qualifications, skills and experience in social research and policy analysis, in social services and other fields.

The SSI has developed its role as a professional division of the Department of Health with three purposes:

- to inspect personal social services provision and organisation and management in order to promote quality standards, improve effectiveness and efficiency, and ensure the safety and well-being of service users

- to provide professional advice to Ministers, the Department and the field on the formulation, implementation and review of social services and health policies, and the effective and efficient delivery of these services

- to facilitate communications between the Department and personal social services agencies in all sectors.

In pursuit of these purposes the SSI has developed systematic, empirically-based approaches to the examination of policy implementation, and to inspection of the management and delivery of social services.

The SSI's empirically-based work has taken two distinct forms, described here as 'inspection' and 'monitoring', and this paper illustrates both approaches. The development of the SSI's methodologies has been informed by parallel developments in evaluative research on social work and social services (notably the work of the Personal Social Services Research Unit at the University of Kent), and in audit of public services (particularly the various 'special studies' of aspects of social services by the Audit Commission). It has also been assisted by, and has directly and significantly contributed to, the development of performance indicators for social services. The first is by the Department of Health which now produces an annual publication 'Key Indicators of Social Services'. The second is by the Audit Commission (England and Wales only – see chapter by Black for position in Scotland) whose publication 'Citizen's Charter Indicators, Charting a Course' (1992) included a number of social services indicators which it is planning to extend and refine. Indicators which are derived from already established collections of statistical data, and which enable comparative analysis, provide an essential foundation for more detailed investigative work, and are therefore invaluable as underpinnings to the SSI's inspection and monitoring projects.

Inspection

'Inspection' is a term frequently used to describe a great variety of quality review and quality control activities. At one end of a spectrum inspection can be a process of 'professional review', for which little if anything is provided by way of structure. In such inspections the processes for obtaining information are loosely defined and informal, and judgements or evaluations are based on professional judgement and experiences, rather than on a carefully constructed evidence base and analysed data. At the other end of the spectrum is an 'audit' approach to inspection, employing structured social research methodologies to produce systematic evidence, on the basis of which judgements and evaluations can be reached. The SSI has increasingly moved towards a structured, empirical model of inspection: a recently published document 'Introducing the Inspection Division' (SSI 1993a) states that 'SSI inspections involve the systematic investigation of the quality of services received by users and their carers, and of the management arrangements for the delivery of these services'.

What does this entail? The SSI inspections are now always based on a clear statement of *standards*, which make explicit the quality of performance it expects an agency to achieve in the particular service to be investigated. Starting from such statements of standards, inspection requires systematic thought by the Inspectorate about the purpose and scope of any particular project, and the application of rigorous investigative procedures alongside effective use of the knowledge and understanding of experienced professionals. Professional judgement is exercised at all stages of the inspection process in the selection of what is relevant, in the collection, analysis and interpretation of findings, and in the validation of findings with those directly involved in the inspection.

Figure 3.1 provides a conceptual map of the inspection process, which has 15 distinct elements. One of the most important is the definition of **standards**, by which the SSI means the quality of performance which it considers is required in the management and delivery of social services, for service provision to accord with legislation, national policy, practice guidance and generally accepted definitions of good practice in health and social care. In some service areas, standards will be more easily articulated than in others where the basis in policy guidance and statutory responsibilities is less clearly defined. Once standards have been defined it is important to be explicit about the **criteria** which will be used to determine whether performance meets the required standards: criteria are

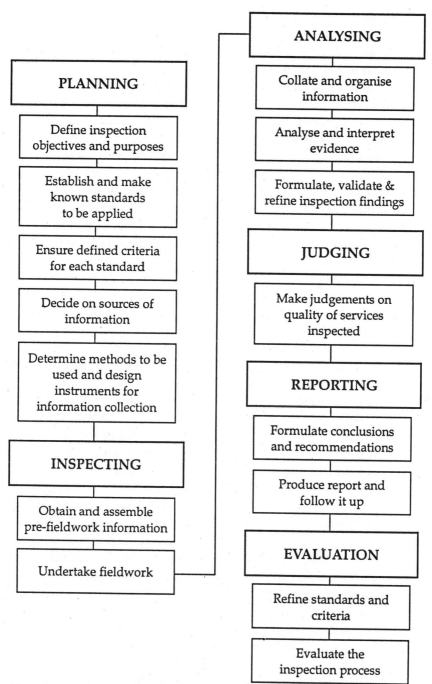

Figure 3.1 A conceptual framework of the inspection process

specific and detailed statements of expectations about particular aspects of performance. They must be capable of being tested against objective information collected in inspections and are the basis for an assessment of whether or not a particular standard is reached.

Careful thought is then required about the potential **sources of information** likely to be most fruitful in yielding evidence about particular standards and criteria. Both prior to and during the fieldwork phase of inspection the SSI uses a variety of methods to collect information from identified sources. This includes the design and application of formally designed instruments (questionnaires, interview schedules, observation checklists, document extraction forms, etc.) for the collection of quantitative and qualitative data. Inspection **findings** are then generated, through a process of analysis and validation of the information obtained by inspectors, in the form of positive or negative indicators of performance for the criteria under a particular standard.

From inspection findings judgements are then required about the quality of performance in the service inspected: essentially, this involves determining whether the standard is met, partially met or not met at all. Inspection findings provide a basis for professional judgements about quality, and it is vital in the inspection process to ensure a clear link between standards, criteria, evidence, findings and judgements of performance. This provides a durable foundation for conclusions, and action recommendations listing those changes deemed necessary in the management and delivery of the services inspected if performance is to be raised to the level of the standards expected and articulated by the SSI.

Inspections by the SSI usually entail visits to, and evaluation of, services provided to users by local authority Social Services Departments or other agencies. Inspections focus first and foremost on service delivery at the point of impact on users and carers, whose views are always included. However, the conceptual framework of a 'standards-based inspection' set out above can equally well be applied to reviewing the performance of other aspects of a social services agency's work than direct service provision. This is illustrated by an inspection of arrangements for the management and resourcing of training in three local authority SSDs, carried out by the SSI in 1992 (SSI 1993).

As well as discovering and reporting on training issues arising from the SSDs' approaches to new qualification structures, and implementation of the NHS and Community Care Act 1990 and the Children Act 1989, a central objective of these inspections was to evaluate the usefulness of a set of draft standards, so that a revised and comprehensive set could be prepared as the basis for future inspections. A set of nine standards for the management and resourcing of training was derived, covering Policy, Strategy and Planning, Managing new Developments, Links with Service and Policy Developments, Workforce Analysis and Planning, Resources, Access, Promotion of Multi-Disciplinary and Multi-Agency Training, and Effectiveness and Impact. These standards were reflected on by the participating inspectors following the three inspections, and revised accordingly. Figure 3.2 sets out the revised standard for Workforce Planning, with five detailed criteria, and Figure 3.3 provides a worked example of how such a standard can be empirically evaluated. This was one of seven revised standards (with between four and eight criteria each) which constituted the revised inspection framework.

Standard

Training activity should be an integral part of an SSD's overall strategy to plan, maintain and develop the skills of the workforce

Criteria

- SSD should understand principles of workforce planning
- SSD should analyse current workforces' skills and knowledge
- SSD should be able to identify current and future workforce requirements and have set workforce targets/goals to inform training and recruitment policies
- Training programmes should take into account workforce goals and plans
- There should be a linked information base between training and personnel functions which informs both

Figure 3.2 The Management and Resourcing of Training: Workforce Planning

---

The two principal sources of information for the inspections were **SSD staff** representing the breadth of interest in training (e.g. staff involved in service delivery and management, as well as in training and personnel, and senior managers), and the SSD's **written materials** (e.g. policy statements, training plans, guidance to staff). These sources provided the basis for the collection and analysis of two main data sets (one in advance of

Sources	* Senior & training managers; training staff; Personnel managers * Workforce: plans, targets, reports * Training: programmes, plans * Information systems: specifications, printouts
Methods	* Document analyses * Staff interviews: SSD, Personnel, IT
Instruments	* Document recording schedules * Interview schedules
Collation	* Data gathered and organised under a series of headings and categories to reflect criteria being used
Analysis	* Analysis of qualitatice data to identify themes and patterns * Integration and cross-referencing of all data between categories and headings
Findings – positive	* SSD training section has a database of staff qualifications, training needs and training received * Information used to inform planning and training programmes * Some overall profiling of workforce by LA * Personnel records are computerised
Findings – negative	* SSD information not linked nor used by Personnel * SSD system is manual but not kept up to date * Personnel records limited to purposes of contract maintenance and payroll * Workforce information is limited and not integrated
Judgements	* This process involves matching of evidence against the standards and criteria and deciding whether the standard has been met * In making decisions about the overall quality of services, weighted judgements need to take account of the number and type of standards which have and which have not been met
Conclusions	* That although SSD does fulfil some criteria is does not meet the standard as stated * Current systems do produce useful information on the workforce but this information is neither processed nor analysed in ways which allow its full potential
Recommen-dations	* The SSD needs to consider and begin to plan its workforce * To do this it needs to build effective bridges between its separate information systems and link these to a common purpose – that of analysing and planning for its current and future needs * Future development will require clear delegated management responsibility to oversee introduction of appropriate processes, goals and systems

Figure 3.3 The Management and Resourcing of Training: Worked Example

Inspectors visiting an Authority and one through fieldwork). Fieldwork consisted of a planned series of structured interviews covering training policy, procedures, management arrangements and the use of training resources with a wide range of staff. As well as an overview report containing the principal general findings, the inspections resulted in a detailed report with specific recommendations to each SSD. Overall, the main findings concerned the need for:

- clearer training strategies, policies and plans
- better understanding by all staff of the managerial, operational and development implications of new qualification structures
- a more robust infrastructure to underpin new training developments
- clarity in setting and monitoring targets for staff and organisational development
- co-ordination of training activity with operational objectives and practices.

Importantly, individual sets of recommendations were given to each SSD inspected, taking account of their particular contexts, and providing local frameworks for practical action which the inspection teams considered should be taken forward.

Monitoring

Although the framework for standards-based inspections set out and illustrated above has potentially wide applicability, it is neither possible nor appropriate for this to be the only approach to empirically-based review of social services agency performance that an organisation with the SSI's wide remit applies in its work. A central government department frequently requires information about the implementation of policies, or the extent of particular policy and service problems in its sphere of interest, which needs to be collected systematically on a short timescale, analysed appropriately and presented succinctly. An example is the significant amount of monitoring of service activity in relation to specific grants (for training, AIDS, mental illness and guardians ad litem) which has been carried out by the SSI since the first such grant (the Training Support Programme) was introduced in 1988/89. Exemplifying what can be involved, the SSI undertook detailed questionnaire-based monitoring of the Mental Illness Specific Grant in its first year of operation in 1991/92.

A report based on SSDs' mental health plans and stated intentions for using the specific grant was published in January 1992 (SSI 1992). The second phase of monitoring moved beyond this to obtaining information about the volume, nature and range of service developments introduced; the contributions which the specific funding arrangements made to the improvement and expansion of social care services for severely mentally ill people; and progress against the priorities and objectives set out in the White Paper 'Caring for People' in 1989.

For the second phase, a questionnaire with 16 general questions (covering expenditure, quality standards, inter-agency collaboration and contracts, and stated 'measurable goals') was designed for completion by each SSD. A second section of the questionnaire requested details about each service development project supported by the Mental Illness Specific Grant. All 104 SSDs in receipt of grant provided completed questionnaires to SSI Regions in the three months after the financial year to which monitoring related. A detailed statistical analysis was carried out centrally and has been reported (SSI 1993b).

Monitoring exercises of this kind cannot be evaluative in the sense of analysing quality and effectiveness of services. However, they can furnish invaluable information to underpin the review of major central initiatives. This particular exercise found that 'the planning and implementation process was characterised by an opportunistic rather than a strategic approach to service development' (SSI 1993b), but the Specific Grant had facilitated inter-agency collaboration so that 'nearly 800 projects have been developed, demonstrating a rich diversity of social care' (ibid). The monitoring exercise also identified deficiencies in the way local authorities accounted for expenditure on specialist and non-specialist mental health services, requiring further investigation by the SSI and the Audit Commission.

A similar questionnaire-based approach has recently been applied by the SSI in monitoring projects covering procedures and practices in residential homes for children following the Inquiry Report on 'pindown' regimes in Staffordshire (Kahan and Levy 1991); the development of local authority arms-length inspection units; the implementation of the Children Act 1989 during its first year; and the extent of the phenomenon of unallocated child protection and child care cases following interest in this problem on the part of the Parliamentary Select Committee on Health during the 1990 and 1991 sessions. Structured questionnaires also provided the basis for regular monitoring by the SSI (in collaboration with

Regional Health Authorities) of progress in implementing the key elements of community care between 1991 and 1993.

Essential features of this approach to monitoring are the wide (often national) coverage of such exercises; and straightforward questionnaires and data sheets facilitating statistical analysis at any level of aggregation, based substantially on 'self-reporting' by the SSD of objective data. Large amounts of data can be assembled and analysed quickly and effectively, although the validity and reliability of some responses requires serious examination. Monitoring exercises provide photographs of performance at a particular time, with varying degrees of accuracy of focus and sharpness of image. Having conducted such exercises, in which there is often limited scope for 'triangulating' questionnaire responses with other data to validate and verify findings, the SSI has an important role in interpreting the findings for policy 'customers' within government, and any external audiences for the material. The keys to effective conduct of monitoring projects lie in the credibility and legitimacy of the SSI when asking searching questions. This has to be sustained by cautious but authoritative interpretation and analysis of the results of such exercises to provide information for Ministers and officials inside Government and also to provide appropriate feedback and information to various external audiences.

Conclusion

The SSI was reorganised in 1992, one objective being to achieve a clearer differentiation between its inspection and its policy work (including monitoring). This paper demonstrates that in both arms of its work the SSI has developed, and is continuing to develop, approaches to the review of performance in social work services which are solidly empirically-based. Generally, the methodologies developed and applied ensure effective use of the knowledge and skills of the SSI's experienced professional workforce in obtaining, analysing, interpreting and drawing conclusions from a wide range of of information about performance in the social services.

The context of 'the new evaluative state' described by Henkel means that questions about *how* systematically and empirically to examine the performance of publicly provided or financed services are increasingly raised. There are no right answers immediately available in the complex field of performance review in social work services. The SSI endeavours to ensure that the methods which it uses are conceptually clear, empirically rigorous, well documented, and allow maximum scope for the exercise of informed judgement by experienced social services professionals in arriving at conclusions. The SSI's methodologies will continue to develop, addressing the challenges set out in the Department of Health consultation paper 'Inspecting Social Services' (Department of Health 1992), particularly regarding the involvement of users, carers and 'lay' people in its national programme of inspections, which is drawn up annually in consultation with the local authority and other important interests. The SSI will also extend collaboration with other bodies concerned with performance review of social services, particularly the Audit Commission, and anticipates that it will be required to carry out systematic monitoring of policy implementation in services for children and adults during the 1990s.

References

Audit Commission (1992) *Citizen's Charter Indicators, Charting a Course*. London: HMSO.

Day, P. and Klein, R. (1990) *Inspecting the Inspectorates*. York: Joseph Rowntree Memorial Trust.

Department of Health (1992) Inspecting Social Services. Consultation Paper. Department of Health.

Henkel, M. (1991) 'The new evaluative state'. *Public Administration* 69 (1), 121–136.

Kahan, B. and Levy, A. (1991) The Pindown Experience and the Protection of Children. Report of the Staffordshire Child Care Inquiry. Staffordshire County Council.

Secretaries of State for Health, Wales, Northern Ireland and Scotland (1989) *Caring for People: Community Care in the Next Decade and Beyond*. London: HMSO.

Social Services Inspectorate (1990) *Inspecting Home Care Services. A Guide to the SSI Method*. London: HMSO.

Social Services Inspectorate (1992) *Mental Illness Specific Grant. Monitoring of Proposals for Use in 1991/92*. London: HMSO.

Social Services Inspectorate (1993a) *Introducing the Inspection Division*. London: HMSO.

Social Services Inspectorate (1993b) *Planning into Practice, Mental Illness Specific Grant, Second Report on Monitoring its Use 1991/1992*. London: HMSO.

Chapter 4

Staff Appraisal and Clinical Audit in the National Health Service

Susan Willoughby

Introduction

Concern for quality of care has always been an important consideration in health service provision in the UK. The original 16th century charter of the Royal College of Physicians listed as one of its objectives 'to uphold standards for the public good' (Normand 1991). From its foundation, the National Health Service has stressed the need to provide the best quality service within available resources. Recent White Papers such as 'Working for Patients' (Secretaries of State for Health, Wales, Northern Ireland and Scotland 1989) and 'Caring for People' (Secretaries of State for Health, Wales and Scotland 1989) are the culmination of a growing recognition of the need to implement modern quality assurance procedures to optimise the quality of care.

The UK is a signatory to the World Health Organisation declaration that 'all member states should have effective mechanisms for ensuring quality of patient care within their health care systems'. This declaration was inspired by three major features of health care provision in recent decades:

(1) the increasing cost of providing health care for the growing dependent proportion of the population

(2) patients' increased understanding of care and awareness of their rights as its consumers

(3) professionals' awareness of the increasing technological and organisational complexity of the care for which they feel themselves responsible.

Since these features are also characteristic of the 'market' for other personal care services, the experience of the NHS in trying to develop effective quality assurance systems may contain lessons relevant to other services.

Quality assurance procedures in the NHS

In a seminal article on quality assurance, Shaw (1986) lists the various internal and external quality assurance mechanisms in the NHS. The list includes traditional internal review procedures (annual reports, member visiting, ethical committees, etc.), external review procedures (community health councils, statutory inspectorates and commissions, the Health Advisory Service and Management Advisory Service, etc.) as well as newer instruments relevant to customer responsiveness such as patient satisfaction surveys (see chapter by Fitzpatrick and Taylor) and complaints procedures, and the two approaches to quality assurance which form the basis of the present chapter, that is, staff performance review or appraisal, and clinical audit.

At the time when I took up a post as a Clinical Psychologist with a District Health Authority in 1989, these two quality assurance mechanisms were beginning to predominate over traditional internal and external quality review procedures.

Performance appraisal in the NHS

The standard form of performance appraisal adopted in the NHS is called Individual Performance Review (IPR). It involves:

- identifying key result areas and objectives of an individual's job which are testable against an agreed timescale
- identifying the individual's learning needs as they relate to key result areas and the individual's current and future job performance, and agreeing the means of meeting those needs.

The IPR process was designed as a blueprint to be used by individual health authorities in developing their own customised performance appraisal systems, for example by modifying the accompanying documentation to suit local needs. The key features of the IPR package are:

(1) an annual review by the post-holder's line manager which includes an assessment of the postholder's work achievements in the current year and identification of the next year's objectives

(2) a numerical rating of performance by the manager

(3) signing of the review documents by two appraisers, a reviewer or 'parent' (typically the line manager) and an equity assessor or 'grandparent' (typically the manager's line manager)

(4) a standardised set of forms for use in documenting the review procedure.

IPR was devised by the NHS Management Executive (NHSME) and introduced to the NHS as part of the extensive development of general management techniques which followed the Griffiths' review in 1983 (DHSS 1983). In 1986, it was made obligatory for all general managers, with the expectation that it would be applied initially to most senior managers and extended in due course to other staff with management responsibilities. By 1991, IPR had been extended to some levels of senior management including senior nurses. Because of its association with the Griffiths' reforms, a major purpose of the IPR system from the beginning was to reinforce the impetus for change by ensuring that the work objectives of individual managers were consonant with the objectives being introduced by the NHSME to the Health Authority's plans and programmes. Increased managerial accountability required devolution of managerial power which, in turn, required the setting of clear objectives at organisational and individual levels. This IPR system was strongly endorsed by the NHSME and general managers.

A major review of the implementation of IPR commissioned by the NHS Training Directorate (IHSM 1991) revealed a picture of performance appraisal working smoothly and contributing to the effectiveness of NHS management, with a majority of the 1600 respondents convinced that they were, in collaboration with their managers, successfully formulating a range of challenging objectives that were related to those of their organisation. Most managers were happy with their ratings in spite of the fact that only a minority understood how these were arrived at or even thought that success in achieving their objectives was measurable. The IHSM study did not address the actual content of objectives, an area of central concern for quality assurance. It did establish that 50 per cent of objectives were concerned with service innovation, 40 per cent with 'maintenance' (of existing services) and only 10 per cent with personal development.

Overall, managers felt that IPR had increased their managerial effectiveness, although it had not contributed to a team atmosphere or increased openness in their organisation. A majority disagreed with the statement that the IPR process had benefitted from the introduction of performance-related pay (PRP). (Only senior NHS managers are eligible for performance-related pay and only up to a maximum of 2.7% of their salary.)

The negative tone of parts of the IHSM report on IPR seems to reflect some preconceived ideas about the likelihood of failure in establishing IPR in the NHS. It was hurriedly imposed by senior management in many Health Authorities without consultation or prior training, and with the numerical rating of performance and the determination of PRP included in the IPR review, despite a commercial sector consensus that these processes are best kept separate.

Three experiences of IPR

The above account gives an overview of how the IPR system operates in the NHS as a whole. My personal experience of IPR within my employing District Health Authority provides an insight into its application at a local level. During three years working as a Clinical Psychologist, I encountered IPR at various levels: first, that of an employee being appraised, then as a manager undertaking training in IPR, and, finally, as a manager conducting an appraisal interview. Each of these experiences highlighted for me different aspects of the strengths and limitations of the IPR system, and each of these is discussed.

Being appraised within an IPR framework

I first encountered IPR in the form of documentation sent to me by my line manager in Psychology prior to my first staff appraisal interview six months after my appointment. Completing the documents gave me a valuable opportunity to structure my future work plans, set myself specific targets and objectives, identify (and feel good about) my successes to date, and troubleshoot any obstacles to success. This is an approach which psychologists use with their clinical clients and in their research, but which they tend to neglect to apply to their own work.

Each of the forms contained in the IPR documentation had its individual merits. The **Personal Preparation Checklist** enabled me to identify the areas of work which I most enjoyed, my special interests and skills, as well as areas which I did not enjoy or where I needed further support or input. The core IPR instrument, the **Performance Plan**, required me to do some planning for all the main work areas of my work, ensuring that some of the less highly prioritised areas such as preventive work and service development were not neglected in favour of the always pressing needs of clinical clients.

The section of the IPR documentation which I found most surprising was the **Personal Development Plan** (PDP). The idea that a large, impersonal employer such as the NHS wanted to discuss my personal career aspirations and share the responsibility for any training needs I might express was both intriguing and gratifying. Since the PDP form required me to state how I would like to progress within the organisation, I was able to list my interest in higher management training at a very early stage in my employment. My manager took seriously his commitment to fulfilling my PDP, and enrolment on an NHS management course followed quickly afterwards. If this topic had not been included in the appraisal interview documentation, it is unlikely that I would have been assertive enough to raise the issue with my line manager.

These benefits resulted from using the IPR framework and documentation to structure my appraisal interview, which might otherwise have been confined to updating my line manager on what was happening in my clinical specialism. I did not experience the 'grandparent' system of equity assessor. This would have been unworkable as the next tier of management in our District Health Authority involved a member of a different clinical profession who, due to the traditional entrenched interprofessional rivalry in the NHS, could not have been relied on to promote the interests of psychologists. Neither did I experience performance rating, since it is linked to PRP which does not apply to psychologists. This process would also have been unworkable, as its rudimentary five-point rating scale would be unsuitable for rating success in complex work tasks such as psychological therapy. In other situations – for example, where the staff and manager came from a single professional discipline and the outcomes of professional intervention were more readily identifiable by other people – the system had greater relevance.

My experience of being appraised under IPR was of a benign and facilitative process which echoed the principles on which the profession of Clinical Psychology is based. However, I am aware that staff from other professions working for the same Health Authority in the same period had very different experiences of IPR. The fact that IPR was being used by the NHS to harmonise organisational and individual work objectives increased the likelihood of its being used in a manipulative or punitive sense, rather than in its benign form as an integral part of a positive system of management by objectives. Many of my manager colleagues from other professions experienced their appraisals as bruising encounters with managers steeped in the traditional, punitive approach to motivating their subordinates. Objectives, while masquerading under the grand title of 'innovation', were heavily biassed towards cost-cutting and the running down of services which involved managers in highly stressful activities such as relocating employees or making them redundant.

IPR training

A welcome counterbalance to the rather predatory management by cost-cutting was provided by the training courses on IPR facilitated by the Health Authority's training and personnel officer. These courses provided a positive interpretation of IPR as a management process which gives employees direction in terms of corporate and individual goals and rewards them for achieving these goals. Attending one of these two-day courses provided me with the additional experience which I needed to equip me to carry out my own staff appraisals using the IPR framework.

The course included practical handouts with appropriate NHS examples and exercises on writing clear statements of job purpose, selecting and drafting work objectives (six objectives is the magic number); setting actions against objectives (four or five actions per objective) and agreeing success criteria ('performance in relation to the objective will be regarded as successful if and when xyz apply'). It also included valuable material on the sophisticated interviewing-cum-counselling approach which is necessary to conduct a successful appraisal interview. We watched an informative and amusing video which demonstrated the new skills in a very accessible form. We then sweated our way through a series of tripartite role plays where an observer commented on our success in mastering the skills appropriate to the various stages of an appraisal interview, for example

- the 'pull' rather than the 'push' style of management

- seeking information, testing understanding, supporting and building on the appraisee's suggestions rather than giving information, proposing, disagreeing or attacking

- dealing constructively with the 'poor performer .

Being an appraiser

My own experience of being an appraiser was more at the empowering than the controlling end of the IPR spectrum. I made good use of the skills learned on the training course to deal with a challenging work situation which involved harnessing the energies of a talented but mercurial employee whose contribution would be crucial to the success of an important new project. The detailed planning of work objectives and actions left my appraisee free to exercise initiative in implementing the chosen targets without becoming too restricted by the petty bureaucratic accompaniments of employment within the NHS.

Peer-review clinical audit in the NHS

As noted above, Shaw's (1986) paper on quality assurance recommended the use of a wide range of procedures to monitor service quality in the NHS. Yet it is significant that the paper provided detailed information only on the procedure of clinical review and accompanied this with examples of its application in a range of areas crucial to the quality of clinical services, for example errors and delays in diagnosis and treatment, complications of surgery and 'critical events' such as cardiac arrest, and communication between consultants and GPs. The overall effect was to create an image of clinical review as a crucial, if not the key, mechanism of quality assurance in health service provision.

Shaw later went on to elaborate the procedure of clinical review in its modern form of medical audit carried out by teams or 'firms' of doctors, and clinical audit carried out by multi-disciplinary teams (Shaw 1989, 1990). The key identifying features of clinical audit are that it:

- is based on peer-review meetings, thus encouraging comparison of practice among peers

- includes topics that have significance for the overall quality of the service either because they are common, high risk or high cost, or as an issue of contention or local interest

- is criterion based, requiring the peer-group to agree on standards of good practice in the area of work under study

- involves the formal agreement and recording of any action required to resolve any discrepancies between recommended and actual practice for review in a later audit.

Medical audit as practised in the NHS typically involves the review of randomly selected patient records or the review of a diagnosis, investigation or treatment protocol to assess the adequacy of medical care, or the review of routine statistics and selected adverse patient events. In order to foster an attitude of critical self- and peer-appraisal, the results of individual audits remain confidential to the 'firm', although annual audit reports outline the areas studied and any significant action recommended. Repetition of the audit cycle brings actual medical practice in line with agreed protocols but also encourages discussion and resolution of divergent opinions on approaches to clinical management.

The launch of medical audit in the NHS (see Irvine's chapter) was given generous support in the form of pump-priming money to fund training courses, district audit committees and new medical posts to coordinate audit, administrator posts to collate audit data, and information technology to computerise the audit procedure which is largely based on the analysis of medical records (see Irvine's chapter). In characteristic NHS fashion, a much smaller sum was provided at a later date to implement audit in the nursing profession and an even smaller amount for other professions, the so-called 'professions allied to medicine' (PAM), thus encouraging dominance of medical audit in the NHS. The arbitrary top-down attempt to structure the organisation of audit in the NHS created its own problems. For example, the audit funds allocated to the PAM group, which included the widely diverging professions of Physiotherapy, Occupational Therapy, Speech Therapy and Clinical Psychology, were allocated to an exercise which tried to determine common standards of practice suitable for multi-disciplinary audit, which was unproductive and unnecessary in the view of many.

Multi-disciplinary peer-review audit

My personal experience of clinical audit was as positive as my experience of IPR. As a member of a multi-disciplinary community mental health team specialising in addiction problems, I anticipated many potential benefits of a peer-review approach to monitoring treatment quality. We implemented clinical audit in the form of monthly meetings to agreed detailed quality standards for key areas of our work. Initial audit topics included confidentiality procedures (very important for alcohol and drug-misusing clients), waiting times, client review procedures and resulting treatment outcomes, and arrangements for communicating with referring agents and canvassing their satisfaction with our service. Because our team had a history of conducting research, we already had a comprehensive computerised client record system and a centre secretary with the necessary skills for recording and collating data relevant to audit, unique at that time in the community mental health unit.

Our team experienced immediate benefits from the audit. The systematic feedback provided by the audit data revealed that we were doing a good job in the majority of cases. Mental health professionals are usually starved of this information as they tend to focus on problematic or 'hopeless' cases which consume a disproportionate amount of their resources. Another benefit was the way in which the process of setting quality standards improved our team functioning. Concentrating on pooling our varied skills to achieve specified outcomes for our clients banished the professional rivalries that had previously sapped our energy and limited our capacity to value each other's work.

An important spinoff of clinical audit procedure was the accumulation of a convincing amount of information testifying to our team's effectiveness, including the results of a questionnaire survey of our local GPs which showed a strong preference for a specialist team to deal with alcohol and drug problems. This information became crucial to our survival as a specialist team when our NHS unit gained trust status in 1992 and began to look around for services which could be 'rationalised' in the interests of short-term savings.

Case study: the benefits of multi-agency audit

My experience of the benefits of multi-disciplinary peer-review audit was later complemented by an opportunity to evaluate formally the benefits of clinical audit. This opportunity arose in 1991 when the South West Regional Health Authority funded a project to investigate the feasability and value of introducing clinical audit across the 18 statutory and non-statutory drug agencies throughout the South West. The Region was anxious to encourage the development of multi-disciplinary clinical audit as opposed to the narrower medical audit, and it also believed that small specialisms such as services to drug misusers should be audited on a region-wide basis. It remained to be established whether the rather formal, clinical records-based procedures of audit could be adapted to the circumstances of non-statutory drug agencies which had a history, and in some cases a policy, of minimising written information about individual clients. Moreover, community drugs projects were particularly underfunded in the clerical support required to maintain a records-based system of quality audit. The funding paid for the costs of bringing project representatives together for audit meetings. It also paid for the salary of a clinical audit officer to organise audit meetings, devise data-collection systems that could be implemented by all the drug agencies participating in audit, and visit and advise agencies on how to adapt or develop their existing record-keeping systems to meet the requirements of audit.

In its first year, audit was introduced to the nine drug agencies in Devon and Avon counties and the evaluation (Willoughby 1992) sought to measure success in terms of the degree of agency participation, completion of individual audits and any resulting improvements in the quality of service delivery, as reported in a questionnaire-based interview with the nine agency managers.

Because of the newness of the service, there is little consensus among drug agencies about what constitutes good practice or minimum quality standards in different areas of service provision. The five topics audited in the first year were therefore notable for the contribution they made towards encouraging different agencies to identify a criterion of good practice that was worth adhering to by all agencies working with drug misusers. Thus, agencies agreed common frameworks for determining their speed of response to referrals; how to ensure that clients received the actual services that they requested; the form, content and administration of confidentiality policy; and how clients could be helped to find a sympathetic GP. All of the audits required additional record-keeping but such was the enthusiasm and rivalry generated by the audit project that not only did agencies record the required information for the audit topic but most decided to continue to record this information on a permanent basis and voluntary agencies which had previously avoided keeping written information on their clients began to devote considerable resources to upgrading their record-keeping systems.

When interviewed, managers of all drug agencies identified both general and specific benefits of audit to the quality of the service delivered by their agencies. General benefits included:

- the opportunity to reflect upon their practice, to review individual areas of practice in detail and to set (and raise) quality standards
- the opportunity to develop trust and rapport with workers in other agencies and to learn from their good practice
- improved team communication systems

- improved record-keeping systems.

Managers were particularly satisfied with the specific benefits resulting from individual audits such as the revision and updating of confidentiality procedures and the setting of standards for primary health care for their agency's clients.

Overall, the major benefit resulting from multi-agency audit in its first year was related to the achievement of consensus and the setting of standards of good practice. Many agencies set up an internal quality audit system during 1991 and saw the regional audit meetings as a valuable external validation of their internal quality assurance efforts.

Conclusions

It is clear from the above account that IPR and clinical audit are powerful complementary tools of performance review and quality assurance. It is equally clear that to maximise their contribution to improving the quality of health care, their application needs to be coordinated. There is currently a striking dichotomy in the application of the two procedures in the NHS, with performance appraisal being used as a quality assurance tool mostly by general managers while clinicians rely primarily on clinical audit. Shaw (1986) endorses this delineation of responsibilities of managers and clinicians by crediting managers with the main responsibility for staff appraisal while stressing that clinical review must remain an internal exercise by professional workers within their own area of expertise. Thus IPR is still largely confined to managerial ranks and has not found ready acceptance among clinically-based staff. Nurses, for example, have argued that the clinical portion of their work does not lend itself to performance appraisal. This attitude is a potential threat to one of the key aims of IPR, namely, that of fostering corporate cohesiveness.

Many trusts have made it a feature of their applications for self-governing status to promise to implement IPR and performance-related pay at all levels, but they may be reluctant to enforce it in the absence of any 'bottom up' enthusiasm from new staff groups seeking to be included in the procedure.

Clinical staff can make impressive gains in the quality of health care using clinical audit. The multi-agency peer-review approach to quality audit described in the present paper has a particularly valuable potential to encourage common standards of quality across services that might otherwise be tempted to skimp on quality due to competitive cost considerations. Because of the cost implications, it is essential that the results of audit are fed into the planning and budgetary priorities of both purchasing health authorities and provider trusts, in a way that has not been achieved in the early years of implementing clinical audit.

Non-health care statutory and voluntary agencies interested to develop quality assurance procedures similar to IPR and clinical audit will be particularly anxious to learn from the NHS how the two procedures can best be implemented to produce coordinated rather than conflicting benefits to the quality of care.

References

DHSS (1983) *NHS Management Inquiry.* London: DHSS.

Institute of Health Services Management (1991) *Individual Performance Review in the NHS.* London: IHSM.

Normand, C. (1991) Clinical Audit in Professions Allied to Medicine and Related Therapy Professions. Report to the Department of Health.

Secretaries of State for Health, Wales, Northern Ireland and Scotland (1989) *Working for Patients: The Health Service.* London: HMSO.

Secretaries of State for Health, Wales and Scotland (1989) *Caring for People: Community Care in the Next Decade and Beyond.* London: HMSO.

Shaw, C. (1986) *Introducing Quality Assurance.* Project Paper No. 64. London: King's Fund.

Shaw, C. (1989) *Medical Audit: A Hospital Handbook.* London: King's Fund publication.

Shaw, C. (1990) 'Criterion-based audit'. *British Medical Journal* 300, 649–651.

Willoughby, S. (1992) South West Drug Agencies Audit Project: An Evaluation of the First Year. Exeter Health Authority. Unpublished internal report.

Chapter 5

Personal Supervision in Social Work

Malcolm Payne

Introduction

The conventional form of management for most social work practitioners is 'supervision'. All forms of supervision in social work are supposed to involve an element of assessment of the competence and achievements of the worker by the supervisor. Supervision is intended to fulfil several aims, usually recognised by the participants as grouped into professional and managerial aspects. This separation creates tensions which, the chapter explains, are usually resolved by the professional aspects receiving greater priority. The managerial concerns are also more likely to be raised implicitly than explicitly. The theory and experience of supervision therefore raises fundamental questions about whether the competence and achievements of the social worker are tested through supervision.

This chapter explores the balance between professional and managerial supervision and the relationship between the components, with particular emphasis on the role of the supervisor. It must be remembered, however, that these are two aspects of a single phenomenon and that the aspects are intertwined: the structure of this chapter reflects this relationship. It is also necessary to note that this chapter does not seek to address all aspects of supervision. For example, most of the examples refer to social workers rather than to other people employed by Social Services or Social Work Departments such as staff in residential or home care settings, occupational therapists and volunteers. Many texts are available on the theory and practice of supervision and the bibliography at the end of this chapter is a comprehensive list.

Supervision in theory

Aims of supervision

Kadushin (1992), in the most comprehensive text on supervision, reviews the history and meaning of the term. He distinguishes social work supervision from an 'orthodox' meaning of the term, which emphasises checking that a job is done 'at a quantitatively and qualitatively acceptable level' (p.19). He identified three aspects of supervision: the administrative or managerial component; the educational component, where the supervisor provides on-going training explicitly or implicitly; and the 'expressive – supportive – leadership function', including maintaining morale, removing discontent which arises from the job and helping supervisees feel worthwhile, secure and belonging to the agency. Other writers link the latter two aspects. In social work either the managerial or professional component is the major aspect of supervision; writers draw a clear distinction, but differ about which aspect is more important.

Managerial supervision focuses on the worker's accountability to the agency and the agency's obligations to its staff – such as providing necessary resources and experienced advice. Caseload management was a frequent concern of many writers in the mid to late 1970s and early 1980s (Glastonbury et al. 1987). A distinction has been made between supervision with its concern about daily functioning in relation to particular cases or episodes of work, and periodic or one-off evaluation of the worker's performance, either as an aspect of performance appraisal or as a contribution to the evaluation of the outcome of social work intervention (Kadushin 1992, Warner 1992).

Professional supervision comprises support for the individual worker and an educative aspect, sometimes seen as a progression from the guidance given to students on practice placements.

An important debate from the 1970s onwards has been about the extent to which supervision needs to be maintained in the face of, or as an integral part of, 'effective management' (Douglas 1990). In other words, is supervision a form of defence by social workers – as staff and managers – of the professional aspects of social work against a managerial concern with effectiveness and concepts such as performance review? Indeed, it is questionable how far there is acceptance within the social work profession of there being a legitimate review of performance.

The balance between managerial and professional supervision might be expected to vary according to the circumstances of the social worker's recent experiences. Most writers have considered the functioning and contribution of supervision, when cases are progressing as expected and the worker and team are not under undue pressures. Here, professional supervision is often presented as the more important aspect. In contrast, some of the strongest endorsements of managerial supervision have been in the official reports of reviews and inquiries following deaths of children under social work supervision or other serious breakdowns of social work practice such as the abuse of children or older people in residential care. Here, supervision has been claimed to be an appropriate and potentially effective means of monitoring standards and raising the quality of the social work response to clients and of supporting and teaching skills to social workers and other staff dealing with difficult cases (DoH 1990).

Another important development has been the creation of a stronger distinction between consultation and supervision, although this some- times leads to confusion about accountability among workers and super- visors. Brown (1984) sees supervision as fundamentally organisational whereas consultation is professional in its focus and excludes managerial responsibilities. He also distinguishes consultation, which is about spe- cific cases and problems, from education, which is about broader devel- opment.

Figure 5.1 provides a detailed list of specific objectives of supervision identified in the professional literature and in various reviews. Some objectives reflect more clearly the managerial or professional focus but most incorporate both aspects.

Supervision and accountability

Most writers, in their own analysis and in reporting the views of social workers, regard the line manager as the most appropriate supervisor. The reasons are that this person is directly accountable for the worker's performance, has responsibility for the team workload and usually has greater professional experience than other members of the team, with the theoretical and practical knowledge to assess performance and give guid- ance. The development of team leadership has led to supervision being linked with teamwork.

Not all writers agree that supervision must be related to the manager's accountability for the worker's performance, however. Rowbottom *et al.* (1974) found many examples where supervision in the educational and supportive sense was carried out by someone who had no accountability for the supervisee's work.

- Enabling social workers to deliver more effective care
- Making sure clients get maximum benefit from agency and related services
- Maintaining standards and morale in social work agencies or units (e.g. residential care, teams)
- Monitoring workload levels (e.g. to ensure fairness, avoid potentially dangerous overloading)
- On-going review and planning of cases by social worker and supervisor
- Objectivity and critical analysis in casework
- Introducing a second opinion
- Preventing or checking inappropriate staff responses to cases
- Opportunity for staff to raise concerns about their own cases or other matters
- Professional development of staff
- Opportunity for staff to get positive feedback
- Enabling social workers to deal with their own feelings (e.g. in difficult or distressing situations)
- Keeping senior staff informed
- Ensuring court orders, statutory requirements and other obligations are discharged
- Maintaining good standards of professional performance
- Giving staff strategies for self management
- Managing change in an organisation

Main sources: Pettes 1979, Collins and Bruce 1984, Cypher 1982, Buckle 1981, DHSS 1978, Parsloe 1982, Payne 1979, 1982. Other sources are not identified here for reasons of space but all are noted in the references elsewhere in this chapter and in the bibliography.

Figure 5.1: Specific objectives of supervision

Forms of supervision

Methods of individual supervision developed during the 1970s and 1980s, promoting forms which are more focused and explicit. An example is Pettes' (1979) 'task-centred' approach in which specific managerial or educational tasks for the supervision session are established, and broader personal support, if offered at all, is given within these. Several writers (Atherton 1986; Parsloe 1978; Robinson 1978; Danbury 1986) propose that a formal 'contract' should be established between the supervisor and worker, covering the expectations of supervision from the points of view of both parties and of the agency.

Payne and Scott (1982) follow the modern convention that supervision should relate to the team or unit rather than individuals and identify a range of possible supervision arrangements involving groups and pairs. They contend that contracts should create an explicit agreement about the focus, content, methods and arrangements for supervision. The objectives of supervision in their view should be:

- consistency of line management with agency functions by monitoring priorities, planning, reviewing and evaluating work in formal supervision sessions, case reviews and through caseload management
- clarification of roles and responsibilities of the supervisor and worker, with the major aim of relieving stress on workers which impairs service delivery
- influencing the agency to develop a suitable climate for practice
- assisting workers' professional development by improving both their skills and knowledge.

Butler and Elliott (1985) review a range of methods used in supervision, which they divide into direct and indirect methods according to whether the worker and supervisor have access to direct evidence of the worker's interaction with clients. Direct methods use, for example, video recordings or viewing of worker-client interactions, and 'live' supervision, where the supervisor is present and gives advice during the course of the interaction. Indirect methods use workers' verbal accounts, agency records or more detailed 'process' records of practice. The availability of new technology has made direct methods of supervision more practicable, but Butler and Elliott found they were not commonly used outside clinical settings.

Summary: supervision and performance review in theory
The literature on supervision indicates that its role in performance review is ambivalent.

- Social work supervision differs from a 'common sense' understanding of supervision in including elements of education and support alongside checking on performance.

- In professional supervision the assessment of the worker's performance is sometimes implicit rather than explicit and in some instances may not occur.

- On the other hand, managerial supervision always involves some form of evaluation of the worker's performance and compliance with agency policies and procedures.

- It is uncertain whether this compliance is about quality of service, or merely about following procedures which may be necessary to efficiency but do not necessarily indicate good standards of professional practice.

- The professional development element of supervision is so dominant that managerial supervision conflicts with this, and social workers – both as supervisors and supervisees – on the whole dislike that conflict.

- Recent developments in supervision tend to emphasise responsibility for co-ordinating work within a team, rather than individual supervision which can address the quality of response to clients and the handling of specific cases.

- Distinguishing consultation about cases from managerial and teamwork aspects of a supervisor's role also suggests that developmental supervision can be separated from checking compliance with procedures.

- Similarly, the 'leadership' aspect of managing change is downplayed in favour of teaching and monitoring, which tends to maintain existing approaches to practice.

What happens in practice within supervision?

So far, we have been concerned with evidence about professional assumptions and prescriptions of practice. How far are these borne out in reality?

Aims and form of supervision

Some general studies of supervision offer a clear perspective on how it is practised. It involves one-to-one sessions between the individual worker and supervisor, supported occasionally by group supervision, emphasising supportive and educative functions. Workers are more dissatisfied with supervision than supervisors, at least partly because they want more critical supervision, and would in certain circumstances accept an element of managerial control. However, supervisors reject or feel uneasy about this managerial aspect. This evidence is consistent over the last 15 years and in several different countries. These findings do not suggest, as the theory discussed above does, that supervision offers a place for evaluation of workers aimed at discovering their achievement of agency objectives in accordance with clear indicators.

The findings of studies show that:

- supervisors report more favourably than workers on the frequency and planning of supervision
- supervisors see their authority stemming from expertise rather than their role in the organisation; workers are more aware of the supervisor's organisational power
- the aspects most valued by workers are competent teaching, an opportunity to share worries, receiving advice and feedback to enable them to improve skills and handling of current cases
- workers look for critical feedback and monitoring of their performance within a supportive setting
- newly qualified staff receive more frequent and more challenging supervision than do experienced staff, who would welcome a return to that type of supervision
- workers attach less importance and value to supervision addressing mainly managerial aspects, including checking on agency requirements
- particularly in the UK, supervisors are less comfortable about managerial aspects when integrated with developmental aspects.

Figure 5.2 draws together the findings of a range of studies on the ways the professional and managerial aspects of supervision are embodied in practice.

Studies in particular settings have found variations within this overall pattern. These can reflect shifts in management practice or expectations over time or different agency policies and cultures. Other reasons for the variations are discussed below. What they confirm is that there is no single approach to supervision or set of views about its value and limitations.

	Professional	*Managerial*
Aims	Support for individual worker	Accountability to agency
	Professional development	Good quality service delivery
	Advice and consultation: • specific cases • wider development	Monitoring workload levels
Form	Task-centred approach	Task-centred approach
	Individual or collective supervision	Individual or collective supervision
Accountability to agency	None or minimal	Low
Who is Supervisor	Experienced professional, who may be line manager	Line manager
Decision-making	Seeking advice or professional second opinion	Approval by line manager of past or intended action (or remedial action) by worker
	Discussion/collaboration preparatory to the decision	
View of Supervisor	Preferred role and form of supervision	Reluctant to manage
View of Supervisee	Helpful	Ambiguous – often reluctant to be managed

Figure 5.2: Supervision in practice: Overview of key aspects

Recent studies and accounts of practice (e.g. Kadushin 1992, Douglas 1990) and descriptions of practice in reviews (e.g. Warner 1992, Borland 1992, Pithouse 1987, O'Connor 1988) suggest that supervision is coming under increased pressure and that there is more cause for concern now. Particular issues are:

- supervision not being done due to other work pressures on supervisor and/or worker; or staff shortages or changes
- greater tendency for it to be rushed and matters considered not to be urgent repeatedly postponed
- supervisors becoming more hesitant about exercising managerial authority and about addressing managerial issues on which, however, they feel under pressure to concentrate
- supervisors describing high levels of concern about workers' well-being and emphasising the need for supervision to provide support
- supervision more commonly being done by people who are not accountable for the supervisee's work – for example, in response to concerns that managerial and development/supportive aspects be kept separate or as a consequence of current organisation of agencies with, for example, specialists working to non-specialists and inter-disciplinary teams
- supervisors not having the skills or training to address all aspects of the worker's role or to give supervision of an acceptable standard
- the extent to which supervision is mainly used – especially by experienced workers – to legitimise practice and to offer consultation rather than test practice in an objective and systematic way.

Reasons for supervision practice

Various findings identify factors that influence the supervisor's response:

- **other pressures:** when supervisors are under pressure from wider responsibilities, they resist regular sessions that their workers want in favour of making consultation available and try to avoid close semi-therapeutic involvement with their workers (Satyamurti 1981).
- **the nature of the organisation and its requirements** (Taverner 1989): an agency with more formal responsibilities will require more managerial supervision than one which is more therapeutic in approach.
- **the nature of the case:** Fisher *et al.*'s (1984) study of mental health work in three social services teams showed that regular supervision broke down except for consultation over crises, and workers resisted the routine managerial checking that regular supervision often involved. Supervisors spent more time on organised supervision of

qualified workers dealing with families with young children mainly because the agency gave greater priority to such work.

- **the formal requirements of job contracts or the type of worker:** in one study (Hadley and McGrath 1984) of a social services team, the supervisor declined to provide supervision because the grade of worker was defined as not requiring regular supervision. The pattern of work in the team thus became one of informal advice, consultation and peer support.

Supervision and child protection

Particular attention has been given to supervision in child protection work, where the tensions between the managerial and professional aspects are particularly acute and where decision-making is under close examination. The need for both aspects has been emphasised in reports of formal inquiries since the early 1980s (DoH 1990), yet evidence to subsequent reviews has shown that these recommendations have not been put into effect by all agencies. As a further distortion of good practice, there is in some agencies a culture which emphasises the process of supervision (as a protection for the agency or for individual staff) rather than the outcome of better child care and more effective response from confident, capable social workers.

Evans's (1990) collation of the experiences of supervisors of child protection team leaders suggests that the growth of procedures and the importance of inter-agency work for which supervisors were not well-prepared leads to a concentration in this field on compliance with formal processes rather than more creative supervision which properly address all its aims. Waters' detailed study (1992) of the process of supervision in complex child protection cases shows that supervision is experienced as unhelpful. The reasons for this lie in a tension between the needs of both groups of staff and conventions about the role of supervisors. As a result, workers felt unable to raise the issue of personal stress they experienced in such cases while the supervisors did not enquire into their workers' need for help. Waters proposes that specialist teams where such conventions could be relaxed would help; alternatively, she proposes separation of management and consultation about cases.

Important events or decisions as cases develop can often be the occasion for supervisory interventions, because it is at such points that a worker is obliged to seek a supervisor's approval for some action. Some commentary (e.g. Douglas 1990) suggests that anxiety about the public consequences of difficult statutory child care decisions has led to systems for involving supervisors explicitly in such decisions. Critical incidents can then form the basis for an attempt at quality control through performance review (Rosen 1993), because a fairly explicit decision subject to clear criteria can be identified and explored on a rational basis. Two studies of child care decision-making in local authorities (Clifford and Powell 1988, Wilkinson 1983) showed that decisions at planned reviews in long-term cases usually involved a supervisor, but in one of the authorities decisions to admit children only involved a supervisor in 30 per cent of cases. In the other authority a supervisor was involved unless the worker was very experienced.

However, such decision-making processes are often quite unlike the processes in conventional supervision. Sinclair (1984) studied decision-making in 292 statutory reviews on children in care in three area offices in a social services department. Reviews in area teams tended to be brief discussions between the supervisor and worker, together with perhaps one other person, while in children's homes, such reviews were like multi-disciplinary case conferences. In both cases the reviews were seen as a separate process from supervision. Vernon and Fruin (1986) studied decision-making on 185 children during admission and retention in care by 11 local authorities. They found that most decisions were made by social workers or by pressure of events and were only legitimated by supervisors, who often did not see it as their jobs to make decisions, but simply checked on the course of events in formal reviews.

Conclusions

Supervision, as described in the social work theoretical and research literature, has two elements; managerial and professional (which combines educational and supportive responses). Carrying out these functions involves supervisors in making judgements about their workers, using those judgements to inform the help that they give, which should in turn improve their workers' functioning. Part of the managerial aspect of supervision is ensuring compliance with agency requirements, which may effect statutory requirements, so that some form of review of the worker's performance against agency policies is implied. The quality of workers' intervention – including the standards and outcome for the client – can also be addressed. However, the research evidence shows that this is not usually done in a systematic way against explicit standards.

Reliance on workers' accounts of their practice and the circumstances in which supervision often occurs – infrequent, rushed, separated from management responsibilities – place further limitations on the extent to which supervision can permit an objective review of performance.

A further limitation is the predominance of the developmental and supportive aspects of supervision. Excessive concern for managerial supervision is resented by both workers and supervisors, who feel that this clashes with support, which is their first priority. Further, supervisors are ambivalent and confused about or resistant to using authoritative power as part of supervision. One other consequence of this tension is that in areas where procedural compliance is crucial, such as child protection, supportive supervision may be lost when it is most needed.

In both theory and practice, supervision does not fulfil its potential and claimed value as a means of reviewing social workers' performance. Social work is an unusual occupation in that provision has been made for a form of detailed support and guidance through 'personal supervision'. Occupations such as teaching, in which mentoring is just being introduced, and other areas of local government where there is only a traditional managerial role, might reasonably be envious. Yet this review of recent experience of supervision shows that its implementation in today's social work services is far from the ideal represented in the professional literature.

The future of personal supervision

If this picture of supervision in the late 20th century is an appropriate one, what might its future be? Three scenarios encompass the possibilities.

The first scenario is a break between the professional and the managerial aspects. Supervision addresses only the professional aspects, and is part of a resurgence of professional consciousness which acknowledges the skilled contribution which social workers are making to action on social problems and a commitment to creativity in exploring social workers' professional roles. One of the central requirements here is the methodology and terminology to enable supervisors to analyse the detail of social work interactions between clients and workers.

In the second scenario, the managerial and professional aspects of supervision are reconciled. Supervisors develop both aspects of personal supervision, combining these with techniques derived from mentoring and other recent developments, and clarify the supervisor's role in relation to more systematic forms of performance review and quality assurance.

The third – and in my view most horrific – scenario is a rejection of the professional aspects of supervision: a descent into unthinking adherence to politically and bureaucratically defined roles, implemented procedurally rather than through professional discretion and creativity, and enforced by managerial sanctions and crude quality assurance mechanisms. Such an outcome offers little comfort to all those who value what social work can offer to the most oppressed and disadvantaged members of society, or to all those who suffer problems and difficulties and who might be helped by the skills and knowledge of social workers.

References

Atherton, J.S. (1986) *Professional Supervision in Group Care: A Contract-Based Approach.* London: Tavistock.

Borland, M. (1992) *The Review of Residential Child Care in Scotland: Evaluation of Statements of Functions and Objectives of Scottish Children's Homes.* Edinburgh: Central Research Unit, Scottish Office.

Brown, A. (1984) *Consultation.* London: Heinemann.

Buckle, J. (1981) *Intake Teams.* London: Tavistock.

Butler, B. and Eliott, D. (1985) *Teaching and Learning in Practice.* Aldershot, Hants.: Gower.

Clifford, B. and Powell, D. (1988) 'Child care practice in the Gloucester area'. *Social Services Research 1.*

Collins, T. and Bruce, T. (1984) *Staff Support and Staff Training.* London: Tavistock.

Cypher, J. (ed) (1982) *The Task of the Team Leader.* Birmingham: BASW Publications.

Danbury, H. (1986) *Teaching Practical Social Work.* Aldershot, Hants.: Gower.

DHSS (1978) *Social Services Teams: The Practitioner's View.* London: HMSO.

DoH (Department of Health) (1990) *Child Abuse: A Study of Inquiry Reports, 1980–1989.* London: HMSO.

Douglas, A. (1990) 'Nothing to lose'. *Community Care,* 4th January, 16–17.

Evans, M. (1990) *Report on the Issues for Front-line Managers in Managing Child Protection Services.* Leeds: National Institute for Social Work.

Fisher, M., Newton, C. and Sainsbury, E. (1984) *Mental Health Social Work Observed.* London: Allen and Unwin.

Glastonbury, B. et al. (1987) *Managing People in the Personal Social Services.* Chichester: Wiley.

Hadley, R. and McGrath, M. (1984) *When Social Services are Local: The Normanton Experience.* London: Allen and Unwin.

Kadushin, A. (1992) *Supervision in Social Work.* New York: Columbia University Press.

O'Connor, G.G. (1988) 'Case management: system and practice'. *Social Casework* 69(2), 97–106.

Parsloe, P. (1978) 'The use of contracts on a social work course', in Stevenson, O. (ed) *Trends in Social work Education*. London: Association of Teachers in Social Work Education.

Parsloe, P. (1982) *Social Services Area Teams*. London: Allen and Unwin.

Payne, C. and Scott, T. (1982) *Developing Supervision of Teams in Field and Residential Social Work*. London: National Institute for Social Work.

Payne, M. (1979) *Power, Authority and Responsibility in Social Services: Social Work in Area Teams*. London: Macmillan.

Payne, M. (1982) *Working in Teams*. London: Macmillan.

Pettes, D.E. (1979) *Staff and Student Supervision: A Task-Centred Approach*. London: Allen and Unwin.

Pithouse, A. (1987) *Social Work: The Social Organisation of an Invisible Trade*. Aldershot, Hants: Avebury.

Robinson, M. (1978) 'Contract-making in social work practice: an experiment in social work education', in Stevenson, O. (ed) *Trends in Social Work Education*. London: Association of Teachers in Social Work Education.

Rosen, A. (1993) 'Systematic planned practice'. *Social Service Review* 67(1), March, 84–100.

Rowbottom, R., Hey, A. and Billis, D. (1974) *Social Services Departments: Developing Patterns of Work and Organisation*. London: Heinemann.

Satyamurti, C. (1981) *Occupational Survival*. Oxford: Blackwell.

Sinclair, R. (1984) *Decision-making in Statutory Reviews on Children in Care*. Aldershot, Hants: Gower.

Taverner, P. (1989) 'Supervision and the nature of the organisation'. *Social Work Education* 8, 25–28.

Vernon, J. and Fruin, D. (1986) *In Care: A Study of Social Work Decision-Making*. London: National Children's Bureau.

Warner, N. (Chairman)(1992) *Choosing with Care: The Report of the Committee of Inquiry into the Selection, Development and Management of Staff in Children's Homes*. London: HMSO.

Waters, J.G. (1992) *The Supervision of Child Protection Work*. Aldershot, Hants: Avebury.

Wilkinson, A. (1983) 'Children who come into care in Tower Hamlets'. *Clearing House for Local Authority Social Services Research*, 1983(1).

Bibliography

Addison, C. (1988) *Social Work Supervision in a Local Authority*. London: Wandsworth Social Services Department.

Austin, L.N. (1963) 'The changing role of the supervisor', in Parad, H.J. and Miller, R.R. *Ego-oriented Casework: Problems and Perspectives*. New York: Family Service Association of America.

Cherniss, C. and Egnatios, E. (1979) 'Clinical supervision in community mental health', in Munson, C.E. (ed) op. cit., 244–257.

Clare, M. (1988) 'Supervision, role strain and social services departments'. *British Journal of Social Work* 18(4), 489–507.

Cockburn, J. (1990) *Team Leaders and Team Managers in Social Services*. Norwich: University of East Anglia, Social Services Monographs.

Cypher, J. (ed) (1982) *Team Leadership in the Social Services*. Birmingham: BASW Publications.

Darvill, G. and Munday, B. (1984) *Volunteers in the Personal Social Services*. London: Tavistock.

Davies, M. (1988) *Staff Supervision in the Probation Service: Keeping Pace with Change*. Aldershot, Hants: Avebury.

Dublin, R.A. (1989) 'Supervision and leadership styles'. *Social Casework* 70, 617–621.

Fineman, S. (1985) *Social Work Stress and Intervention*. Aldershot, Hants: Gower.

Goldberg, E.M. and Warburton, R.W. (1979) *Ends and Means in Social Work: The Development and Outcome of a Case Review System for Social Workers*. London: Allen and Unwin.

Hall, A. (1975) 'Policy-making: more judgement than luck'. *Community Care*, 6th August, 16–18.

Hayes, L.S. and O'Connor, M.R. (1982) 'Emotional aspects of supervision: an eap workshop'. *Social Casework* 63(7), 408–414.

Hurlbert, D.F. (1992) 'Changing the views of social work supervision: an administrative challenge'. *The Clinical Supervisor* 10(2), 57–69.

Kakabadse, A.P. and Worrall, R. (1978) 'Job satisfaction and organisational structure: a comparative study of nine social services departments'. *British Journal of Social Work* 8(1), 51–70.

Kadushin, A. (1979) 'Supervisor-supervisee: a survey', in Munson, C.E. (ed) op. cit., 244–257.

Kadushin, A. (1992) 'What's wrong, what's right with social work supervision?' *The Clinical Supervisor* 10(1), 3–19.

Ko, G.P. (1987) 'Casework supervision in voluntary family service agencies in Hong Kong'. *International Social Work* 30, 171–184.

Lewis, S. (1987) 'The role of self-awareness in social work supervision'. *Australian Social Work* 40, 19–24.

Munson, C.E. (ed) (1979) *Social Work Supervision: Classic Statements and Critical Issues*. New York: Free Press.

Munson, C.E. (1979) 'An empirical study of structure and authority in social work supervision', in Munson, C.E. (ed) op cit, 286–296.

Nixon, S. (1982) 'The need for working agreements: social workers' expectations of their team leaders in supervision', in Cypher, J. (ed) *Team Leadership in the Social Services*. Birmingham: BASW Publications.

Orme, J. (1987) 'Workload management in the probation service', in Glastonbury, B., Bradley, R. and Orme, J. *Managing People in the Personal Social Services*. Chichester, Hants: John Wiley.

Saari, C. (1989) 'The process of learning in clinical social work'. *Smith College Studies in Social Work* 60, 35–49.

Smith, P.B. (1984) 'Social services teams and their managers'. *British Journal of Social Work* 14(6), 601–613.

Thigpen, J.D. (1979) 'Perceptional differences in the supervision of paraprofessional mental health workers'. *Community Mental Health Journal* 15(2), 139–148.

Thoburn, J. (1986) 'Quality control in child care'. *British Journal of Social Work* 16(6), 543–556.

Vickery, A. (1977) *Caseload Management: A Guide for Supervisors and Staff.* London: National Institute for Social Work.

Webb, N.B. (1988) 'The role of the field instructor in the socialisation of students'. *Social Casework* 69(1), 35–40.

Whitmore, R. and Fuller, R. (1980) 'Priority planning in an area social services team'. *British Journal of Social Work* 10(3), 277–292.

Yodefet, Y., Yaakovson, Y. and Pinto, M. (1978) 'The relationship between the social worker and his supervisor: dependence or independence?' *Society and Welfare*, August.

Part 2

User Perspectives

Chapter 6

User Perspectives on Community Care Assessment

Sue Brace

Introduction

This chapter looks at how users and carers are likely to define 'quality' in the new arrangements for assessing people's individual community care needs from April 1993, and at what 'user participation' may mean in practice. It takes as its context the Government's wider plans for public care services in the 1990s, and the specific government guidance to local authorities on implementing assessment and care management. The 'seven stages of assessment' proposed in the guidance are used as a framework for evaluating how users and carers might be involved in and evaluate the quality of their own assesssments and care plans.

Assessing people's community care needs: changes in the law

New arrangements for assessing people's community care needs in Britain spring from the NHS and Community Care Act 1990, implemented in stages from 1991-1993. Born out of the Griffiths Report (Griffiths 1988) which led to the Government's White Paper 'Caring for People' (Secretaries of State 1989), and closely allied in terms of policy to the proposals for changes in the National Health Service outlined in the White Paper 'Working for Patients' (Secretary of State for Health 1989), the legislation involves the following related changes in how individual needs are assessed and services planned:

- Since April 1993, local authorities have had the lead role for ensuring the appropriate assessment of people's individual needs, for the procuring of non-health care services to meet each person's assessed needs and for coordinating individual care plans. Unmet care needs must be noted and aggregated as a basis for planning better area services.

Local authorities have been given the lead role in the coordination and planning of community care services in their area, but must work closely with other agencies, in particular with Health Boards/Health Authorities. From 1992 an annual Community Care Plan must be produced for each area.

The assessment of people's individual need is described in 'Caring for People' as the 'cornerstone of quality care'. Good assessment is seen as having two important functions. First, it should provide an accurate picture of what each person wants and needs as the basis of their own 'care plan', with a clear mechanism for complaints if the person is not satisfied. Second, information on what cannot be provided for individuals ('gaps' in services) should be logged and aggregated in order to plan better and more flexible future services. If the theory is correct, then the ultimate effectiveness of community care policy will depend on the quality of individual needs assessments, linked to local planning mechanisms.

This chapter focuses solely on the arrangements for assessing people's community care needs. Written just as the 1990 Act was being fully implemented, the chapter anticipates how the assessment model may work in practice. Major current concerns about the resources available for community care are not directly addressed, although for users and carers the availability of actual services to meet their assessed needs will be a significant factor in their judgement of local assessment and care planning arrangements.

The wider context: promoting quality in public services

The professional principles and political motivations behind the new arrangements are complex and relate only in part to improving quality and consumer satisfaction; regulating costs is known to have been equally important in prompting the new legislation. The new arrangements for community care are thus part and parcel of a wider set of explicit government plans to shape public services in the 1990s. The broad objective is to separate purchasing from the provision of services, with public sector care agencies increasingly acting as purchasers and enablers rather than direct providers. Much more diverse services are expected from 'independent' trusts in health care, and for private and voluntary organisations in social care. It is argued that the creation of competition through a 'mixed economy' of care will improve both the range of services and their value for money and, through this, user choice.

So far as achieving consumer satisfaction in public services is concerned, the government urges that local authorities do this by improving the range and therefore choice of services for users, explicitly stating standards of service and ensuring that there is a clear plan for community care service developments in their area. A procedure for complaints and suggestions is made a statutory duty (Griffiths 1988, DOH/SSI/SWSG 1991a, b). (Complaints procedures are fully discussed in the chapter by McClay.) Thus 'Caring for People' talks at the outset of 'promoting choice and independence' in social and health care and promises that the changes will 'give people a greater individual say in how they live their lives and the services they need to help them to do so'.

In addition to these specific aims for community care, a series of high profile government charters for consumers of public services has been produced in the past two years, headed by the 'Citizen's Charter' (Prime Minister 1991). All pledge that consumers will have better information about services, fair treatment and openness in their dealings with public sector services and explicit standards. John Major believes that the Citizen's Charter 'gives more power to the individual citizen' (Prime Minister and Chancellor of Duchy of Lancaster 1992), but in fact the Charter does not in itself offer people basic, enforceable entitlement to services, nor the right in law to fair treatment of their needs (Coote 1992). There is also no charter specifically for social or community care services. (This, and wider aspects of the relationship of the Citizen's Charter to social care, are discussed in the chapter by Black.) Users must instead look for local definitions of minimum standards for community care services, including assessment, and to enforcement, if necessary, through the NHS and Community Care Act 1990 and the Disabled Persons (Services and Representation) Act 1986. For the government view on how these broad principles are to be put into practice in community care we must look to its own guidance to local authorities.

Government guidance: quality in assessment and user/carer involvement

Government guidance to local authorities on the new assessment arrangements has come from a number of sources. In 1989 broad aspirations for standards were outlined in the White Paper 'Caring for People' (DOH/SSI 1989) which said that:

- users and carers must have adequate information about services and about the assessment process
- assessment must be timeous, as simple and effective as possible, and multidisciplinary wherever possible
- carers' needs should be assessed separately
- people with complex needs should always have a care plan with a care manager whose job it is to coordinate the plan
- a record of the person's unmet needs should be made to inform service planning.

The White Paper introduces the principle of the user's and carer's 'proper participation' in assessment. The meaning of this term is crucial to users and carers and has been much debated. It is not, however, defined in detail in the White Paper, which says that assessors will simply 'take into account the wishes of the individual and his or her carer'. This approach seems to be confirmed in a recent widely advertised government leaflet in which users and carers are told that Social Services/Social Work Departments will assess what help they need, will take into account their wishes and will then 'decide what help can be arranged for you' (DOH/SWSG 1993). For many user and carer groups this would not rank as 'proper participation'.

The White Paper also stresses that assessment of need will have to operate 'within available resources', with local definitions of eligibility and priority both for assessment and services. The public are reminded of this in the same leaflet which says that the changes will mean 'using the money that Social Services Departments and the NHS have to spend to best effect'.

The broad terms of reference of the White Paper were followed a year later by more detailed guidance for local authorities on assessment and care management. This came in the shape both of specific government circulars (e.g. SWSG 1991) and more substantially through the SSI/SWSG 'Practitioners' Guide' and 'Managers' Guide' (DOH/SSI/SWSG 1991a,b). These outline the 'shared values' which should govern how users and carers experience community care assessments and services. These are the **rights of citizenship, independence, privacy, dignity and individuality, individual choice, and realisation of individual aspirations and abili-**

ties. The Guides accept that these may not be straightforward in application but propose that the quality standards by which assessment and care management are evaluated should be firmly rooted in these principles.

The assessment model

The Practitioners' Guide proposes a seven-stage model of individual needs assessment. The stages are:

(1) Publishing information about services

(2) Determining the level of assessment

(3) Assessing need

(4) Care planning

(5) Implementing the care plan

(6) Monitoring the care plan

(7) Reviewing the care plan.

This framework is used in the remainder of this chapter to examine how 'quality' in assessment might be defined at each stage by users and carers. For each stage there is a brief description of what is involved, followed by general comments and finally a summary of the key 'quality' pointers for users and carers.

1. Publishing information

Good information about what services are available should be in a form which is readily accessible and takes account of different sensory impairments, communication difficulties, language and cultural needs. This is seen by users and carers themselves as a fundamental requirement. Research studies in community and health care have consistently documented how lack of information, and confusing or conflicting information, can compound the difficulties which people face (Willcocks *et al.* 1982, Bland and Bland 1985, Hudson 1990, Samuel *et al.* 1991, Allen *et al.* 1992).

The 1990 Act requires local authorities to consult on and publish their area Community Care Plan – giving users information about general services, strategies and policies. It also requires them to establish and publicise a complaints procedure. Both requirements are of crucial importance to users and carers, and are closely linked with assessment of individual need. (Elements of both are dealt with in detail in the chapters by Barnes and Wistow, and McClay.)

The government also requires local authorities to publish specific information on their assessment and care management arrangements (DOH/SSI 1989, SWSG June 1991). The practice guidance described above fully recognises the importance of the information itself and of involving users and carers in preparing it (DOH/SSI/SWSG 1991a,b). The Managers' Guide, for example, calls information 'one of the most effective ways of empowering users and carers' and advises a range of publicity material which takes account of different audiences (for example the public, professionals and care agencies and elected members), using a variety of media. The material should clearly explain what the eligibility criteria are for assessment and services, and promote realistic expectations about community care.

More detail was provided in the report 'Getting the Message Across' (DOH/SSI 1991) – a step-by-step guide to developing publicity material for community care. This suggests involving user and carer groups and minority ethnic groups in development work, and sharing ideas and drafts with users and carers at appropriate stages.

Few would argue with the desirability of these proposals, but how achievable are they in practice? Involving people in any meaningful way with the development of publicity material requires particular thought. There are a variety of options: large planning meetings can be off-putting and smaller working groups may be needed; professionals may go out by invitation to existing organisations; user and carer groups may be given a budget to develop their own material. Approaches may also be needed to individuals who are not part of a group (most housebound older people, for example). At a practical level, translators may be needed, carers may need sitting arrangements for the person they care for, some users may need special transport arrangements and reimbursement for travel costs. It takes time, effort and resources to build up the trust needed for a real partnership (Harding 1993, Ellis 1993).

Whilst many local authorities, user and carer groups have embarked on innovative work, there may be difficulties in achieving these standards widely. Hard-pressed local authorities must balance spending on information for users against resources for services and need to have achievable publicity strategies which have the involvement and support of users, carers and minority ethnic groups and the full backing of local councillors.

In summary, community care publicity will be judged by different users and carers on:

- whether it is widely available and easily understood
- whether it tells people what they really want to know
- whether it is available in different formats – for example on tape or in Braille
- whether it has been translated into other, minority ethnic languages
- whether it is updated regularly
- whether it seems to be value for public money
- whether the local agencies make a commitment to a publicity strategy which involves users and carers and which has the understanding of the general public and the support of councillors.

2. Determining the level of assessment

The next key stage in the assessment process is the initial response made to the user. Aspects of this include appropriate reception of enquiries; user requests for assessment; and how these are acted on.

Asking for help is not easy for many people; clear information about who is eligible for an assessment of need, and who has priority for a full assessment, is essential for users and carers. In any locality this will be influenced by the definitions of 'need' used by the local authority.

The government guidance describes need as a 'dynamic concept, the definition of which will vary over time' (DOH/SSI/SWSG 1991a). It also suggests that need must be defined at a local level, taking into account local factors including those of current resources, and acknowledges that 'no two individuals will perceive or define their needs in exactly the same way'. This open-ended definition means that whilst users and carers can legitimately say what they require, this will always be interpreted through local policy and met if possible 'within available resources'. The 1990 Act does not mean an abandonment of limited budgets and priorities, as many users' and carers' national pressure groups were quick to recognise when the legislation was unveiled.

At a practical level, each person's experience of asking for help can be coloured significantly by what happens when contact is first made with an agency or organisation – for example by the state of the waiting area and interview rooms; the attitude of the receptionist; how long it takes for the phone to be answered or to be seen or put through to someone who can help; and the attitude and helpfulness of this person (SWSG 1991). The importance of these basic, practical considerations cannot be over-emphasised. Even a first rate assessment service may find it hard to compensate for an unsatisfactory reception.

Once past the initial contact, users and carers need to know whether their request for assessment is to be accepted and, if so, how quickly. 'Screening' will determine the type of assessment which will follow (simple/complex/specialist etc.), and recommend how quickly action should be taken and by whom. This is the first point at which 'eligibility' and 'priority' criteria will be formally applied; users and carers will want to know quickly whether the answer on each count is 'yes' or 'no'. Feelings are likely to be influenced by how well the criteria are publicly understood; how they have been explained to the user or carer in particular; and whether the user or carer feels that the rules have been fairly applied. If the user considers the outcome unfair, then the ease of challenging the decision and the speed with which the local authority responds to the complaint will all be major measures of quality from the consumer's perspective. People who are disabled have a right to a comprehensive assessment under the 1990 Act, 'irrespective of the scale of need that is initially presented' (DOH/SSI/SWSG 1991a). Under the Act, disabled people can strongly challenge any refusal of assessment.

Many people are referred to Social Work/Social Services Departments by other professionals – for example by their general practitioner or district nurse. Good reception, clearly understood criteria of eligibility and priority, and quick and effective decision-making are equally important to referring professionals. Clear feedback to the referrer on the outcome of the request will be essential, and good working relationships between key local professionals and services will also enhance the quality of the user's experience by preventing misunderstandings and disputes in which the user becomes a pawn; users and carers will judge the assessment service at second hand when someone is acting on their behalf.

In summary, users and carers will judge the quality of their first contact with social care agencies according to:

- whether the office waiting area and interview rooms are welcoming and pleasant or dingy and depressing
- how long it takes for the phone to be answered
- the attitude of the receptionist or telephonist

- how long it takes to be seen or put through to someone who can give advice
- whether the staff understand their language
- the attitude and knowledge of the person who eventually sees or speaks to them
- whether the eligibility and priority criteria for assessment are fully explained
- whether other professionals referring on their behalf work closely with community care assessors, understand any criteria operating and get quick feedback on their referral
- whether the request for assessment is accepted, and how quickly.

3. Assessing need

In this third stage of the process, assessors should seek 'to understand the user's needs, to relate to them and to any agency policies and priorities, and to agree the objectives for any intervention' (DOH/SSI/SWSG 1991a). The Practitioners' Guide further comments that 'a significant change in attitude and approach' will be needed by most practitioners in order to separate the assessment of need from the known availability of services, and to ensure the active participation of users in their assessments. This comment is supported by research in this field (e.g. Bland and Bland 1985; Hunter *et al.* 1987, Brace 1988, Buckley 1989, Samuel *et al.* 1991, Allen *et al.* 1992) which has documented the current approach to assessment of social and health care professionals.

All the social and health care professions emphasise the need to observe people's individuality, and in recent years the 'empowerment' of users and carers has been keenly discussed in the social work profession in particular. However, ensuring users' active participation in an assessment process previously 'owned' by the professional does present challenges. Some individual professionals will embrace user participation more quickly than others, and the culture and expectations of some professional groups may make it difficult for them to put user participation comfortably and fully into practice. It will be problematic for users and carers if different professions work to different assumptions about 'participation' and its desirability. Joint training opportunities for people who work together and which involve users and carers may provide the most effective way to clarify the local approach and mutual expectations

(Harding 1993; Mitchell 1992). Even so, the culture shift required will not be achieved overnight or without difficulty (Parsloe and Stevenson 1993).

Local authorities are also urged to make assessment timeous, simple and informal, to negotiate the scope of the assessment with each person and to enable a separate assessment of the carer's needs where appropriate. Users and carers have already indicated that these are important quality markers in a number of studies (e.g. Allen *et al.* 1992, SWSG 1991). Where the needs of the user and carer differ or conflict – for example, where the carer no longer feels able to provide care and the user is reluctant to consider alternative help – then each will need separate support and it may become untenable to have only one assessor holding both sets of reins.

Some users will have difficulties in being actively involved in their assessment. There may be communication problems (for example because of a stroke or severe hearing impairment), or poor comprehension through impaired insight (for example due to an acute mental health problem, profound learning disability or dementia). Specialist communicators may be needed, or an advocate recruited to ensure that the user's perspective is fully represented. Family members or others who know the person well may help to interpret the person's speech or special ways of communicating. This may all take time when others are urging quick action. Ensuring 'quality' of assessment from the user's perspective will sometimes be at the expense of speed – an important quality measure for others, including many family carers and professionals.

Difficulties in communication or in ensuring that cultural background is fully understood may also arise for users and carers from minority ethnic groups. Their satisfaction with the assessment service will be closely linked to its ability to understand and reflect different cultural and religious needs, and to ensure the availability either of assessors from different minority ethnic groups or of translators.

Assessing need effectively will require contact with others who know the user or carer. Sometimes there may need to be a formal request (for example for medical information), or a case conference. People have a clear right to a confidential service from the professionals, health and social care organisations consulted. Community care assessors must seek the user's permission to make contact with others in all instances bar the exceptional.

Finally, the assessment of need must be recorded and users should, if they wish, receive a copy of the final assessment. They will prefer forms and documentation which avoid jargon and which are laid out clearly. By this stage the options for a care plan should be clearer, the user's preferences noted and any charges for possible services advised. The user or carer must know how to complain if they are not satisfied with the outcome.

In summary, the main quality measures for users and carers at this stage of the assessment will be:

- a clear understanding of what 'user participation' means, accepted by all professional groups involved
- a timeous response to the request for assessment
- simple processes, informally conducted
- separate, formal consideration of the carer's needs where appropriate, sometimes involving a second assessor
- effective involvement of people where communication is difficult, using an advocate where appropriate
- assessors who understand the needs of people from minority ethnic groups, involving translators where necessary
- a confidential service
- clear recording of the assessment, with a copy provided to the user
- an effective and fair complaints procedure for the user if not satisfied.

4. Care planning

The care planning stage of the process involves negotiating and agreeing the kind of plan needed. The user's and carer's preferences and choices must be taken into account, but the overall plan must be within available resources. Any costs to the user must be clearly stated, the care plan recorded and made available to the user and, with their permission, to others involved. Unmet needs should be logged and used for future planning purposes – although, stemming from several government directives, letters and comments, there is considerable confusion at the time of writing as to how local authorities should do this.

Not all people who have an assessment will need a formal care plan; for many, a one-off service or action will suffice. Care plans will, however, be needed when continuing services or supports are to be put in place. Some will be simple and others very complex, for example involving many services, frequent changes of plan, a high degree of risk or family stress. Starting with the abilities rather than the disabilities of the user and carer, the assessor must discuss all the options available and their costs.

Users and carers will judge the outcome on the following measures:

- whether they feel that their needs have been adequately recognised in the care plan
- whether they feel that their preferences have been taken into account
- whether carers are being asked to provide more support than they feel able to offer
- whether the costs are likely to be affordable in their view
- whether services are going to be available to meet their needs, or whether many needs will be unmet, and if the user is disabled, how quickly the local authority will be able to meet its statutory duty to provide or procure services to meet essential needs.

5. Implementing the care plan

Once the care plan has been agreed it must be implemented by an identified care manager. The guiding principle outlined in the Practitioners' Guide is 'to achieve the stated objectives of the care plan with the minimum intervention necessary'. Users and carers should have 'as active a part in the implementation of their care plan as their abilities and motivation allow'. A key worker may be identified as the day-to-day contact for the user. A care manager must be given the central coordinating role by all the services and professionals involved.

It will be crucial for many users to have the maximum control over their own care plan, perhaps even acting as their own care manager. Others will prefer that the care manager orchestrates a variety of acceptable supports and coordinates these effectively. As at the assessment stage, the ability of the professionals to make absolutely explicit any priorities or 'rationing' and to take account of each person's individual wishes will be important determinants of the user's satisfaction. This will require a high degree of skill, professional maturity and credibility on the part of the care manager as inter-agency negotiator, purchaser, counsellor, budget manager and coordinator.

The key measures for users are likely to be:

- whether the plan meets their needs as they see them
- whether the cost is acceptable
- whether the care manager and key worker are acceptable to them

- whether their own wish to control the care plan can be accommodated
- whether the care manager has all the skills required of them to negotiate, set up and coordinate the plan to everyone's satisfaction
- whether other services and professionals are prepared to give the care manager the central coordinating role.

6. Monitoring the care plan

Stage six involves supporting the care plan over time and adapting it to the changing needs of the user. Users and carers should be given 'every encouragement to play an active part in the process' (DOH/SSI/SWSG 1991a). Some will wish to have a much greater direct say in this than others, and some will need an advocate to ensure that their views are represented. Measures of user satisfaction with monitoring will include:

- the relationship with and ease of contacting the care manager
- the relationship with the key worker, and their effectiveness at contacting the care manager
- the speed of response of the care manager and the ease with which minor changes to the plan can be made
- the preparedness of other professionals and agencies to work within the care plan and to give the key worker and care manager their place as coordinators
- for those acting as their own care managers, the flexibility of the local authority in enabling adjustments to the plan and access to the budget.

7. Reviewing the care plan

Reviewing the care plan is the final stage of the care management process. It means reassessing the person's needs and the care plan at intervals and revising the care plan if necessary. The care plan review is a formal process, the frequency depending on the circumstances of each person. All the participants in the plan – user, carer and providers – should contribute and sometimes a formal meeting may be held. Users and carers may need an advocate or other representative.

The word 'review' is in daily use by professionals but to users and carers can spell the potential withdrawal of valued supports. The success of the review stage may depend on users and carers understanding fully and in advance what the process entails and feeling able to say what they really think about the services and supports involved in the plan.

Users and carers will measure the success of the review stage on:

- whether it comes at the right time
- whether it is held in a way which makes it easy to participate
- whether in their view the right people are asked to contribute
- whether their views seem to be heard
- whether any changes are welcome or not
- whether the conclusions of the review can be challenged.

Conclusion

The arguments for community care services to be responsive to the views of those who use them have been well-rehearsed over the past twenty years and are incorporated into the stated principles of the new community care legislation. By ensuring that individual needs assessment focuses on the person rather than on current services it is claimed that users and carers will enjoy better quality assessment and more responsive services. This chapter has examined how users might define quality in the different stages of needs assessment and care planning.

Endorsing the basic principle of participation in community care is easy, but ensuring the full and active participation of all users and carers in their assessments, either directly or through advocacy, will represent a major culture shift for many social and health care workers and professions. Some may find this 'handing over' of power difficult, particularly when resources are limited.

Users and carers have changing expectations too. Whilst some have been waiting a long time for the opportunities offered by the new legislation, others may be less comfortable with the new approach. Time and effort will be needed to develop mutual understanding between assessors and users, and to promote the more active participation of users. Useful and innovative work has already been reported and could provide models for others to follow or adapt.

Despite the problems which will undoubtedly arise, the new assessment arrangements do establish more clearly than before the rights of users and carers to be fully involved in their own assessments, and the routes to challenge these. This presents opportunities which could be maximised by both individuals and groups.

Major current concerns about resource levels for community care have not been addressed in this chapter which has concentrated on how user participation in the new assessment model may work. However, without the resources – new or recycled – to meet needs identified in assessments in which users and carers have an increasing say, disillusion may set in. At the end of the day, users and carers are likely to judge community care assessments more on their outcome than on how they are conducted.

References

Allen, I, Hogg, D. and Peace, S. (1992) *Elderly People: Choice, Participation and Satisfaction*. Policy Studies Institute.

Bland, R. and Bland, R. (1985) *Client Characteristics and Patterns of Care in Local Authority Old People's Homes*. University of Stirling.

Brace, S. (1988) *Responding to Old People: A Study of Older People Referred to Social Workers in Three Area Teams*. Lothian Regional Council.

Buckley, G. (1989) The Health Assessment of Older People at Home. M.D. Thesis, University of Edinburgh.

Coote, A. (1992) 'Charter Blight'. *Social Work Today*, 12.11.92.

Department of Health (1989) *Working for Patients*. London: HMSO.

Department of Health, Social Services Inspectorate (1991) *Getting the Message Across*. London: HMSO.

Department of Health, Social Services Inspectorate/Social Work Services Group (1991a) *Care Management and Assessment: Practitioners' Guide*. London: HMSO.

Department of Health, Social Services Inspectorate/Social Work Services Group (1991b) *Care Management and Assessment: Managers' Guide*. London: HMSO.

Department of Health/Social Work Services Group (1993) 'Community Care Changes in April 1993'. Booklet.

Ellis, K. (1993) *Squaring the Circle: User and Carer Participation*. York: Joseph Rowntree Foundation.

Griffiths, R. (1988) *Community Care: an Agenda for Action*. London: HMSO.

Harding, T. (1993) 'The user speaks'. *Community Care*, 11.3.93.

Hudson, H. (1990) *The Process of Care for Dementia Sufferers in West Lothian*. West Lothian Interagency Group/Lothian Regional Council.

Hunter, D. *et al.* (1987) *Patterns and Pathways in the Care of Elderly People*. Unit for the Study of the Elderly, Aberdeen University.

Mitchell, D. (1992) 'Running out of excuses'. *Community Care*, 10.12.92.

Parsloe, P. and Stevenson, O. (1993) 'A powerhouse for change'. *Community Care*, 18.2.93.

Prime Minister (1991) *The Citizen's Charter: Raising the Standard*. Cm 1599. London: HMSO.

Prime Minister and Chancellor of Duchy of Lancaster (1992) *The Citizen's Charter: First Report: 1992*. London: HMSO.

Samuel, E., Brace, S., Buckley, G. and Hunter, S. (1993) *Process and Preference: the Multidisciplinary Assessment of Older People*. Edinburgh: Scottish Office Central Research Unit.

Scottish Office Social Work Services Group (1991) *Assessment and Care Management: circular SW11/1991.* Edinburgh: SWSG.

Scottish Office Social Work Services Group (1991) *Community Care in Scotland: Getting to Know You.* Edinburgh: SWSG.

Secretary of State for Health (1989) *Working for Patients.* London: HMSO.

Secretaries of State for Health, Social Security, Wales and Scotland (1989) *Caring for People: Community Care in the Next Decade and Beyond.* Cm 849. London: HMSO.

Willcocks, D., Ring, A., Kellaher, L. and Peace, S. (1982) *The Residential Life of Old People: A Study of 100 Local Authority Homes.* Vol. 1. Research Report No. 12. Survey Research Unit, Polytechnic of North London.

Chapter 7

Involving Carers in Planning and Review

Marian Barnes and Gerald Wistow

Introduction

Local Authority Social Services or Social Work Departments now have a statutory responsibility to consult with users and carers in the preparation of their community care plans. Evidence from the analysis of the first round of plans in England and Wales suggests that this responsibility is being undertaken with varying degrees of commitment, understanding and sophistication (Bewley and Glendinning 1992, Wistow, Leedham and Hardy 1993). In part, such findings reflect the range of starting points from which users and carers, no less than local authorities, are operating in terms of the knowledge and skills they can bring to the consultation process. In addition, a distinction needs to be drawn between consultation on the content of plans and involvement in the process of planning. From the latter perspective, the preparation of an annual plan is merely an intermittent output in a continuous cycle of activity in which monitoring and review are integral elements. The impact of carers and users on planning will, therefore, depend upon their ability to contribute effectively to all stages of that process.

We suggest that there are at least three levels at which user and carer inputs to planning are necessary if such input is to be effective. First, there are the formal and less formal structures and processes through which the various elements of plans are developed and refined. Perhaps significantly, attempts to develop more pluralistic planning structures and processes were among the first steps taken in a small group of authorities as they geared up for the first planning round. There is also evidence from other authorities of large scale consultation exercises being undertaken to produce broadly-based inputs from users and carers to the planning process (George 1991).

A second level at which involvement is important arises from the community care White Paper's emphasis on both planning and service delivery being needs-led. This has the concomitant requirement that users and carers should be fully involved in individual care planning and also in the aggregation and interpretation of data from that level to the overall community care plan (Secretaries of State for Health, Social Security, Wales and Scotland 1989).

Involvement in monitoring and review provides the third necessary level of involvement. One way of achieving this is through involvement in reviewing the effectiveness of individual care plans. Another is in the wider process of performance review which, as Barnes and Miller (1988) have pointed out, includes securing 'user perspectives of what constitutes a good service in the definition of what information needs to be collected and what indicators generated'.

We have discussed elsewhere how the involvement of users and carers in the research process must affect the conduct of research (Barnes and Wistow 1992a, Barnes 1993). One of the basic principles we, and others, have advocated is that people who use services should not be viewed solely as 'respondents', as they are in satisfaction surveys (Barnes 1992, Beresford 1992, Davis 1992 and chapter by Connor and Black), but as participants who have a role in defining the questions to be asked. Similar principles apply in considering how users and carers might be involved in planning and review processes.

The implementation of such an approach poses certain general questions:

- How do you ensure 'representativeness' – and do you need to?

- How feasible is it to engage with service users in a continuing way as opposed to collecting information from them on a one-off basis?

- What are the appropriate vehicles for involving people in planning and review processes?

- Are people able to contribute to such processes over a period of time?

In this chapter we consider two ways in which carers were invited to contribute at different stages of the planning and review process, as part of a wider initiative in which Birmingham City Council and the local health authorities sought to develop a more 'user-oriented' approach to community care. In reviewing each of these mechanisms we focus on three issues: who was involved?; how were they involved?; and what were the outcomes of that involvement?

The Community Care Special Action Project

The Birmingham Community Care Special Action Project (CCSAP) was a three-year initiative, launched in 1987 with a remit to develop a user-oriented, inter-agency approach to community care. The authors were funded by the Department of Health to undertake an evaluation of the CCSAP and have provided an overview of the project elsewhere (Barnes and Wistow 1991).

The CCSAP was a multi-faceted initiative which sought to involve people with learning disabilities, disabled people, people with mental health problems and informal carers through a range of different mechanisms. The most extensive area of CCASP's work, and that which attracted most interest both locally and nationally, was the carers programme (see Jowell 1989, Jowell and Wistow 1989, 1990, and Prior, Jowell and Lawrence 1989, for descriptions of this programme). Central to that programme was a series of public consultations to which anyone who identified themselves as looking after an elderly or disabled relative or friend was invited.

Through these consultations, and other initiatives developed or supported under its remit, CCSAP sought to obtain information from service users, and more particularly their carers, in order to inform service planning. It sought to do this before the publication of the White Paper 'Caring for People' (Secretaries of State 1989) and hence there had been considerable experience in Birmingham (council and health authorities) of consulting with people prior to the requirement to consult about community care plans. This meant the city was potentially in a better position than some others to carry out those responsibilities. One indication of the head start the city had in consulting about community care was its establishment of a series of discussion groups and wide distribution of a booklet describing the changes to be introduced by the NHS and Community Care Act. This contained a self-completing questionnaire seeking views on the changes to be returned by anyone who was interested. The Council and the health authorities also had the results of the earlier consultations to draw on in producing its plan.

The research objectives included an element of action research. Specifically, one of its aims was to develop quality and performance measures based on criteria defined by users and carers. Hence we sought to involve carers in monitoring the outcomes of the original consultations. That experience demonstrated how involvement in monitoring also enabled carers to make a more detailed input to service planning. In this chapter, therefore, we identify the consequences and implications of involving carers in both planning and review processes. We draw on already published material as well as our final reports to the Department of Health on this aspect of the evaluation. This material is referenced in the bibliography at the end of the chapter and we do not repeat the references throughout the text. The material derives from the following sources:

(1)   Analysis of questionnaires sent to all carers who attended the CCSAP consultation meetings. A total of 318 questionnaires were returned from 531 sent out.

(2)   Interviews with 17 carers out of a random sample of 20 who returned questionnaiares.

(3)   Material generated by the Carers' Panels which are described below.

(4)   Group interviews with members of the two Panels and a review of the research team's experience of working with the Panels.

Consultation as a contribution to service planning
Who participated?

The CCSAP consultations were advertised by word of mouth through service providers who were in contact with carers; through posters in service outlets, libraries, neighbourhood offices and the like, and through advertisements in the local press and radio. Some carers were helped to attend through the provision of transport organised by groups of which they were members. Some were thus encouraged to attend, but by and large they were a self-selected group. It is important to remember that the purpose of consultation is different from that of a research survey which may require a representative sample from a population with known characteristics. By contrast, the aim of the Birmingham consultations was to learn from hearing carers' experiences at first hand, and to have their voices heard directly by those with major responsibilities for service planning and provision. Representativeness is not a pre-requisite for those purposes, but it is important to understand who does and who does not respond to open invitations of this type.

From the questionnaires we were able to find out some basic information about the carers who attended the meetings and who they were caring for. From these data, we identified a number of 'carer groups' who were probably under-represented in the original meetings (Barnes and Wistow 1992b). These were: Black and minority ethnic carers; people who had only recently become carers, including parents of disabled children; carers who do not live with the person they care for (Green 1988); people caring for someone with a mental health problem; and people caring for someone with a physical disability who was not elderly.

The absence of detailed local information about the numbers of carers and who they care for means that we cannot talk of under-representativeness in a statistical sense. However, it is likely that the particular circumstances of the above groups were not as well reflected in the discussions as those of, for example, parents of adults with learning disabilities or daughters living with and caring for elderly parents.

In addition to differences associated with the characteristics of the person cared for, the nature of the caring relationship can be affected by factors such as: the nature of the relationship before the caring role was taken on; the capacity of the person being cared for to make decisions on their own behalf; and the extent to which the caring relationship was entered into voluntarily or under pressure. These factors are indicative of the range of differing needs among individual carers which the planning process ought to reflect. Whilst carers as a group have common concerns which need to be reflected in service planning, the differences between such groups also need to be drawn out. This may indicate a requirement for both general and specialist approaches to carer participation in order to ensure that the perspectives of all groups are included. It may also be more appropriate to think in terms of establishing a range of different mechanisms to secure involvement, rather than seeking 'representativeness' within any one mechanism.

The process of involvement

When CCSAP was initiated, interest in 'user involvement' was just beginning to occupy a place on more mainstream agendas of health and social care services. At that stage, few users or carers had much experience of 'being involved' in or by those services. It was not surprising, therefore, that carers did not know quite what to expect from the consultation meetings. We found that some went along out of interest, with an open mind, or with general feelings that they might obtain something of benefit from attending. Others had more specific needs which they hoped might be met: needs associated with sharing their experiences, 'getting things out of their system', or obtaining information which would be of use to them.

The latter was a widespread perception of what the consultations could offer. Whilst 'having your say' was identified in response to our questions as the most important of four purposes by most of the carers attending the consultations, 'finding out about things which could be important to you' and 'an opportunity to get out and meet other people in a similar position to yourself' were identified as the most important aspect of the meetings by a substantial proportion of those attending. Moreover, our interviews and experience with the panels showed that finding out from other carers was at least as important as finding out from service providers.

In addition, some carers clearly hoped that the consultation meetings would provide an opportunity for individual problem solving. Approximately one-third of those attending the consultations said that they did not think the consultation had helped in any particular way. Interview responses also indicated that some people felt they had not been able to deal satisfactorily with a particular problem which had in part prompted their attendance.

A general conclusion from this finding is that the intentions of the providers in setting up the consultation meetings did not entirely coincide with the carers' reasons for attending them. As we have put it elsewhere:

> '... providers wanted to aggregate data from individuals to secure a more general overview of patterns of need, while carers were more interested in their own individual cases and particular needs. Perhaps significantly, only two of the 17 carers interviewed were able to identify any previous experiences which could be described as pressure group activities. Thus, carers' past experiences may make them less likely to understand consultation processes as an opportunity to exert generalised pressure on service providers rather than to pursue their own individual needs.' (Barnes and Wistow 1992c)

This is not to say that carers were uninterested in contributing to a process through which services as a whole might be improved for them and their fellow carers. It would be wrong to ignore the significance of altruism as a motive influencing participation. Some respondents were aware that the link between involvement and change was at best uncertain and indirect.

In addition, both solicited and unsolicited questionnaire responses showed that carers were prepared to participate in activities which might not secure immediate individual benefits but which might produce improvements of future benefit to other carers. These findings indicate, therefore, the importance of understanding the different motivations which prompt people to participate in such exercises, and also of ensuring that they provide direct benefits which make participation worthwhile.

This point can be further illustrated by contrasting the respective positions of providers and carers in the consultation process. The former are paid for their time and may be expected to adopt a specifically task-oriented approach to planning. However, the latter are not normally paid for their participation, and their time and energies are substantially taken up with their caring responsibilities. Thus, they can legitimately expect to have some of the time involved devoted to meeting their needs for sharing experiences with other carers, and for obtaining information which may, for example, make it easier for them to access services. This was illustrated in carers' comments about what they liked about the way in which the consultation meetings were organised. They welcomed opportunities for informal conversations with other carers, as well as information provided to them.

Content and outcomes

Two broad themes were proposed to guide discussions at the meetings: 'Help at home' and 'Getting a break'. However, the discussions were allowed to follow topics raised by the carers themselves rather than being determined by a detailed set of questions posed by the discussion group leaders. The discussions were recorded and transcribed and the transcripts analysed to produce what became known as the '11 Action Points', 11 key issues which were raised throughout the consultation programme.

- the need for better information about services
- respite care
- concerns about the future
- difficulties with transport services
- day care services
- a wish for help in taking holidays
- problems obtaining equipment and adaptations
- how to get help outside office hours

- social isolation
- concern about late or un-notified changes to services
- professionals who were visitors to carers' homes not leaving calling cards which would enable them to be contacted later.

The 11 Action Points became an 'agenda for action' which was adopted by the city council and the health authorities. An inter-agency Performance Review Group was established with the task of ensuring that the consultation process achieved tangible outcomes in response to those issues raised by carers. This initiative was seen to be vital by both carers and officers in the city. From the start, therefore, consultation was seen to be the start of a process which should lead to action.

The 11 issues were considered to be a robust reflection of carers' main concerns because of the frequency with which they were repeated in different meetings. However, responses to our questionnaires suggested that other important issues raised by carers did not appear on the action point agenda. There were five such issues which we identified from carers' questionnaire responses:

- financial problems associated with caring
- specialist help needed to deal with a particular illness or disability
- the attitude of professional staff
- the stress of caring
- the need of carers to be cared about.

We can only speculate about reasons why these were not identified as action points. It may be that an unconscious process of selection went on which filtered out issues which were felt to be too difficult to deal with. It may be that the process of categorising issues meant that particular concerns became conflated with others and their individual significance was thus lost. Alternatively, it may be that carers were telling us what they wanted to talk about, but they had not been able to express themselves in a way which had led to these concerns being identified from discussion transcripts. Whatever the reason, the general point to be made from this finding is that any 'action agenda' derived in this way is unlikely to be a complete reflection of concerns which require a response. Also, issues identified from one-off consultations with any group will not reflect changing needs and difficulties. The agenda itself needs to be dynamic.

The nature of the individual Action Points also varied. Some reflected carers' concerns with specific aspects of services received (or not received), others related to the experience of caring. There is likely to be a relationship between the two. For example, it is not unrealistic to suggest that a relationship exists between carers' uncertainty and concern about future care and the perceived unreliability of services received in the present. The responses required of service providers were also of very varying nature and complexity and it was unsurprising, therefore, that progress in responding to the 11 issues was extremely varied. Nevertheless, the consultations were the start of a process through which carers' concerns relating to their experiences of caring and of using services were translated into a programme of action. In the next section of this chapter we report on experiences of involving carers in monitoring and reviewing the action which flowed from the consultations.

Carer involvement in the review process

The Performance Review Group was originally an officer-only group. Later a carer became a member of the group and thus had direct input to decision making in respect of the action strategy. However, the main carer input at this stage was through two Carers Panels which were established as part of our research project. These had three broad aims: identifying criteria carers would want to use to judge the action taken in response to the 11 issues; enabling carers to become involved in monitoring that action; and enabling carers to take an active part in reviewing services which were the subject of action in response to the concerns raised.

Who was involved?

We noted above that the carers attending the consultations were largely self-selected. The carers participating in the panels were invited by the researcher. Those invited were identified as having already demonstrated an interest in being involved in the work of CCSAP beyond the initial consultation programme. Some had prior experience of presenting their views, or had volunteered to join the project. Some had contributed to a presentation at a national social services conference and had participated in consultation meetings with two Ministers of Health who visited CCSAP. Others had written to the project team indicating that they wished to be involved in follow ups to the original consultation meetings, or had volunteered to be interviewed by the local media about their role as carers. It was envisaged that such individuals would both be more likely to respond to an invitation to join the panel and would also approach its work with some degree of confidence about their capacity to participate.

As intended, the panels eventually involved carers of people with different types of needs. However, no attempt was made to select a panel which would be representative of all those involved in the consultation meetings, who were, in any case, not fully representative of carers as a whole. Rather, the intention was to seek to engage carers who the researchers thought might be both willing and able to participate in the experiment. The experience of the panels does, of course, need to be viewed in the light of this selection process. We return to this issue below.

The process of involvement

The responses of the 24 carers who agreed to participate in the panels revealed that some would find it easier to meet during the daytime and others in the evening. Consequently, two panels were established, meeting monthly for an initial period of six months, which participants subsequently agreed to extend for a further six months. The two groups were different in size and composition. The style of the morning group was influenced by the presence of two carers who had experience of pressure group activity, were knowledgeable about service systems and had some sense of tactics and bureaucratic politics. As a result, meetings had at least something of the flavour of a traditional voluntary sector committee meeting. By contrast, the evening group was less experienced in such matters and, consequently, had a style which was closer to that of a mutual support group meeting in which participants shared personal experiences with each other. It was in this rather than in the balance of functions that they differed.

However, participation in the panels was a learning experience and some members without pressure group experience did start to develop this. Hence, the style of the meetings also varied over time, and in response to the current needs and competencies of participants.

The meetings of both groups lasted for approximately two hours and, although a small number of members in each group made only limited contributions, by and large members appeared to experience little difficulty in contributing to panel discussions. Most of the panel members had not met together before, but they evolved a common identity and sense of purpose over time which facilitated frank and open discussion, even about sensitive personal matters.

One of the purposes of the panels was to fulfil our research objective of contributing to the empowerment of users through involvement in the evaluation process. 'Empowerment' is a term which can have many meanings. Peter Campbell and Peter Beresford have argued that only by involving people directly in decision-making and service provision can empowerment be unambiguously attained (East Sussex CC, Brighton HA, MIND 1988). Such a view reflects a concept of empowerment as attaining power over services; it relates to power as control. Implicitly it assumes that power needs to pass from one place to another if empowerment is to be achieved.

Another perspective on empowerment does not view power as a 'zero sum' but as a process of personal growth in which an increase in the power experienced by one person does not necessarily diminish the personal power, or more appropriately 'strength', of another. Involvement in the panels was in that way an empowering experience for at least some of the carers involved. One spoke of a growing realisation that she could express her views about services to elected members and be taken seriously in a way which she would not previously have expected. Another said:

> 'I think this is the first time in a lot of respects that we have been treated as experts… and we *are* experts.'

This example does, however, also illustrate that, while conceptually distinct, in some circumstances the two notions of empowerment identified here may be seen to be interdependent, since personal growth may be a precondition for involvement in decision-making processes.

Content and outcomes

The main purpose of the panels was to monitor the implementation of the 11 Action Points. In order to contribute to this developing sense of being taken seriously, it was important for carers to see that they were achieving some specific outcomes in relation to these issues. Two examples will be used to reflect specific outcomes from the work of the panels.

One of the 11 Action Points related to concerns about **how to access help outside office hours**. The Carers Panels began by identifying the circumstances in which the need to obtain help outside office hours would arise. There was a general agreement that the need was not for a sympathetic ear, but for immediate practical assistance at times of crisis. The panels went on to define the key characteristics of a service which would meet their needs for out-of-hours services. They also responded to an initial report by the officer responsible for dealing with this issue. This officer met with the panels and received feedback from them which enabled him to clarify the circumstances which create the need for help, and the desirable features of a relevant service.

Subsequently, the panels received details of proposals to extend and develop a Helpline service which met most of their requirements, if in a rather different way from that which they had envisaged. A remaining issue was the way in which such a service might be funded. After our work with the panels had ended, they became involved in applying for and administering grant aid for the development of the service.

Respite care provides a different example of the way in which the panels operated. In this instance little action was evident and so the panels took the lead in defining the characteristics of a 'quality respite care service', producing a 'Respite Care Quality Checklist'. This had the potential of being used by carers to assist them in choosing a home which they would find satisfactory, and to contribute to the inspection process alongside inspectors employed by the Social Services Department. (This checklist is included in Report No.3 referenced at the end of this chapter.) Thus, this initiative provides a clear example of the panels as a mechanism through which carers could define criteria to be applied in performance review.

Both these examples demonstrate the value of engaging with carers over time rather than in a single consultation event. Encouraging people to contribute their stories; making use of those stories to identify key aspects of service weaknesses; what would make things better, and what criteria should be used to assess services; then reflecting that analysis and checking out that these interpretations make sense – all these activities require effective co-working and time to develop. By providing a forum for discussion, the panels enabled their members think about what information they had received and discussed, and then return with ideas they may not have thought of in a one-off discussion. As we have demonstrated above, their involvement in monitoring action extended beyond simply keeping tabs on what was happening to making an active and constructive contribution to the development process. They also served as a stimulus to action by providing a reminder to the officers concerned that they were waiting for information about progress.

Further direct outputs from the panels included: development of a monitoring form intended to record users' experiences of special transport services provided by the Social Services Department, and identification of criteria to judge this service; and detailed feedback on the content and design of the 'Birmingham Information File' produced to respond to the inadequacy of existing information services to assist access to services, and criteria to assess its effectiveness.

In addition, through analysis of panel discussions we were able to identify a number of general and specific criteria which carers used to evaluate services. We also identified issues which had not been picked up through the original consultation process and which were sufficiently significant to be referred to the Performance Review Group for addition to their agenda for action.

However, there was very uneven progress in respect of action being taken on the 11 issues and some of the carers involved were frustrated by this.

> '... what's the progress? No progress whatsoever at the moment. Well we've been here 12 months. What can you say? You can't say nothing to them.'

Nonetheless, progress towards specific service changes was not the only motivation for carers' continuing involvement in the panels. In addition to the general feeling that they were being taken seriously for the first time through the methods studied earlier, we identified five benefits which carers experienced from their involvement:

- an opportunity for carers to provide and receive personal **support** from each other, including expressions of understanding and sympathy, and also suggestions about how to handle difficult caring situations

- carers provided each other with **information and advice** about benefits and services and how to access them

- carers got to know each other better, the panels appeared to provide a **safe environment** within which they could talk about experiences and feelings which they had not publicly talked about before and which they might feel were not the 'right' feelings to have

- for some, the panel meetings appeared to provide an opportunity for **companionship and a break from caring**

- in some instances, particular **problems,** issues or concerns were taken up on behalf of carers **and information** was given to them to which they would not otherwise have had access.

Issues and Lessons

In order for carers to be able to experience these benefits, the panels had to have certain characteristics of a support group as well as a task group. There was, however, something of a tension between the necessity for achieving task-related outcomes within the research timetable, and of responding to the various needs and motivations which affected carers' willingness to participate in the panels. Such tensions could also be expected to arise in panels established to meet the needs and agenda of providers.

In spite of the frustration about slow progress on some issues, carers felt that it was important for the panels to continue to meet, and emphasised the importance of direct contact between the panels and senior managers to convince them that they were being taken seriously. Carers had learnt about some of the requirements for influence:

> 'You can't be influential unless you're in the system and you know what goes on behind closed doors.'

This learning was another important output. If participation is to be effective, both service providers and service users must learn how to relate to each other in different ways. Providers need to learn how to listen to carers' stories and be imaginative in considering their implications for services. Service users will need to understand more about how services work and who is responsible for what, in order to reach decisions about how best to influence them.

However, an important dilemma arising from the experience of this initiative is the potential for the creation of a group of 'elite participant' carers or users. Not all carers or users will want, or be in a position, to make the level of commitment that panel involvement required. One way of dealing with this limitation is to encourage panel members to act as a voice for other people. This was recognised by one of the carers involved:

> 'Basically I think what we've achieved is speaking up for other people, we've come forward... to represent the majority of people who can't come forward and say what they think.'

But a further implication is that panels alone will be an insufficient mechanism for securing carer or user input to review processes. The checklists and monitoring forms generated by the panels should be the start of a further process to secure feedback from a wider number of people, and to check out how broadly based are the views expressed by the much smaller number of panel members.

Conclusion

Elsewhere (Barnes and Wistow 1992b) we have emphasised the importance of viewing consultation as a precursor to action. Reflecting on the experience of the carers panels emphasises the importance of seeing involvement in monitoring and review as a necessary part of involvement in planning. Our experience of working with carers has demonstrated the feasibility and the benefits – as well as the limitations – of involving carers in both planning and review processes. Securing involvement at the initial stage creates an expectation of follow-up – providers who consult only about their community care plan are likely to find that they cannot stop here.

The carers involved in the panels wanted to continue meeting after the research input had come to an end. Exactly how they should operate, and what their remit should be, was then something they needed to determine and negotiate with the city council officers who were to support them. At a general level the panels have continued to be a mechanism through which carers can feed back their views on community care developments. Some of the carers have also become involved both in inspections and in chairing complaints committees.

There are dangers in giving insufficient thought to whether meeting the needs of the service planning system, and meeting the needs of users and carers who become involved in that system, are compatible. Providers should be sensitive to the demands they are placing on people whose lives are already complex and demanding. They should be ready to ensure that people derive some direct benefits from participation, as well as ensuring that that participation is justified by the outcomes it achieves.

References

Barnes, M. (1992) 'Beyond Satisfaction surveys: involving people in research'. *Generations Review* 2 (4), 15–17.

Barnes, M. (1993) 'Introducing new stakeholders: user and researcher interests in evaluative research. A discussion of methods used to evaluate the Birmingham Community Care Special Action Project'. *Policy and Politics* 21 (1), 47–58.

Barnes, M. and Miller, N. (eds) (1988) 'Performance measurement in personal social services'. *Research, Policy and Planning* 6 (2).

Barnes, M. and Wistow, G. (1991) *Changing Relationships in Community Care: An Interim Account of the Birmingham Community Care Special Action Project.* Nuffield Institute for Health Services Studies, University of Leeds.

Barnes, M. and Wistow, G. (1992a) 'Research and user involvement: contribution to learning methods', in Barnes, M. and Wistow, G. (eds), *Researching User Involvement.* Nuffield Institute for Health Services Studies, University of Leeds.

Barnes, M. and Wistow, G. (1992b) 'Consulting with carers: what do they think?' *Social Services Research*, No.1, 9–30.

Barnes, M. and Wistow, G. (1992c) 'Putting words into action'. *Community Care*, July 23, 16–17.

Barnes, M. and Wistow, G. (1993) 'Relative values'. *Health Service Journal*, 14 January, 26–28.

Beresford, P. (1992) 'Researching citizen involvement: a collaborative or colonising enterprise?', in Barnes, M. and Wistow, G. (eds), *Researching User Involvement.* Nuffield Institute for Health Services Studies, University of Leeds.

Bewley, C. and Glendinning, C. (1992) *Involving Disabled People in Community Care Planning.* Social Care Research Findings No. 27. York: Joseph Rowntree Foundation.

Davis, A. (1992) 'Who needs user research? Service users as research subjects or participants', in Barnes, M. and Wistow, G. (eds), *Researching User Involvement.* Nuffield Institute for Health Services Studies, University of Leeds.

East Sussex CC, Brighton Health Authority, MIND (1988) Report of Common Concerns. International Conference on User Involvement in Mental Health Services.

George, M. (1991) 'The initiation process'. *Community Care*, 28 March.

Green, H. (1988) *Informal Carers: General Household Survey 1985.* London: HMSO.

Jowell, T. (1989) 'More care for the carers'. *The Guardian*, September 20, p.27.

Jowell, T. and Wistow, G. (1989) 'Give them a voice'. *Social Services Insight* 4 (7), 22–24.

Jowell, T. and Wistow, G. (1990) 'The total service?' *Social Services Insight* 5 (5), 22–23.

Prior, D., Jowell, T. and Lawrence, R. (1989) 'Carer consultations: towards a strategy for consumer led change'. *Local Government Policy Making* 16 (2), 17–25.

Secretaries of State for Health, Social Security, Wales and Scotland (1989) *Caring for People, Community Care in the Next Decade and Beyond*, Cm. 849. London: HMSO.

Wistow, G., Hallas, J. and Swift, J. (1991) 'Community care planning workshops'. *Caring for People Newsletter*, No.8, 14–16.

Wistow, G., Leedham, I. and Hardy, B. (1993) *Community Care Plans: A Preliminary Analysis of a Sample of Community Care Plans.* London: Social Services Inspectorate, Department of Health.

Research reports describing the carers' programme

These are all written by Marian Barnes and Gerald Wistow. They are unpublished, but are available from the Nuffield Institute for the cost of copying and postage.

(1) The Carers' Programme and the Role of the Performance Review Group.

(2) Coming in from the Wilderness? Carers' Views of the Consultations and their Outcomes.

(3) Partnership and Empowerment: Involving Carers in Monitoring the Outcomes of the Consultations.

(4) Overall Conclusions to the Carers' Programme and its Outcomes.

Chapter 8

Service Evaluation by People with Learning Difficulties

Andrea Whittaker

'I enjoyed it. It was a challenge. I'd never done this sort of thing before. I learned a lot about myself – my strengths and weaknesses – got to know myself a bit better from it. It gave me a big boost doing the evaluation.'

'Although it's been hard and tiring sometimes, I've enjoyed it. I'd do it all over again if I was asked. I really felt smashing and important. I know one thing, I wouldn't have missed it for anything.'

Thus Simon Gardner and Joyce Kershaw described their experience of carrying out an evaluation of residential services for people with learning difficulties in the London Borough of Hillingdon. Simon and Joyce are members of People First, the national self-advocacy organisation run by people with learning difficulties. They were doing pioneering work because, as far as the author knows, this was the first time ever – either in the UK or overseas – that people with learning difficulties had been asked to undertake, and be in control of, an evaluation of services to their peer group.

This chapter tells the story of that evaluation, who was involved, and how it was conducted. It sketches briefly the historical background, considers the conditions that were in place to enable the evaluation to happen and poses questions for the future development of user-led evaluations. A detailed description and report of the results of the evaluation is given in Whittaker *et al.* (1991).

What is self-advocacy?

Self-advocacy is speaking up for yourself as a person rather than letting others speak or act on your behalf. It involves being aware of what your rights are, developing the skills to express your needs and trying to ensure that those needs are met.

Historically, it has been the practice for other people to advocate for people with learning difficulties, who were believed unable to make decisions for themselves and therefore dependent on others for protection from the stresses and strains of ordinary life.

Self-advocacy by people with learning difficulties began in Sweden in the 1960s where the focus was on teaching people the skills of decision-making, committee work and voting, particularly to enable them to run their own social and leisure clubs. Over the next 20 years or so it spread to many other countries, particularly Canada and the USA. It became established in the UK in the early 1970s when many training centres set up their own representative committees (Crawley 1988). The achievements of the self-advocacy movement since its beginnings in this country clearly demonstrate that people with learning difficulties, given the opportunity to acquire the appropriate skills, can speak for themselves, make choices and decisions and take the responsibilities that go with those decisions.

Self-advocacy can be on an individual or group level. The first involves a person pursuing his or her own interests, being aware of his/her rights and taking responsibility for tackling infringements of those rights. The second involves joining with others to pursue the interests of the group and of people with learning difficulties in general (Whittaker 1991, Whittaker *et al.* 1991, Appendices).

The development of People First

The People First movement began in the United States of America in 1973 and in the UK in 1984 after British self-advocates attended the first international People First conference in Seattle, USA. Now there is a UK-wide network of People First groups which campaign and advocate strongly for people with learning difficulties on a variety of issues. Their London office is staffed by people with learning difficulties as well as support workers and people with learning difficulties form the Management Committee. The London office also runs a national newsletter and acts as a contact point for groups in the UK. The background and role of

People First are described in Whittaker *et al.* 1993; see also Shearer 1991, pp.50–55.

Background to the evaluation

The evaluation arose out of a programme which moved people from institutions to ordinary houses in the community as part of a hospital closure programme. The study focussed on two group houses in Hillingdon which together provided homes for seven people with learning difficulties. The houses were jointly funded by North West Thames Regional Health Authority and the London Borough of Hillingdon Social Services Department (SSD) and managed by the SSD. Additional back-up support was also provided by Hillingdon Social Services Department.

The work was commissioned by the Regional Health Authority (RHA) in collaboration with SSD. The RHA wanted a service-users' view of the service needs and lifestyles of people with learning difficulties now moving into the community. They asked for a down-to-earth evaluation to cover several matters: a look at services from the point of view of a person using the service; what was happening in people's lives at that time; how they felt about their lives; what quality of life and opportunities they want in the future.

When People First was invited to do this evaluation it had accumulated six years of experience in advocating on behalf of people with learning difficulties, although this was the first evaluation they had undertaken. As an independent organisation it could give an independent opinion of services. Its members know from personal experience what they are talking about and they can relate to people with learning difficulties in a way which is not possible for either staff or professional researchers.

Simon Gardner and Joyce Kershaw were the consultants who undertook the evaluation. They were supported by Andrea Whittaker, a Senior Project Officer in the Community Care Group at the King's Fund Centre. Other members of People First were also involved in planning for the study: this is discussed further below.

Hillingdon Social Services Department was a very appropriate third partner in the initiative as the borough had already demonstrated its commitment to including service users. It had been active in encouraging people with disabilities to say what they wanted from services and backed this up with resources – for example, money to help develop a local People First group.

Why this evaluation is important

Valuable work has been done by those who fund and undertake research both here and abroad on how to make the views of service users an integral part of creating quality services. However, most of this work has been done by researchers taking the lead on methods and interviewing. The fundamental difference was that in this evaluation people with learning difficulties were given the task – with the necessary back–up resources – of undertaking an evaluation of services to their peer group. People with learning difficulties themselves drew up the questionnaires, carried out the interviews and agreed the conclusions. More important still, they had a conventional role in setting the terms of reference for the evaluation and the criteria against which the services were to be assessed. The conduct of this evaluation put service users 'in the driving seat'; calling on support and skills from other people as needed.

This evaluation was an important recognition of the value of the opinion of people who use services and the unique contribution they can make in monitoring and evaluation.

Because of the potential value of the approach for future evaluations and for other settings, it was also agreed by the RHA and People First that the evaluation should itself be evaluated – in terms of its own objectives and values, possible alternative approaches and the standards of conventional research methodology. It was also decided that this element should be built in from the outset. This evaluation was done by Libby Cooper, Director of Charities Evaluation Services, and her assessment is part of the published report of the evaluation (Whittaker *et al.* 1991).

Setting up the evaluation: consulting People First members

The evaluation process began with a consultation meeting in February 1990 between the evaluation team and other members of People First, all of whom had experience of living in a group home. Information collected at this and subsequent meetings formed the basis from which the questionnaires were developed. The People First members talked about what was important to them in their own lives and what they felt the consultants should consider when looking at the lives of the residents in Hillingdon. Participants came up with the following list of topics which they felt were important to include in the evaluation:

- living with other people
- visitors/friends/families/neighbours

- privacy
- rotas/rules/rights
- having a job
- relating to staff
- organising leisure activities.

Several further sessions with People First members resulted in a total of 25 different topic areas covering all aspects of a person's life. The questionnaires were then developed from this material. The questionnaires for residents covered all these topics and the lists for staff focussed on the same topics, but in less detail. (The questionnaires are reproduced in full in Whittaker *et al*. 1991.) In developing the questionnaires for staff, People First members had very clear ideas about what they wanted to ask. For example, they were conscious of the need for staff to be properly supported, they wanted to ask questions relating to people from minority groups; and they wanted to know how far service users were involved in interviewing and appointing staff.

The methods used were formal interviews, informal interviews and observation. Simon Gardner and Joyce Kershaw interviewed all the residents and spent time with them in their day centres and leisure activities including evening activities. They also interviewed residents' relatives and 11 staff – five working directly with the residents, two day centre managers, two hostel managers and one senior manager in charge of services.

Interviewing

Simon and Joyce shared the interviewing. Sometimes they were both involved in interviewing one person: sometimes one or other did an interview on their own. Joyce developed considerable skill in using the questionnaires to record information. Simon did not do any writing, but was particularly skilled in asking relevant supplementary questions. Andrea sat in on the interviews and also filled in a questionnaire.

Joyce and Simon became adept at explaining questions to people when necessary – perhaps when the question was too abstract or the person didn't seem to understand what was being asked. Sometimes they 'acted out' an example to help make it clearer. Both consultants recorded additional impressions and opinions outside the interview situation – Joyce writing notes and Simon using a dictaphone.

Simon recorded the following account of interviewing a young man with few verbal communication skills:

> 'I felt physically and mentally drained from this interview, because I haven't got the skills to sign in Makaton. I had to make the questions a little bit simpler so that I could make Paul understand what I was trying to ask him. I had to show him one thing – it was about privacy – like if someone was in the bathroom, having a bath or was on the loo, about knocking on the door and a resident was in there. I think he understood that question after I had physically showed him what I meant, rather than explaining it to him.'

> 'Half way through the interview, Joyce took over because I was beginning to feel shattered and Joyce finished the interview. When she had finished, she looked shattered as well.'

Gathering the information: what worked well – and what could have been better

The following list gives a summary of how the evaluation team – Simon, Joyce and Andrea – felt about the work. Some of the points are discussed in more detail later in the chapter.

Summary of strengths and challenges

WORKED WELL

We worked together as a team

Recording the information

Helping people understand the questions

Practical organisation

- support at King's Fund Centre
- support at Hillingdon

We all enjoyed it!

COULD HAVE BEEN BETTER

Parts of questionnaires

- some questions too complex
- abstract questions

We needed more time to get to know people in the houses before we interviewed them

More preparation time needed, for example to draw up question-naires and to work out different ways of interviewing

Number of interviews with family members

Travelling

- driving
- not knowing the area

Analysing the information

The evaluation team now needed to bring together the information gath-ered to consider what this showed about how well the current services were suited to residents' circumstances, future needs and wishes.

In analysing the results, the evaluators adapted a way of looking at people's lives which was developed by John O'Brien, an American who works for better lives for people with learning difficulties (O'Brien 1986). He identified five important areas of people's lives to consider when judging services. These are community presence, relationships, choice, competence and respect.

The Independent Development Council for People with a Mental Handicap has publicised O'Brien's approach, drawing attention to the principles which underpinned the evaluation criteria and the importance of these factors for people with learning difficulties (IDC 1986). Their description of the principles is reproduced below:

'1. **Community presence.** People with learning difficulties have the right to spend their time in the community, not segregated in resi-dential, day or leisure facilities which keep them apart from other members of society.

2. **Relationships.** Living in the community is not enough. People also need help and encouragement to mix with other non-handicapped people in the course of their daily lives. [Services] should be creating opportunities for people to form valued relationships at home, at work, in education and in community and leisure activities.

3. **Choice.** An important feature of the quality of life is the degree of choice that people can exercise. This can apply to small, everyday matters like what to wear or what to eat, and to major life decisions like who to live with or where to work. A high quality service will

give priority to enhancing the choices available to people and to protecting their human rights generally.

4. **Competence.** In order for people with learning difficulties to live a full and rewarding life in their local community, many will require help in experiencing a growing ability to perform useful and meaningful activities with whatever assistance is required. This increase in competence should be directly relevant to people's life situations, helping them to develop relationships and achieve greater choice and independence.

5. **Respect.** People with learning difficulties often have an undeserved bad reputation and are seen and treated as second-class citizens. Services can play an important part in helping people to be seen and treated with the same status as other valued members of the community.'

The evaluation team looked at all five aspects of the qualities identified by O'Brien. In the end, they decided to leave out the last area – respect. They felt they could not make a judgement here because during the two weeks at the house there were not enough opportunities to observe people interacting with ordinary members of the public. For detailed results on each aspect of the residents' lives, readers need to consult the full report (Whittaker *et al.* 1991).

Consequences of the evaluation

The report of the evaluation was presented in July 1990 to the Regional Health Authority, which had commissioned the study. In Hillingdon the RHA and SSD work closely together and the report was aimed at both organisations. A conference was held to publicise the study. The report (Whittaker *et al.* 1991) was published by the King's Fund Centre and has been widely circulated. It is seen as an extension to on-going ways in which staff listen to users and work with them to improve services (see Introduction to Whittaker *et al.* 1991).

One of the aims of the publication was to encourage other people to consider user input to evaluation. David Pashley, Director of the Community Care Office of North West Thames RHA, wrote in the Foreword:

'What I hope this report does is to stimulate you into devising your own ways of putting service users at the at the heart of service design and evaluation. We did it one way in Hillingdon. There will be many other ways which service users themselves will discover as they gain expertise in evaluation.' (1991)

Two years on John Spargo, Divisional Director of Hillingdon SSD, described the effect of the evaluation as follows:

'Most, if not all, of the practical steps recommended in the evaluation have now been taken, and the world and lives of the people directly involved in the study have moved on, as one would expect. But the model of the evaluation and its positive and successful outcome has given Hillingdon a range of insights which have been built into the thinking about service inspection and standard setting, and the way in which service users can and should be involved in a very central way to these processes.

Actual examples include:

- A user/carer forum planning the future shape and form of daytime services.
- User groups working alongside Inspectors in the arms-length inspection of residential homes.
- A user group working alongside officers to look at the way respite services are provided.' (in Whittaker *et al.* 1991)

Assessment of the evaluation

This evaluation was an extremely important 'first' because it took the involvement of people with learning difficulties in assessing the quality of services further than it had ever gone before. A great deal can be learned from the experience in Hillingdon which will strengthen this involvement. A list of the elements which the experience of this study showed are essential to any service-user-led evaluation is attached as an Annex to this chapter. The ways in which this evaluation fits in with the range of initiatives aimed at achieving and maintaining high quality services by reflecting the needs and wishes of people who use those services also needs to be considered. There are several issues which need to be explored further in order to develop this work in a positive way.

Using professional research skills

One of the important issues for consideration for the future is how much professional expertise should be included. In the case of this evaluation, it is true that more professional involvement at the design stage of the questionnaires, for example, would have resulted in fewer inappropriate questions from a professional researcher's point of view, but how much of the freshness and enthusiasm of People First's ideas might have been lost – or at least 'watered down' – in the process? Perhaps, at least on this pioneering occasion, it was a good thing that the balance of input weighed heavily on People First's side.

Training for people carrying out evaluations

It is necessary to build in time and resources to enable users carrying out an evaluation to have relevant training. One example is interviewing techniques – asking supplementary questions, when to keep probing for an answer and when to stop, avoiding leading questions.

On the other hand, it is not the aim to turn users and their advocates into quasi-researchers. Given the long history of services casting people with disabilities in a patient/pupil role, it would be all too easy to try to turn people into role models which would be acceptable to professionals but which could blunt the uniqueness of their personal contribution.

How do we get the balance right?

Making a balanced judgement

In this evaluation the service providers were asking for the service users' point of view, but to what extent can/should we help people to take into account a broader range of views and information before making a judgement? To what extent might the lack of this skill weaken the validity of the judgement? Are there certain areas where this might be important and others where it is less important?

How can we involve users effectively in service evaluation at the senior level as well as grass roots level?

As Libby Cooper pointed out in her assessment of this evaluation (in Whittaker *et al.* 1991), the parts of the evaluation which proved most successful in terms of quality of the questionnaires, the interviews and observation, and the judgements made, were those which related to people's everyday lives – home, work, day centre, leisure – and this is perhaps to be expected because it is based on service users' direct experience.

The part of the evaluation which she identified as less successful was that involving staff, particularly service managers and senior staff. To the extent that the questionnaires to managers and staff were made up of the questions which People First members wanted to ask, they achieved their purpose. The consultants were able to use the information gained to supplement their knowledge of the residents' lives and to help make judgements about the services in general. They gave a service user's view of some staff and management issues. Also, by addressing less commonly raised questions issues such as equal opportunities for staff and users, the consultants took managers by surprise on more than one occasion and made them think afresh. On the other hand, Libby Cooper noted in her assessment of the evaluation that the evaluation did not take sufficient account of the management of services and some matters raised by staff could have been pursued further.

Service users have shown that they can contribute to the monitoring and evaluation of services at the management level as well as at 'grass-roots' level. If the approach is to have the greatest possible impact, we need to consider how that contribution can be further strengthened. Perhaps in this area it will be made most effective by working alongside professional researchers.

One way forward might be for service user consultants to carry out interviews with senior managers who have responsibility for the services and those who planned new developments, in partnership with a researcher who has the necessary degree of skill to probe deeply. The roles and boundaries of each member of the evaluation team would need to be defined: the more experienced interviewer would need to be somebody skilled in working in partnership with the service user in order not to become dominant at the interview.

Another suggestion would be to use small discussion groups of not more than six people – perhaps three with learning difficulties and three senior managers – led by a skilled facilitator. Discussion would take place in the setting to be evaluated, and would be loosely structured around broad areas of living rather than specific questions as in a formal questionnaire.

Keeping 'ownership' with the service users

However these issues are tackled in the future, support should be given in a way which enhances the partnership with service users and does not supplant the unique contribution which they can make from their own life experience.

This evaluation has shown that people with learning difficulties can take part in the external monitoring and evaluation of services in a very direct way. Now there is a base line from which to explore how to develop and strengthen their involvement in such work in the future. But true ownership will also require a say in commissioning the evaluation – when it is needed, what is covered by the initial remit – and afterwards in deciding what will be done to take forward the results of the evaluation.

Conclusion

This evaluation was requested by service providers to help them improve services in the way users wanted. John Spargo of Hillingdon SSD summed up the value of this evaluation:

> 'The People First Evaluation required a radical re-think of the way we look at services, the language and jargon we often use, and at how inaccessible many of our traditional planning approaches are to people who use our services.
>
> The People First Evaluation led the way in challenging traditional models, stereotypes and assumptions. It applied a refreshingly human and outcome-led philosophy to the business of looking at quality and has given us all a very clear reminder that our services are about people with very strong views about what they like and do not like, and that by ignoring the crucial information within these personal views and opinions, we ignore a way to develop services which properly meet the needs and wishes of the individuals for whom they are intended.' (in Whittaker *et al.* 1991)

In September 1993 People First began another evaluation. Funded by the Joseph Rowntree Foundation, this work will take place in two London Boroughs and will look at what happens to people in the transition period before leaving hospital as well as their life out in the ordinary world. The work should be completed in 1994.[*]

---

[*]   For more information on this and other People First activities contact: People First, Instrument House, 207–215 King's Cross Road, London WC1X 9DB.

Annex: Key elements for success in a service-user-led evaluation
This is a summary of the aspects which the evaluation team felt were the most important points to consider in undertaking similar work.

* Commitment from service managers
Securing commitment from people at all levels in the service to be evaluated is the vital first stage in any work of this nature. Words are not enough. They must be backed up with resources, support, and a commitment to take action on the findings.

This evaluation would not have happened without the commitment and enthusiasm of key senior managers in Hillingdon Social Services Department and North West Thames Regional Health Authority. These people were prepared not only to work together across service boundaries to reach agreement in principle to such a new undertaking, but to back this up with appropriate financial and other resources – for example, fees, expenses, office accommodation.

* Commitment from 'grassroots' staff
The fact that Hillingdon had a well-established policy of involving service users, demonstrated in practice, meant that staff supporting people in their day-to-day lives welcomed this initiative and were ready and willing to co-operate with the evaluators.

* Involve service users right from the start
It is crucial to involve people with learning difficulties at every stage. This is a basic principle underpinning this work, since it is important to make sure that the 'ownership' of the work remains with the service users.

* Training for the consultants
It is likely that people with learning difficulties who are going to be involved in evaluating will already have some of the necessary skills (e.g. experience at speaking up for themselves, the ability to get on well with people; interest in other people and what they think and feel). But they will need additional skills particularly relevant when evaluating. They need to learn interviewing skills. They need to work out which method of recording information will suit them best (e.g. writing; using a dictaphone; having someone else write their comments for them).

* Provide the right support

PERSONAL/ADVISORY SUPPORT

It is essential that anyone providing support to service users who are involved in evaluations should be experienced in enabling people to express their own views. The supporter needs to work in such a way as to ensure that his or her views do not intrude – that the possibility of him/her influencing the service users is minimised as much as possible. The supporter needs skills in giving 'neutral' advice. For example, being able to suggest various options for asking questions, leaving the choice of options to the consultants.

PRACTICAL SUPPORT

Transport, meals, accommodation, secretarial back-up, office space – a place that the evaluation team can call their own – for storage, for reviewing progress, for recording impressions and results, for quiet thinking and relaxing!

* Allow plenty of preparation time

The amount of preparation time needs to be planned carefully. With hindsight, the evaluation team felt they needed more preparation time, although they became aware also that a balance needs to be struck between allowing enough time to prepare properly and not spending so much time preparing that it spoils the enthusiasm and dedication to the work.

Preparation time is needed

- to devise questionnaires – allowing enough time to prepare first drafts, to get some help from a questionnaire 'expert' and finally to revise them

- to prepare the consultants and their supporter

- to get to know the people with learning difficulties who will be interviewed.

Although the evaluation team had a profile of each person – their weekly activities, what they did in the daytime, what they did in the evenings, what they usually did at the weekend, and a certain amount of information about their ability to communicate – this was not sufficient to prepare the team for some of the difficulties they encountered with people whose ability to communicate verbally was very limited.

Teamwork

It is important that the service user consultants and their supporter work well as a team. Doing this work can be physically and emotionally tiring and if you don't get on well, it is unlikely you will do a successful piece of work.

References

Crawley, B. (1988) *The Growing Voice – a Survey of Self-advocacy Groups.* Campaign for People with Mental Handicap (now Values into Action).

(IDC) Independent Development Council for People with Mental Handicap (1986) *Pursuing Quality – how good are your local services for people with mental handicap?* London: King's Fund Centre.

O'Brien, J. (1986) 'A guide to personal futures planning', in Bellamy, G.T. and Wilcox, B. (eds) *A Comprehensive Guide to the Activities Catalog: An Alternative Curriculum for Youth and Adults with Severe Disabilities.* Baltimore, Maryland: Paul H Brookes.

Shearer, A. (1991) *Who Calls the Shots? Public Services and How They Serve the People Who Use Them.* London: King's Fund Centre.

Whittaker, A. (ed.) (1991) *Supporting Self-Advocacy.* London: King's Fund Centre.

Whittaker, A., Gardner, S. and Kershaw, J (1991) *Evaluation by People with Learning Difficulties.* London: King's Fund Centre.

Whittaker, A., Wright, J. and Bourlet, G. (1993) 'Setting up for self advocacy', in Booth, T. (ed) *Better Lives: Changing Services for People with Learning Difficulties.* Social Services Monographs.

Chapter 9

User Evaluation in the National Health Service

Bridie Fitzpatrick and Rex Taylor

The evolution of user perspectives in the NHS

In its formative years the National Health Service was primarily concerned with issues relating to the provision and distribution of health services. Equity was more important than quality. Indeed, it was assumed that quality flowed naturally from provision and that it was assured by the routine activities of the medical profession. The years of formation and consolidation were followed by a decade and a half of expansion and planning. Throughout the 1960s and early 1970s the main task was to define and achieve medically determined national norms. The district general hospital was a basic unit for the delivery of services and within each district there was an attempt to achieve nationally determined levels of service provision. It was assumed that if these levels were achieved, quality would naturally result. This assumption was challenged by a number of enquiries, the best known being the Ely report (DHSS 1969), which suggested that poor quality of care had as much to do with inadequate internal arrangements as insufficient provision. The UK Hospital Advisory Service was established in 1969 and it was followed in 1974 by the appointment of a Health Services Commissioner or Ombudsman. His task was to investigate and adjudicate complaints about the services, but issues involving clinical judgment were specifically excluded from his remit. Responsibility for quality remained primarily with the medical profession.

Local Health Councils were created throughout the NHS in 1972 to represent the interests of the public and to give consumers an opportunity to express their views on health service provision. They were entitled to be consulted by health boards on any major development in local services. From their inception, they had mixed fortunes but generally they failed to make much impact and were paid scant attention by most health boards. Consumers remained peripheral; indeed, writing of this period, Klein has described them as 'the ghosts in the NHS machinery' (Klein and Lewis 1974).

Throughout the 1980s and up to the present, the NHS has been increasingly incorporated into the market economy. Health has become a commodity and the major concerns of the NHS have become indistinguishable from those of a business organisation – levels of service, quality of product, meeting budgets, cost improvements, productivity, motivating and rewarding staff (DHSS 1983). The appointment of the Chief Executive of Sainsburys to head a small team to advise the Secretary of State for Health and Social Services was highly significant and symptomatic of this move towards commodification.

The central thrust of the first Griffiths Report (DHSS 1983) was for a more clearly defined managerial role. While he called for greater involvement of clinicians in management, his report marked the beginning of a progressive transfer of power from clinicians to managers. The titles of the 1989 White Papers – Working for Patients and Caring for People – were symptomatic of a further shift. Managers still retained ultimate responsibility for defining the nature and quality of provision but this responsibility was to be devolved as close as possible to the consumer. The NHS and Community Care Act 1990 formalised these proposals and there have been a number of subsequent developments which have attempted to strengthen the role of patient-as-consumer.

Both the Citizen's Charter (Prime Minister 1991) and the subsequent Patient's Charter (DoH 1991) outlined how the NHS (and other public services) were to become more consumer oriented. The Patient's Charter specifically enjoined health authorities to 'expand their use of questionnaires and surveys to find out what [consumers] think of the current services and to get suggestions of how things could be done better' (DoH 1991, p.18). The national Patient's Charter has been followed by local charters, mission statements and applications for NHS Trust status, all of which purport to give the patient a greater voice in the NHS. In most there is explicit recognition of the new-found status of users, for example

'The Trust will recognise that our users are the judge of the services provided, measurement of patient satisfaction, reviews and performance monitoring will be integral aspects of Trust activity.' (Ayrshire and Arran Health Board Application for Community Health Care Trust 1992)

Within health boards, individual posts and sometimes whole departments have been given a quality remit and designation. Similar developments are taking place in local authority social work departments following the publication of community care plans (see chapter by Leckie).

While there is a good deal of rhetoric in these developments, it would no longer be appropriate to describe the consumer as the ghost in the NHS machine. Indeed, it is possible to detect a sense in which the patient has become the expert in the appraisal of health services (Steele 1992). The stage is set for the patient-as-consumer to play a decisive role in determining the quality of health services. The attention must now shift to methodological issues involved in eliciting consumers' views. The main part of this paper describes dominant and evolving approaches to this task.

The dominant approach: patient response to service-determined criteria

The use of questionnaires based on criteria defined by service providers is undoubtedly the most common approach in eliciting patients' views of health services. A variety of approaches are taken: self-completion or administered by an interviewer, either at the time of service delivery, on discharge or posted at a later date. The questionnaires themselves sometimes consist only of structured (closed) questions which limit the information recorded, or sometimes of unstructured (open) questions which allow free unprompted information to be recorded. More often, they contain both structured and unstructured sections.

An early example of a questionnaire survey which included a combination of structured and unstructured questions was carried out by Raphael (1977). This study used a self-completion questionnaire which contained 28 questions covering five areas of hospital life: the ward and its equipment, sanitary accommodation, food, activities and care, and overall contentment. Patients were also invited to add comments and to record what they liked best and least about their stay in hospital. The study was conducted in 68 hospitals between 1970 and 1974.

The results showed that overall satisfaction was high. The highest satisfaction rates related to the delivery of care. Patients also expressed satisfaction with hospital food. The highest dissatisfaction rates related to toilets and the lack of privacy. The chief complaint about wards was that they were uncomfortably hot, stuffy and noisy at night. Boredom and early waking times were also identified as problems. Patients were also critical of the lack of information about the nature of their conditions and investigative tests. Analysis of the positive comments revealed that 93 per cent made reference to human or organisational aspects of their care, 49 per cent to physical factors. Similar analysis of the negative comment revealed that 46 per cent cited human or organisational factors as aspects they liked least. The questionnaire used in this study has been utilised in countless subsequent studies.

A more recent example of the same approach, and one of the largest ever conducted, was a Scottish Office national survey to ascertain public satisfaction with the NHS in general and also with their experiences of the care delivered (Scottish Office 1989). The research was conducted on four separate but interrelated groups each including over 1000 individuals in one or more of the following: hospital inpatients, hospital outpatients, general practitioner (GP) patients, and the 'general public'. The sample groups were designed to represent the elderly, maternity patients, parents of child patients and other adults. The method employed was interviewer-administered questionnaires containing mainly structured questions, but some unstructured questions were included. Respondents were interviewed in their own homes.

The results showed that general attitudes to the NHS were favourable across the six health boards. The 'general public' rated the NHS, along with the police, as the best run out of eight public services. The three patient sample groups also expressed high levels of overall satisfaction when asked about different areas of the service; only six per cent of inpatients, six per cent of outpatients and four per cent of GP patients were in any way dissatisfied.

For hospital inpatients, the highest satisfaction rates were related to the way the hospital was run, the standard of nursing care, attitude of doctors and nurses, standard of medical treatment and visiting arrangements. The highest dissatisfaction rates related to hospital food, facilities available for passing the time, and transport arrangements. Hospital outpatients were most satisfied with the helpfulness and attitude of staff/nurses and the standard of medical treatment received. They were most dissatisfied with facilities in waiting areas, time spent waiting at hospitals for appointments and transport arrangements. GP patients were most satisfied with the standard of medical treatment and the understanding attitude of the doctor. They were least satisfied with the time taken to get an appointment and the time waiting at the surgery.

Despite anecdotal evidence to the contrary and general disquiet within the health professions regarding the quality of the services they provide, these and similar studies have consistently shown high satisfaction rates. The commonly held explanation is that patients' loyalty to the NHS refrains them from expressing negative views about any particular aspect of the service. Recently this conventional explanation has been challenged by Jones (1989) who argues that studies based on service-determined criteria are unlikely to be sensitive to the valid concerns of patients. The inclusion of an open comment section in which additional patients' concerns can be recorded does not entirely overcome this problem since many people may have difficulty in thinking of concerns outwith the structure of the questionnaire.

Alternative approaches: using patient-determined criteria to evaluate services

Review of formal complaints of the service is probably the simplest means of using unsolicited data to evaluate service performance from the patients' perspectives. However, such data can never be representative of all dissatisfaction since formal procedures may inhibit many people from registering dissatisfaction. Furthermore, review of these data can describe only the negative side of the service in that complaints give no indication of which aspects of the service give the consumer satisfaction. These data could be counterbalanced by reviewing the contents of unsolicited letters of praise from patients and family members. However, the task of collating and analysing the hundreds of such letters received by any institution is likely to be administratively cumbersome.

Comment cards on which patients record complaints or praise about their health care experience is a quick and relatively inexpensive method of soliciting unstructured patient feedback. They can be left in a prominent position at the point of service delivery. Alternatively, they can be administered to all or to a representative sample of patients at the time the service is being utilised (e.g. when the person is in hospital), on discharge, or posted out at a later date.

A study using this method was carried out in York District Hospital by Learmouth (1990). In this study, 193 patients were contacted at home by post shortly after attending the outpatient department. Each patient was sent an explanatory letter which stressed anonymity and invited criticisms as well as praise, a complimentary pen, a sheet of paper headed 'My comments on the outpatient department', and a reply paid envelope. Rather surprisingly, in view of the low return from most exercises of this kind, 62 per cent of the study population returned comments. Consistent themes were then identified. Waiting times and the importance of nursing quality were frequently mentioned, but the facilities in waiting rooms figured in very few replies.

Interviews conducted on a one-to-one basis or in the form of focus groups, which elicit the collective views of a group of individuals, are commonly used to obtain unstructured views of patients. Pryce Jones (1988) used the 'Critical Incident Technique' to conduct individual interviews with patients in an outpatients department to identify their good and bad experiences of the service. They were encouraged to relate 'critical' incidents which caused them to form an opinion of the service. The highlighted incidents were then classified according to areas of common interest, the majority were found to relate to communication.

Buckenham (1986) used group interviews as a method of eliciting views in four groups of patients in acute wards in order to investigate their perceptions of nursing care. The patients were shown a card from a pack of alphabet cards and asked to identify functions performed by nurse beginning with that letter. The majority of the patients' responses related to attitudes and interpersonal relationships rather than to activities of care. Most patients were reluctant to criticise nurses and the majority of the comments made were positive. Their negative comments were particularly related with inadequate service provision and unsatisfactory service provision such as poor communication.

The above approaches are undoubtedly useful in providing qualitative data which highlight patients' concerns. However, their use in evaluating services is limited since they do not quantify the extent to which these concerns are representative of all users.

MacDonald *et al.* (1988) used a combination of structured and unstructured methods to survey long-stay patients in a large London psychiatric hospital. A questionnaire based on criteria elicited from both patients and staff was administered to patients by a trained interviewer, who in addition recorded all spontaneous comments to the questions. The interview schedule covered the following eight issues: fearfulness, isolation and apathy, lack of individualisation, unsatisfactory surroundings, lack of autonomy, unsatisfactory personal hygiene arrangements, lack of status and recognition, and restriction of actions. The respondents were also invited to comment on the best and worst aspects of being in hospital.

With this approach, utilising patient and staff criteria, the authors found higher levels of dissatisfaction than commonly found in studies using only staff criteria. Analysis of the responses to the most and least satisfactory aspects of hospital showed that 70 per cent of the best and 80 per cent of the worst aspects related to human factors such as personal and professional relationships, whilst only 30 per cent of the best and 20 per cent of the worst aspects related to physical factors such as the ward, food, grounds and buildings.

Space precludes a full description of all the innovative approaches which have been developed to identify patients' views. An NHS Management Executive paper (1992) provides a useful summary of techniques which have been devised by 19 English health authorities. These include the use of user/carer forums, public meetings, focus groups and telephone 'hot-lines'. The paper also makes useful suggestions as to how consumer opinions can and should be integrated into all stages of the contracting process. It is as yet too soon to assess the success of individual techniques and there is scope for rigorous evaluation.

Study of patient priorities in one Scottish Health Board

Method

The remainder of this chapter describes experimental research carried out by one of the authors (BF) to develop tools to evaluate service performance reliably from a user perspective. The research was funded by Ayrshire and Arran Health Board in the form of sponsorship of a research fellow in the Department of Social Policy, University of Glasgow.

The initial focus of the research was on people in long-stay wards for the elderly but the intention was to develop consumer-based methods which would be applicable across the Board's activities. The research aims were:

(1) to elicit the criteria by which patients in long term care for the elderly judge a good service

(2) to compare these criteria with those of others traditionally used as patient advocates; and

(3) to measure service performance against the patient criteria.

The method employed was a modification of the Nominal Group Interview Technique devised by Delbecq *et al.* (1975). This technique enables a group to generate ideas and reach consensus on the criteria above through a structured process. Patients were asked for their own priorities, while visitors and nurses were asked which features they thought were valued by patients.

Findings

KEY REQUIREMENTS DETERMINED BY PATIENTS

Table 9.1 lists the top 13 criteria, one half of all the criteria patients thought essential for a good service. Each item has a potential score of 120. The other 13 items not listed in Table 9.1 scored less than 20.

Table 9.1 The top 13 ranked criteria for a good service as ranked by patients in long-stay wards for the elderly

Patient Criteria	Score
Nurses attentive/cheerful/listen	82
Visitors	75
Company/chance to make friends	45
Cleanliness of wards	45
Church services	42
Knowing the purpose of medication	38
Privacy/dignity	37
Permanent place in the ward	36
Eating at a table	35
Occupational therapy	29
Food – variety and choice	28
Visiting times	28
Concert parties	26

Source: Fitzpatrick, B. (1992) Towards Comprehensive Quality Assurance. Unpublished report. Ayrshire and Arran Health Board.

As found in most surveys, personal attributes of nurses were clearly the most valued by patients. A surprising result not found in previous work is the importance patients attach to visitors. A majority of the patients' criteria (7) focus on organisational aspects of their care – having a choice and variety in food; company/chance to make friends; eating at a table; church services; having a permanent place in the ward/not being moved; visiting times; and concert parties. Only two criteria related to management of care for the individual – privacy and dignity; and knowing the purpose of medication. Patients selected as important only one criterion relating to their physical environment (cleanliness of the wards), and only one criterion which might have resource implications (occupational therapy).

KEY REQUIREMENTS DETERMINED BY RELATIVES
Although relatives accurately identified the importance which patients attach to the personal qualities of their carers, they did not identify their own importance to patients. The majority of the relatives' criteria (5) related to management of care for the individual – privacy and dignity; continuity of care/same staff; carers with a vocation for work with the elderly; patient toileting; and personal grooming. Relatives were also more likely to focus on resource-related criteria – physiotherapy; safe and appropriate aids; more nurses (trained and untrained); and sustained medical treatment. Two criteria related to the patients' physical environment – the cleanliness of the wards and patients having their own clothes and toiletries. In contrast to the patients' criteria, only one of the relatives' criteria related to the organisational aspects of patient care (having a choice and variety of food).

KEY REQUIREMENTS DETERMINED BY NURSES
The nurses were clearly aware of the importance which patients attached to their personal qualities and although they recognised the importance of visitors, their ranking of them was much lower than the patients' ranking. The majority of the staff criteria (5) related to the patients' physical environment – own clothes and toiletries; decor and furnishings; personal belongings; TV/radio/books; and warmth and lighting. Two criteria related to care management of the individual – patient privacy and dignity; and personalised care (defined by the nurses as care which respects the individual's personal habits). In contrast to the relatives' criteria, only two of the staff criteria might be directly related to resources – toilet facilities; and safe and appropriate aids. In contrast to the patients, only one of the staff criteria related to organisational aspects of patient care (choice and variety of food).

THE EXTENT OF AGREEMENT ON THE KEY REQUIREMENTS

Figure 9.1 illustrates the extent of concordance between the 13 top ranked criteria of patients, relataives and staff. Three items (i.e., less than a quarter of the patients' criteria) were held important by all three groups. These were: nurses who were attentive/cheerful and who listened, having variety and choice of food, and patient privacy and dignity.

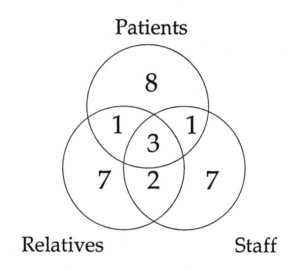

Patients

Relatives   Staff

Figure 9.1 Relationship between the top 13 ranked criteria of patients, relatives and staff

There was strong agreement on the importance of the personal attributes of the nurses and it was the top-ranked criterion of the three groups. The importance which patients attach to privacy and dignity was overestimated by the relatives (ranked 2nd) but accurately identified by the nurses (ranked 7th). On the other hand, the relatives were more accurate in ranking the relative importance of food-choice and variety.

In addition to the above, relatives agreed with patients that the cleanliness of the wards was important and nurses appreciated the value of visitors to patients. There was greater concordance between relatives and staff. In addition to agreeing on the importance of nurses being attentive/cheerful and who listened; choice and variety of food; and privacy and dignity, both groups believed that patients would have prioritised safe and appropriate aids; and own clothes and toiletries.

The comparison of the different sets of criteria permits an assessment of the implications of using others as patient advocates. In this exercise, the consequence of using either relatives or nurses to represent patients would result in identifying less than one third (4 of 13) of the patients' own criteria.

Further investigation
In order to test the robustness of the method employed in eliciting consumers' views, the exercise was repeated with groups of patients, relatives and nurses in long stay wards for the young mentally ill. The findings of the previous study were substantially replicated: nurses and relatives were successful in identifying only one third of the criteria which the patients thought the most essential for a good service.

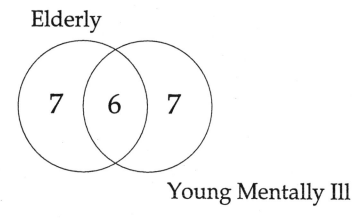

Figure 9.2 Relationship between the top 13 ranked criteria of patients in long stay wards for the elderly and young patients in long stay wards for the mentally ill

As in the previous study, the individual groups had quite different concerns. The patient criteria mainly related to interpersonal relations with staff and others, relatives focussed on patients' physical environment whilst staff believed that patients would value empowering aspects of patient care or the opportunity for patients to self-regulate their daily activities. Comparison of the two sets of patient criteria revealed that the level of agreement achieved between these two different groups of long-stay patients is much higher than that achieved by their respective groups of advocates, relatives and carers (Figure 9.2). Both patient groups identified three identical criteria – personal attributes of nurses, patient privacy and ward cleanliness. A further three criteria were strongly related: (1) 'meaningful work option' and 'occupational therapy', (2) 'safe medication' and 'knowing the purpose of medication' and (3) 'good food' and 'food-choice and variety'.

These findings suggest that despite differences in age and nature of health problem, patients in long stay wards have common values and that the best patient advocates are other patients.

Evaluation of the service against the patient criteria

The criteria identified by the patients in long stay wards for the elderly and the young mentally ill were subsequently the basis of two questionnaires which were used to assess patient satisfaction with their lives in their respective care settings. The questionnaires contained a series of closed questions with varied range of response categories. They were administered by an interviewer so that all spontaneous comments to the questions could also be recorded.

Whilst the majority of patients were satisfied with the majority of aspects of their care which they themselves had identified as essential for a good service, significant levels of dissatisfaction were reported in relation to the organisation of the delivery of care, and those which were directly related to interpersonal relationships with nurses. The levels of dissatisfaction reported on these aspects were substantially greater than commonly reported in conventional surveys.

Conclusion

The research was successful in evaluating the quality of a service from the user's perspective. However, in initiatives such as this the consumer's voice is limited to expressing opinions on services which are provided on the basis of decisions made by others. If purchasers and providers of health care services are to provide services which are more responsive to the needs, views and preferences of the people they serve, they will be obliged to involve consumers in larger issues such as strategic planning and service development. In line with these nation-wide developments, the authors are building on the above work in which the focus shifts from the conventional approach (one-off consultation measuring service outcome) to developing methods of consumer participation throughout the whole purchasing cycle (assessing needs for health services; determining service development; and measuring service quality).

References

Ayrshire and Arran Health Board (1992) Application for Community Health Care Trust.

Buckenham, M. (1986) 'Patients' points of view'. *Senior Nurse* 4 (3), 26–27.

Department of Health and Social Security (1969) *Report of the Committee of Enquiry into Allegations of Ill Treatment of Patients and other Irregularities at Ely Hospital.* London: HMSO.

Department of Health and Social Security (1983) *NHS Management Inquiry.* London: DHSS.

Department of Health (1991) *The Patient's Charter.* London: HMSO.

Delbecq, A.L., Van de Ven, A.H. and Gustafson, D.H. (1975) *Group Techniques for Programme Planning: A Guide to Nominal Group and Delphi Processes.* Glenview, Illinois: Scott, Foresman and Company.

Jones, L.M. (1989) 'The Chief Scientist Reports – The consumer's voice: learning how to listen'. *Health Bulletin* 47 (5), 258–265.

Learmouth, M. (1990) 'Please speak your mind'. *Health Services Journal* 100, 1035.

Klein, R. and Lewis, J. (1974) *Local Health Councils: The Politics of Consumer Representation.* London: Centre for Studies in Social Policy.

MacDonald, L., Sibbald, B. and Hoare, C. (1988) 'Measuring patient satisfaction with life in long-stay psychiatric hospital'. *International Journal of Social Psychiatry* 34 (4), 292–304.

NHS Management Executive (1992) *Local Voices – the Views of Local People in Purchasing for Health.* London: Department of Health.

Prime Minister (1991) *The Citizen's Charter: Raising the Standard.* Cm 1597. London: HMSO.

Pryce Jones, M. (1988) 'Not how many but why – a qualitative approach to customer relations'. *Health Service Management* (December), 175–177.

Raphael, W. (1977) Patients and their Hospitals. London: King Edward's Hospital Fund.

Scottish Office Central Research Unit (1989) *Consumer Attitudes to the National Health Service in Scotland.* Vols I and II. Edinburgh: Scottish Office.

Secretaries of State for Health, Wales, Northern Ireland and Scotland (1989) *Working for Patients.* London: HMSO.

Secretaries of State for Health, Social Security, Northern Ireland and Scotland (1989) *Caring for People.* Cm 849. London: HMSO.

Steele, K. (1992) 'Patients as experts: Consumer appraisal of health services'. *Public Money and Management* (October–December), 31–37.

Part 3
Implementation

Chapter 10

Quality Assurance in Social Work

*Tom Leckie**

Introduction

An Eastern sage once said something along the lines of 'there is more than one path to Nirvana'. He wasn't referring to quality assurance, but he might have been. Quality assurance sometimes seems to promise perfection, and it can be pursued in a vast variety of different approaches. Social work service agencies have been following these many paths to this potential heaven with increasing vigour recently. But where on earth (or Nirvana) does this impetus spring from?

Quality in this context can be defined as 'the totality of features and characteristics of a product or service that bear on its ability to satisfy a given need' (James 1992). Those responsible for planning, developing, managing and delivering social work services would argue that their work is constantly and consistently about improving the services to clients (or users or consumers) within the resources available. Central Government's view is that the quality of services could be further improved, and in 'Caring for People' (Secretaries of State 1989) it set out methods by which this improvement might be achieved in the field of care in the community.

The methods focused on in 'Caring for People' were:

- community care planning
- registration and inspection
- complaints by users
- assessment and care management

---

* All views expressed in this chapter are those of the author.

- service specification through commissioning and purchasing.

Through these initiatives, services should be targeted at those most in need, the quality of services to these clients should be specified and monitored, and there should be procedures outlined for dealing with services found to be unacceptable.

Central Government has also promoted the improvement of quality through the introduction of the Citizen's Charter (Prime Minister 1991), with its emphasis on publication of standards of service and performance against those standards, clear information about services, the setting and achieving of targets, and lay involvement in inspection.

Most people would agree that improvement of quality is a 'good thing', yet reaction to the development of quality assurance in social work services has been somewhat mixed. Why should this be?

First, there has been a genuine suspicion about the acceptance of a concept so clearly originating from, and rooted in, manufacturing industry, and seemingly so distanced from social care. The British Quality Association's Social Care Agencies Sector Committee has produced guidance for social care agencies on the interpretation of BS5750 (BQA 1987) – which sets out facets of organisational practice that should be addressed to ensure the maintenance of agreed standards.

Second, and related to the first concern, is the feeling that while the concept propounded by one of the gurus of quality assurance that 'quality is free' (Crosby 1979) may be viable in product industries, and perhaps in service industries, it would not be true in social care. It is perhaps significant that in 1991, at a time when quality and quality assurance were being seriously debated in social work, the title of the annual conference of the Association of Directors of Social Work in Scotland was not 'Quality is Free', but 'The Cost of Quality'.

Third, there has been an understandable ambivalence about the introduction of quality assurance initiatives at a time when significant change, in part brought about by the community care developments highlighted above, was already taking up much of the energy of local government social services and social work departments and of voluntary agencies. An alternative view is that since quality assurance is about constant change, as it is about constant improvement, then periods of change offer a fertile medium for the introduction of quality assurance.

Finally, the scepticism concerning the introduction of measures to develop quality may lie in the confusion surrounding the language about quality, and the understandable reluctance of organisations and individuals to commit themselves to something ill-defined and not fully under-stood.

What 'quality' means

This is an appropriate point to try to clarify some of the terms associated with quality assurance. A useful place to begin is the 'Purchase of Service' practice guidance issued by the Social Services Inspectorate (SSI) for England and Wales in 1991 (SSI 1991). It offers the following definitions:

> '**Quality assurance** is used to refer to those processes which aim to ensure that concern for quality is designed and built into services. It implies commitment on the part of local authority social services committee members and senior managers to a systematic approach to the pursuit of quality and will be demonstrated by an explicit statement of policy, setting out agency expectations and standards. Systematic and comprehensive arrangements to ensure that the re-quired standards are achieved will be evident throughout organisa-tional procedures and will include processes for verification and feedback.'

It is useful also to note the SSI's definition of **quality control**, which

> 'refers to those processes of verification, and will include systematic monitoring, including statistical and other management informa-tion, recurring and one-off audits and inspection activity designed to establish whether standards are being achieved. Quality control is one aspect of quality assurance. It should provide objective feedback to line managers who have continuing responsibility for quality, about what is actually being achieved.' (*ibid*)

It is important to note the difference between quality control and quality assurance, because it is not uncommon for local authority social work or social service departments to base their quality assurance initiatives only on quality control mechanisms, specifically registration and inspection and complaints procedures. The statutory timetable required by the NHS and Community Care Act for the introduction of community care initia-tives, with the introduction of registration and inspection units and complaints procedures in the forefront, perhaps encourages this ap-proach. One Scottish social work department's 1992 Community Care Plan clearly identified that its quality control mechanisms did not provide a quality assurance system (Dumfries and Galloway Regional Council 1992).

Returning to a good working definition of quality assurance, Ann James suggests that the SSI definition of quality assurance above 'needs to be broadened beyond a description of service delivery processes to include the centrality of user views on defining quality' (James 1992). This view is echoed and expanded upon in the Scottish Office Social Work Services Group's discussion paper, which states:

> ...the development of quality assurance in community care focuses on:
>
> - the user receiving a service which meets his/her needs;
> - achieving this by setting appropriate standards, monitoring those standards and measuring the outcomes;
> - ensuring the above by a quality assurance process;
> - implementation by management, staff and users.'
>   (Scottish Office 1991)

It goes on to say:

> 'Quality assurance needs to be developed from senior management, with freedom to develop and experiment at unit level. Quality assurance systems include quantative techniques such as checklists, schedules, procedures and information, but they also focus on qualitative aspects such as relationships between staff and management, between staff and users, team building, and so on. There are already being developed systems which can be used by social work departments either on a department-wide basis or for aspects of service delivery.' (*ibid*)

Developing quality assurance

Before examining some of these initiatives, it would be useful to look at the components which together might make up a quality assurance process. These include:

- consumer surveys
- the setting, monitoring and developing of standards (input, process, output and outcome standards)
- information systems

- staff training, development and supervision
- a quality policy
- quality control mechanisms, such as inspection units and complaints procedures
- user involvement.

These components reflect the variety of ways in which local authority social work and social services departments and voluntary agencies have introduced quality assurance measures – the paths to Nirvana. These include using quality control mechanisms to lead the process (usually through registration and inspection units, whose remit is almost exclusively for residential establishments), developing quality through service specification when contracting out services, improving quality by the use of audits (independent examinations of quality to provide information and appraisal), using one or more projects as pilots for quality assurance, developing a 'customer care' approach, developing quality by standard setting at local level, and adopting a 'whole organisation' approach using a system such as BS5750. There are others, I am sure, but for the moment I would like to exemplify some of the above approaches which are already in use in the United Kingdom.

I will begin by considering quality assurance through registration and inspection. This is a sensitive area. Some social service and social work departments have placed registration and inspection units within quality assurance in the organisation. I earlier cautioned against confusing the two, or substituting control for assurance. James found cause for concern in practice:

'In some cases there was, for example, much talk of intended work in quality assurance, but when we looked at the workload of inspection and its aftermath it became clear that most staff were, and would remain, primarily inspectors for the foreseeable future. Indeed, we found that staff in quality assurance units were generally called inspectors either formally or colloquially. Moreover, where the inspectorate and the quality assurance units were not distinguished from each other it was often left to individual staff within units to work out any potential conflict between policing standards and what might broadly be termed a developmental, change agency or internal consultant role.' (James 1992)

She identified three risks in approaching quality assurance (QA) through the medium of inspection. First, those involved may begin, and continue, to equate QA with the correcting of mistakes identified through inspection rather than the celebration of success on which good quality assurance focusses. Second, the responsibility for QA is seen as belonging to the inspection unit rather than to everyone in the organisation. Third, inspection and QA are often confused in the minds of those working in both areas.

While three of the five agencies studied by James had resolved these dilemmas by separating inspection from quality assurance, others attempt to deal with possible difficulties from within a unit with joint responsibilities. One organisation which seems to have resolved matters well is Berkshire Social Services Department, where quality assurance inspectors become involved in helping individual projects develop quality for themselves, by using their skills to help staff think through quality problems, such as setting standards and defining training requirements.

It is clear then that while there are risks to the development of QA through an inspection route, it can be a successful way to use the impetus created by the care in the community agenda.

Another approach is a care audit system such as the one adopted by Birmingham Social Services Department (James 1992). This approach is akin to inspection, with visits by teams of auditors – seconded social work staff, co-ordinated from the department's Performance Review Section – but differs slightly in that the care audit process helps staff generate their own information bases from which they can measure the performance of their own unit. Working from agreed standards derived from national and local documents, the auditors record their evaluation of care in an establishment, based on observation, interviews and examination of records, come to an agreement with the staff about changes needed, and timetable these changes, including a future review. This system seems particularly useful in helping staff take responsibility for setting and developing their own standards, and placing and retaining responsibility for quality squarely within the line management structure.

Cleveland SSD has also developed a quality assurance programme which similarly employs audits and standard setting as essential elements, but also has incorporated quality management training for managers. Cleveland's standards are developed by staff with the views of service users and carers being taken into consideration. Audits of units then take place, the audit team being made up of a quality assurance officer and staff from other units. The audit team interviews staff and users, reviews documents and prepares a report. It is expected that managers of units visited will prioritise issues from the reports and develop action plans to improve quality. This system also allows unresolved local issues to be taken to senior managers and elected members for action.

The application of BS5750 (British Standards Institution 1986) is yet another method chosen to introduce quality assurance to social care agencies in Great Britain. There has been some scepticism about applying BS5750 to social work because its requirement for a quality policy and clearly defined procedures throughout all the processes of an organisation has major resource implications, and may in any case not lead to improvements in outcomes in services for users. Nevertheless, three successful examples are already in place, two covering whole social services departments and one a single residential establishment.

The two departments are Norfolk and Gloucester. Over the last decade Norfolk has been developing a quality assurance system based on the adoption of a quality policy, clear organisational responsibility and accountability, inspections, good procedures, and a particular focus on training in quality for staff. This approach was led by top management, and an account of this has been prepared by two of the senior managers involved (Cassam and Gupta 1992).

Gloucester Social Services Department took a more unusual route in introducing quality assurance (Gloucester SSD 1990a). Its approach might be seen as 'project' based, and was initiated by piloting four projects to identify issues for further development of quality assurance, with a 'quality assurance officer' allocated to lead each project. This project approach focuses intervention at a local level, enables staff to have a significant say in the process, and begins to seek ways to involve 'customers' (a term used locally to include a wider group than users) more fully. These pilots were carried out in a variety of social work settings, helping to confirm the appropriateness of quality assurance measures throughout social work.

One of Gloucester's projects, of particular interest in the light of the changes in community care in April 1993, is the Tewkesbury Care Management Project for which an associated quality manual was developed (Gloucester SSD 1990b). This focusses on the method necessary to ensure that the project identified and met to appropriate standards the needs of those it served.

The residential establishment, which is for older people, is Napier House in Newcastle, which was the first personal social services residential establishment, including nursing homes or any personal care enterprise anywhere in the UK or Europe to be registered as a 'quality assured' home under BS5750.

There are three important factors, related to the use of BS5750 in these agencies that are worthy of note. First, this method can be applied to a whole department or to one project. Second, service provision is independently assessed, accredited and monitored. And third, it can involve consumers in the process. As Cassam and Gupta (1992) point out, objectives were defined in Norfolk SSD to ensure that the service provided a client focus, client satisfaction by way of client involvement in the process, a prompt and appropriate response to client requests, and the best use of available resources for clients' benefit.

Humberside Social Services Department has opted for yet another way into quality assurance, which also places a heavy emphasis on the views of users in implementing quality measures (Lynch and Pope 1990). This is achieved through standard-setting exercises. Individual interviews to ascertain the preferences of users are employed to develop standards, and these preferences are aggregated by way of a computer system to set targets for each quality standard. The process is taken forward through a method termed a 'diagonal slice', which entails the forming of project teams composed of staff members from various levels of the department from top management to support workers as well as users. One element of this procedure that is of crucial and increasing importance is that it has been developed jointly with East Yorkshire Health Authority, thus addressing the thorny problem of different standards being set or accepted by local health and social service agencies.

This joint social work/health service approach is echoed in the use of the 'Enquire Quality Assurance' system (Richards and Heginbotham 1990) to examine mental health services in Mid Glamorgan (Mid Glamorgan SSD and Health Authority 1992). This initiative, undertaken by Mid Glamorgan County Council Social Services Department and Mid Glamorgan Health Authority, is a practical approach to quality assurance through examination of service delivery by the creation of an observation team. This comprises the staff providing the service and social work and health care staff external to the service being assessed. The team's purpose is to look at structure, process and outcomes; interview managers, staff and service users; analyse these observations and discussions; develop action plans for the improvement of the service in conjunction with staff and management; and establish processes to monitor the implementation of the action plans.

Summary of approaches described

Many if not all of the systems itemised above have monitoring and review processes which ensure that proposed changes do in fact take place, and regular reviews are built into the systems, but the question of exactly who 'quality assures' the quality assurance systems remains. BS5750 is a system with a defined external monitoring process, and for monitoring to be objective and influential it is clear that it should be performed by agents external to the system being monitored. Cassam and Gupta (1992) identify some of the possibilities for what they term 'an external MOT'. They include the Social Services Inspectorate (or in Scotland, the Social Work Services Inspectorate) taking on the role; reciprocal arrangements between agencies which have quality assurance systems; a system of trained external auditors (which is being considered by the British Quality Association and Norfolk County Council); and contracted consultants. There is understandably still some way to go in developing this important aspect of the quality assurance process.

Thus, despite anxieties, scepticism, defensiveness, and a plethora of other changes to incorporate, social care agencies are on the way to encompassing and developing quality assurance systems. As can be seen from the examples above, which are not comprehensive, they are doing so in ways which fit with their values, structures, staff and relationships with other agencies as much as with the validity or solidity of any model or system introduced.

It is perhaps early to identify many trends in quality assurance in social service agencies, but the following seem to be emerging:

- the increasing use of systems, such as BS5750, which delineate a quality assurance process and are externally validated

- the secondment of staff from one part of an organisation to work with external quality assurance agents in reviews of other parts of the organisation, thus developing expertise

- attempts to involve users in the quality assurance process

- joint quality assurance projects with health.

The way ahead

So much for the way we are. What about the way we might be? The SSI suggests some methods for developing systems (James 1992), to which I have added. These include:

- listening attentively to 'stakeholders'
- recognising and encouraging good quality wherever it is to be found
- investing in people
- making quality high profile within the organisation
- investing in management information systems which are user friendly, quick and accurate
- involving users in standard setting and service design
- creating a culture which encourages innovation
- working with health, voluntary organisations, private agencies, housing agencies and others
- using available Quality Assurance systems and adapting them to fit
- developing mechanisms for reviewing practice
- quality assuring the Quality Assurance system.

In conclusion, assuring the quality of services in social care is not easy.

> 'In the case of services that deal with people's bodies or minds, where the nature of the problem is constantly shifting and is difficult to define it may be particularly hard to define the nature of the actual or intended outcome and therefore to make any judgement of quality.' (Walsh 1991)

But this should not stop us from trying. Nor has it. The improvement of the quality of services is a major preoccupation of those engaged in social care. But the development of a systematic approach to ensuring, improving and monitoring quality throughout an organisation is taking longer and meeting with more resistance, because of some of the factors outlined above. However, initiatives are being pioneered by the agencies exampled above, and many others. And the numbers are growing apace. It has been said of manufacturing and service industry enterprises that by the end of the century if a company is not quality assured, it will not survive as a company. This may not apply to social care in general (though it may apply to elements of social care) but in a world where the purchasing and providing of services is to be increasingly split then quality assurance will be increasingly important if not essential.

There is no 'one way' to quality assurance. We have seen several approaches introduced by a variety of routes. The Social Services Committee of the House of Commons (Social Services Committee 1990) recommended 'that the Government investigate the feasibility of developing a detailed quality assurance system for use by local authorities, with appropriate skills training programmes'. While there is some worth in this suggestion, it may be more appropriate for local authorities, and other agencies, all of whom have developed their own particular approaches to organisational development, to create and refine quality assurance systems which suit them. Perhaps these systems should grow from within the organisations, rather than be imposed from above.

Examples of non-prescriptive guidance have been published by the Social Work Services Group at the Scottish Office and the Department of Health. In its Discussion Paper it is stated that 'The SWSI will wish to work with local authorities in developing quality assurance across the whole range of social work services'. The Department of Health set up a working party on Inspection and Quality Assurance, which commissioned the King's Fund to undertake a study (James 1992), describing it as 'a description and analysis of emerging practice'.

The future of quality assurance in the social services will be decided by a combination of external changes and internal decisions on how to respond to these changes. It is likely that some of the more important future developments will be:

- the development of joint approaches, not only with health, but with housing agencies

- the increasing use of contracts to specify clearly not only the quality of services to be delivered, but also how these services will be monitored, and perhaps to insist on a quality assurance system being in place before a contract is agreed

- the development of staff training in aspects of quality assurance so that staff can understand quality assurance and take part in peer group monitoring

- the use of external agencies to monitor quality assurance systems.

In an example of the last of these, the SSI has recently inspected the quality assurance sections of two social service departments and produced reports on them (SSI 1992a,b). These inspections were carried out at the request of the departments involved.

So much for the possibilities. However carried out, the task for the future is to ensure this process spreads, that it is monitored and improved, and that the focus is on the end product – a continual improvement in the quality of service offered to those who use the service.

References

British Quality Association Social Care Agencies Sector Committee (1987) *Guidance on the Interpretation of BS5750: Part Two: With Reference to Social Care Agencies.* London: British Quality Association.

British Standards Institution (1986) *Quality Assurance.* B.S.I. Handbook No. 22. London.

Cassam, E. and Gupta, H. (1992) *Quality Assurance for Social Care Agencies.* London: Longman.

Crosby, P.B. (1979) *Quality is Free: The Art of Making Quality Certain.* New York: McGraw Hill.

Dumfries and Galloway Regional Council (1992) Community Care Plan.

Gloucester Social Services Department (1990a) Quality Assurance Pilot Projects.

Gloucester Social Services Department (1990b) Tewkesbury Care Management Project: Quality Manual.

James, A. (1992) *Committed to Quality: Quality Assurance in Social Services Departments.* London: HMSO.

Lynch, G. and Pope, B. (1990) *Involving clients and staff in the development of a quality assurance system: Social services and quality assurance.* Manchester: Social Information Systems.

Mid Glamorgan Social Services Department and Mid Glamorgan Health Authority (1992) Quality Assurance Through Observation of Service Delivery: A Practical Approach Undertaken in Mid Glamorgan.

Prime Minister (1991) *The Citizen's Charter: Raising the Standard.* Cm 1599. London: HMSO.

Richards, H. and Heginbotham, C. (1990) *The Enquire System: A Workbook on Quality Assurance in Health and Social Care.* London: King's Fund College.

Scottish Office, Social Work Services Group (1991) *Discussion Paper: Improving Quality Assurance in Community Care.* Edinburgh: Scottish Office.

Secretaries of State for Health, Social Security, Wales and Scotland (1989) *Caring for People.* London: HMSO.

Social Services Committee (1990) *Community Care: Quality, Seventh Report: Social Services Committee, Session 1989–90: Together with the Proceedings of the Committee.* London: HMSO.

Social Services Inspectorate (1991) *Purchase of Service: Practice Guidance and Practice Materials for SSDs and Other Agencies.* London: HMSO.

Social Services Inspectorate (1992a) *Inspection of the Quality Assurance Division, East Sussex Social Services Department.* London: Department of Health.

Social Services Inspectorate (1992b) *Inspection of the Quality Service Unit, Hampshire Social Services Department.* London: Department of Health.

Walsh, K. (1991) 'Quality and public services'. *Public Administration* (69), winter, 503–514.

Chapter 11

Performance Review and Quality in General Practice

Donald Irvine

Quality in British general practice is like the curate's egg. Some practices are strongly motivated to try and improve standards. Others are quite uninterested, and this shows both in their standards of practice and in their lack of involvement in educational and other quality improving activities. Most come somewhere between these extremes. There is thus a very broad spectrum of performance, reflecting widely differing attitudes to both the functions of primary health care and the responsibilities of being a professional person. This wide variation helps to explain the difficulties inherent in introducing quality assuring and quality improving policies in a public service in which there is a strong tradition of individual professional independence and autonomy; some 35,000 family doctors function as independent contractors and are widely dispersed in small units throughout the United Kingdom.

This paper outlines progress to date in the implementation of quality initiatives in general practice and looks ahead to further developments. It begins with those landmarks in the history of general practice which have had significant quality implications, and so provide the context within which current policies should be set.

Early landmarks

When the National Health Service (NHS) was established in 1948, most general practitioners worked single-handed. Standards of care varied enormously, a fact documented in meticulous detail by Joseph Collings (1950) in his famous reconnaissance of general practice. Collings sought to establish the suitability of general practice to continue as the main provider of primary medical care in the new health service. His study amounted to a general condemnation of the standards then prevailing, and not surprisingly it produced a robust reaction from the medical profession. More thoughtful general practitioners recognised that something had to be done. In 1952 they founded the College of General Practitioners – later to become the Royal College of General Practitioners – in order to seek standards for general practice where hitherto there had been none (Horder 1992).

The second landmark was structural and political, and was embodied in the Charter Contract of 1964 (British Medical Association 1965). This new contract between general practitioners and the NHS provided a package of incentives which encouraged group practice, and made it more possible for doctors to afford new buildings and equipment, and to employ receptionists and secretarial staff to support them in their work. At about the same time innovative general practitioners saw the value of working more closely with district nurses and health visitors, and so the 'attachment' of local authority nurses to practices was established. The overall result of these changes was to improve the quality of the environment for care where practitioners chose to invest appropriately, and to lay the foundations for modern team working where doctors and nurses decided to work more closely together. It had the perverse effect, however, of widening the gap between innovators and the traditionalists who did not make the full use of the new opportunities.

As the 1960s drew to a close, the Royal College of General Practitioners (RCGP) completed its arrangements for vocational training. This new development was to have important consequences for quality and standards. Thus, vocational training forced the newly selected trainers to describe their discipline for the first time (e.g. RCGP 1972, Freeman and Byrne 1976), and in so doing to abandon the traditional concept of general practice as simply the sum of a number of specialties practised at a fairly superficial level. Teaching and learning in small groups led by general practitioners was introduced. Continuous assessment was built into the best programmes and an examination (Membership of the RCGP) was established as a final assessment indicating optimal competence in general practice for those who chose to take it. Most significant of all, teaching practices were established. These practices and their designated trainers, all volunteers, were for the first time expected to meet external quality standards, in this case set by the College and implemented through the new university-based regional postgraduate organisations. Trainer appointments were for three years only, and were renewable on the basis of continuing demonstrable performance. Over time a national system for accrediting teaching practices has been progressively refined; today this assures the quality of teaching in such practices (RCGP 1990).

Overall, vocational training may be said to have brought the ethos of standard setting to a significant segment of general practice for the first time. However, there are two important qualifications. First, although the system for accrediting teaching practices works and is capable of being extended to all practices, it is in fact still confined to these self-selected teaching practices because there is not yet either the professional or governmental will to extend it generally. Second, trainees can choose whether or not to be assessed. Although the British Medical Association supports the principle of assessment on a voluntary basis, it is still not ready to acknowledge that a national standard of competence for new entrants to general practice is needed to protect the public even though professional opinion is now moving in that direction (General Medical Services Committee 1992).

Towards audit: initiatives from the profession

In 1975 the RCGP, in another major innovation, introduced a system for assisting interested members to audit various aspects of their work, notably practice activities such as, for example, hospital referrals (RCGP 1978a) and home visiting profiles (RCGP 1978b). The RCGP's Birmingham research unit helped doctors with data collection and undertook the analysis and feedback to show where a practitioner stood in relation to his or her peers. The system faltered partly because the standard setting and change management aspects of the audit cycle were never adequately addressed, but mainly because audit was not on the profession's main agenda (Merrison 1979). Now, as the profession is required to implement audit in the NHS, the relevance of this approach is being rediscovered.

In 1983 the RCGP, responding to growing professional and public concern about the standards of care in some general practices (Irvine 1983), launched its Quality Initiative (RCGP 1983). The Council of the College invited all members explicitly to describe their current work and the services available to their patients, to define their objectives for care, and to audit their personal performance against these. Enthusiastic members responded. Two years later, in a major policy statement on quality in general practice (RCGP 1985), the RCGP for the first time began to see medical audit not only as a way of enhancing a doctor's professional development through education, but even more as an essential tool of quality management in practices intent on improving patient care. Today, the principles of the Quality Initiative live on, especially in the growing number of practices which are interested in the total quality approach to their service.

In the 1980s there were two methodological developments of significance. First the RCGP launched its 'What Sort of Doctor?' method (RCGP 1985) in parallel with the Quality Initiative. This approach to quality assurance used a structured practice inspection by a visiting team of peers (a development of teaching practice inspections) which assessed four areas considered to be indicative of performance – professional values, accessibility, clinical competence, and ability to communicate. The method exposed a practice to outside scrutiny and influence, and required the practitioners and staff to explain and justify their policies and results to local colleagues.

Second, in the late 1980s, the North of England Study of Standards and Performance in General Practice (Irvine, Russell and Hutchinson *et al.* 1986) brought 92 trainers together in small groups to set standards for five common conditions in childhood. The clinical performance of the trainers was assessed before and after standard setting, using data abstracted from clinical records. This study provided valuable experience of peer led standard setting on a fairly large scale, and reassuringly it demonstrated significant changes in doctor behaviour in the direction indicated by the standards set (North of England Study of Standards and Performance in General Practice 1992a,b). At the same time general practitioners in the Netherlands began a comparable exercise (Grol, Mesker and Schevellis 1988) using externally generated standards; this provided a valuable opportunity for comparing and contrasting the internal and external approaches.

Arrangements imposed by government
These developments were accompanied by a growing number of published single practice audits, the nature and content of which were fully reviewed by Baker in 1988(a). Nevertheless, despite these activities, the government concluded that reliance on a wholly self-regulating approach to quality assurance in general practice would not succeed in raising standards overall because of the persisting problem of engaging the interest and commitment of all practitioners (Secretaries of State for Health and Social Services 1986). Consequently, in 1990 the government

introduced the new contract for general practice (Secretary of State for Health and Welsh Office 1989) in order to increase the public accountability of doctors for more clearly specified services, and decided that by 1992 medical audit should become an integral feature of clinical practice for all general practitioners working in the NHS (DOH 1990).

Summary of current practice

Today there are several approaches to quality assurance and quality improvement in British general practice. Medical audit is currently the most prominent, but the link between quality and the NHS contracting process is becoming as important in its own way. The accreditation and re-accreditation of practices and the certification and re-certification of the competence of individual doctors are coming onto the agenda (Gray 1991), as is standard setting for the Patient's Charter (Secretary of State for Health 1991). Furthermore, the General Medical Council (GMC)(1992) is to introduce new procedures to enable the medical profession to deal with registered medical practitioners whose competence and performance are thought to be seriously impaired.

The approach to quality through audit

Despite professional innovation in both general and specialist practice, medical audit was introduced in the 1989 White Paper 'Working for Patients' as a new principle for the NHS (Secretaries of State for Health 1989). It was seen by government as probably the most important approach for improving quality in individual practices, and was the only part of the NHS reforms which the medical profession supported wholeheartedly. In the paper the government defines audit as 'the systematic process by which doctors continually assess and evaluate their clinical practice, the organisation of services, their managerial function and educational activities.' Medical audit is thus seen as a cyclical standard setting and monitoring activity through which doctors critically examine their own and each other's practice, and then apply the lessons learned to improve their professional practice and enhance the quality of care.

General practice uses the concept of quality proposed by Donabedian (1966). He conceived quality as having three interrelated components which he called structure, process and outcome. He used the term structure to describe the physical features making up the environment for care; such characteristics could include, for example, the number of health centres, doctors, nurses and practice records. The term process describes what happens to patients, what is done for them and how well. Process variables include, for instance, examinations undertaken, prescriptions ordered, tests carried out, advice given – indeed, all the activities involved in a consultation. Donabedian defined *outcome* as the effects of care on patients, that is, those changes in a patient's health status that could be attributed to antecedent health care.

In 1991 the Department of Health established Medical Audit Advisory Groups (MAAGs) to implement government policy on audit throughout England and Wales. There are comparable arrangements in Scotland and Northern Ireland. MAAGs are committees of Family Health Service Authorities (FHSAs) which are exclusively medical and which are charged with the responsibility of introducing the culture and habit of audit to every general practice (Department of Health 1990). Today MAAGs are still settling in, deciding on their best ways of working, forging links with individual practices (Humphrey and Hughes 1992) and, in Oxford, developing criteria for auditing their own effectiveness (Derry, Lawrence, Griew *et al.* 1991).

In this early stage of general implementation, audit is still regarded by the organised medical profession primarily as an educational activity rather than as a management tool for assessing, evaluating and improving standards of patient care (SCOPME 1989). However, ideas are changing. It is now becoming accepted that audit has to embrace the whole practice team, and that the relevant concept is therefore of 'clinical audit' involving all health professionals concerned with the care of a patient rather than 'medical audit' limited to doctors only. This development gains impetus from the fact that nurses are also developing their own approach to quality assessment (Kitson, Hyndman, Harvey and Yerrell 1990). Some innovative practices, imbued with the quality philosophy, are already moving even further, to see quality assuring and quality improving activities as an inseparable part of practice management (RCGP 1983, Irvine 1990, Irvine and Irvine 1991, Irvine 1992).

Performance review methods

The following are the main methods used in general practice today.

1. Practice activity analysis

Practice activity analysis is the term used in general practice to describe process audit by practitioners. It is the commonest type of formal audit in use today (Crombie and Fleming 1988). Individual practice audits have tended to focus on aspects of clinical care in common, chronic conditions. It is also usual for practices to monitor the quality of their record keeping using this approach (Baker 1988b, Fleming and Lawrence 1981). Most often the audits are episodic, but there is growing interest in continuous activity monitoring, especially where contractual obligations are involved as in achieving targets for immunisation or cervical cytology (Irvine and Irvine 1991).

The outstanding feature of most published practice activity audits is that the practitioners carrying them out have tended to see the data in isolation, describing current practice but not relating that to pre-existing standards or as the basis for creating new standards, or systematically to use the results to bring about appropriate change. This tendency not to complete the audit cycle is now becoming better recognised, particularly as practices become more aware of the need for practice guidelines and protocols, and for management procedures and systems which will enable them consistently to handle the results and so effect change.

2. Criterion-based review

Criterion-based review requires the development of explicit criteria and standards for the diagnosis, investigation and management of patients presenting with specific diseases or symptoms, and in assessing a doctor's performance against these standards. Aggregated data are collected, analysed, and compared with the standard after which appropriate changes in practice are made. The cycle is then repeated. This approach, still exceptional in general practice today, is classic standard setting, and is by far the most effective method of effecting change when done rigorously (North of England Study 1992a,b; Grol, Mesker and Schevellis 1988).

Criteria and standards are normally presented as clinical guidelines – national statements of good practice – and clinical protocols, which are guidelines adapted for local use. The effectiveness of guidelines and protocols in general practice and the practicalities of implementing them have both been the subject of recent comprehensive reviews (Russell and Grimshaw 1992, Grol 1992).

3. Critical incident review

The purpose of critical incident review is to enable members of the practice team to meet and review adverse outcomes in the care of individual patients in their care such as case fatalities, complications and patient complaints (Irvine and Irvine 1991). Such reviews, although long regarded as a valuable part of specialist clinical practice, are still uncommon in general practice.

Critical incident review is an important building block in developing the culture for assuring quality because it identifies and clarifies problems and raises questions, all of which may be explored further through focussed audit. It also lays the foundation for critical event monitoring through which critical incidents can be aggregated over time to reveal trends (Hart, Thomas *et al.* 1991) – for example, the pattern of unexpected deaths (Hart and Humphreys 1987).

4. Patient surveys

The fourth method is based on the patient survey, and in the general practice setting this has been used infrequently and only recently. Surveys are interesting mainly because of the opportunities they provide for assessing patient satisfaction (North of England Study 1992b, Baker 1990), and also for eliciting patient observations on the outcomes of care (North of England Study 1992b).

Implementation of Audit

As noted above, MAAGs have been set up with NHS support to implement audits with considerable freedom as to how best to go about this task. The medical profession has insisted that MAAGs should be doctor-led, and that in particular there should be no direct link with the FHSA. Yet, on the other hand, the FHSA appoints the members of the MAAG, provides its money, and legally the MAAG is accountable to it. So there are tensions which have yet to be resolved.

Without exception, MAAGs have elected to follow the educational approach preferred by the profession. This has had the effect of seeming to detach audit from everyday clinical practice; consequently, audit tends to be seen as an add-on for which no time has been allowed in the doctor's contract, rather than as an integral part of providing patient care.

The following have been the main implementation activities.

1. Raising awareness and motivation

The first task has been to raise awareness with the local profession, both about the MAAGs' status and role and about audit and its new place in medical care. As said earlier, some practices are already engaged in audit, others know about it but have done nothing, and a minority find it difficult to believe that the new government policy will affect them directly. MAAGs have gone for a battery of activities to establish contact with practices including local meetings, the distribution of circulars and news-letters, visits by members of the MAAG to local practices, and the appoint-ment of facilitators.

The visits to practices have been particularly important, providing an opportunity to explore audit in depth with partners and at the same time offering the chance of finding out how far a practice has already gone in implementing audit. Interest has varied widely, from the keen to the frankly hostile, but anecdotal feedback from chairmen suggests that in the main the message has been well received (Humphrey and Hughes 1992, Newcastle upon Tyne Medical Audit Advisory Group 1990). Neverthe-less, doubts remain about the value of audit, and in particular whether it is to be an essentially helping or a potentially threatening activity.

Looking beyond the first year, it is already becoming clear that MAAGs will have to prioritise their activities strictly. For example, should they concentrate on helping practices develop their own internal methods and capacity for self audit, or should they begin to carry out extended audits amongst groups of practices on subjects which have a particular clinical interest? Should they focus on practices which are willing and able to implement audit, to get the method firmly established, or should they devote their main effort to the traditionalists who as yet see no merit for them in audit? At this early formative stage it will be important to allow MAAGs to decide for themselves, for as yet there are no clear answers to these and similar, equally difficult, questions.

2. Confidentiality

In most parts of the country confidentiality questions have loomed large in the minds of doctors. There are two aspects, the first concerning the confidentiality of patient records and the second about the confidentiality of information gained by the MAAG on the performance of individual doctors.

With regard to patients, the question has turned out to be relatively straightforward. The GMC (1992b) has published advice saying that data about patients can only go beyond the practice with their explicit and informed consent; where this is not obtained, data must be anonymised.

The question of confidentiality and doctors is more sensitive, espe-cially for those whose performance is being assessed. What doctors fear most is that information about them will be passed by the MAAG to the FHSA, and may then be used in a contractual context. The MAAGs, with the full support of the profession's own organisations, have gone to considerable lengths to assure individual practitioners that there will be a 'Chinese wall' between each MAAG and the FHSA, and that therefore potentially sensitive material will not be passed on. This said, a grey area remains, for obviously any visitor to a practice coming into possession of information which suggests that a practitioner is putting patients at risk, by virtue of seriously impaired clinical performance, is morally obliged to act on that information. Indeed, the GMC's guidance to the profession (1992b) requires that action.

3. Training

Even where practitioners are positively disposed towards audit, there remains the huge educational task of equipping doctors with the necessary knowledge and skills to carry out audit effectively. NHS money has been made available for the training aspects of implementation, and this is channelled throughout the regional postgraduate organisations and their regional advisers in general practice.

The North of England Study (1992a) gave a valuable forewarning of what might be required, particularly where practitioners were gathering together in small peer groups to set standards. That study identified the need for skills in three areas:

- skill in the construction of guidelines
- knowledge and skill of the clinical subject under discussion
- skill in the management of small group activities.

Within the past two years several starter books on audit have been published, and these are listed in an appendix to this paper since the methods may well be of interest to those in the social work services as well as to doctors and nurses. This reading material has been implemented by a plethora of local courses on method.

The RCGP Audit Programme has facilitated local educational activities by providing a series of courses for MAAG members and in particular for teachers. As often is the case with new developments, some of the teachers are just ahead of the learners themselves!

More generally, one important aspect of the relationship between the education of the doctor and audit is becoming clearer. Audit, whether internal or external, is bound to raise questions about continuing competence in specific areas of practice. By providing a practitioner with direct feedback on performance, it could – indeed should – lead to more focused continuing education designed to remedy gaps in knowledge and skill.

4. Standards

Another sensitive issue is about standards, whether those should be internal or external. Internal standards, set by those whose performance is to be assessed, promote learning and understanding through the direct participation of practitioners and by conveying a sense of ownership which may enhance compliance (North of England Study of Standards and Performance in General Practice 1992a,b); on the other hand, they encourage diversity and may lack rigour. External standards, devised by those whose performance is not under scrutiny, are more likely to reflect best practice and may carry the added bite of an external review.

Actually, both have their place. The ideal is probably a light, external framework comprising a few well chosen standards within which practitioners can set their own working standards on a much broader scale (Irvine 1990).

Other approaches to quality

Whilst audit provides the main thrust, other approaches to quality are unfolding.

1. Contracting for quality

Aside from audit, one of the principal innovations in the NHS Reforms has been the introduction of contracting as a means for improving quality in general practice. Two examples are given below:

First, targets were introduced in the New Contract (Secretary of State for Health and Welsh Office 1989) to improve the immunisation status of patients on practice lists, and to improve the uptake of cervical cytology. Doctors were paid by results, with those coming nearest to a defined optimal standard receiving most money, and those falling below a prescribed minimum standard receiving none. Even in the first year of operation this form of quality incentive led to a quite dramatic improvement in the immunisation status of the community.

Fundholding is the second example. Fundholders are already beginning to introduce quality standards when purchasing hospital care and nursing services. Building on this, there is growing interest in the development of fundholding practices as providers with the practice – rather than individual practitioners – contracting with a health authority to deliver a defined range of services of an agreed quality and cost (Irvine 1993). Patients registering with such practices would see the practice as their source of total care, some provided by the practice itself, and some commissioned by the practice on their behalf from hospitals or the specialised community health services and the social services. Through contracting, the practice would thus have a continuing responsibility for the quality of commissioned care. Not surprisingly, practices which are exploring this road have a fundamental interest in developing quality management procedures and quality assuring and quality improving methods.

2. Accreditation

Accreditation is the process whereby standard-setting organisations, which may be either professional or public bodies, explicitly identify, or accredit, individual practices or individual practitioners who comply with their standards. In the case of general practice, the accreditation of both practices and practitioners is being established on a selective basis.

The regional postgraduate organisations continue to accredit and re-accredit teaching practices in accordance with their published requirements (JCPTGP 1992) and there is some evidence that the profession as a whole would see this as the preferred way of accrediting all practices (General Medical Services Committee 1992). Meanwhile, the King's Fund is also developing organisational standards for practice accreditation and several general practices have recently achieved the British Standards Institution indicator of quality (BS5750).

3. Citizen's charter

The Patient's Charter has its application in general practice, and at the time of writing the first standards for this are just appearing. The Charter is a form of external standard setting. It offers the public yet another way of assuring quality, but obviously its effectiveness remains to be tested.

4. General Medical Council: performance procedures

Obviously, for most practices the emphasis is quite rightly on helping and encouraging good practices to become even better. This is the essence of the philosophy of quality improvement. Nevertheless, it has become painfully obvious in recent years that some general practitioners are incompetent, and that the GMC's machinery for dealing with this is inadequate.

The GMC (GMC 1992) has just completed an extensive discussion with all interested parties and has now taken proposals to Parliament for completely new procedures, designed specifically to detect and handle serious deficiencies revealed in the pattern of a doctor's practice. It is hoped that these new procedures will become operational within the next three years or so, and so provide yet further protection for the public by requiring doctors who are found to be seriously deficient to undergo further training, or by removing from medical practice altogether those who will not or cannot improve.

Looking ahead

The future of quality assurance and quality improvement in general practice is closely tied up with the development of practice itself. In this regard a consensus is emerging, reflected in a wide spectrum of both professional and NHS publications, that the key to effective primary health care in future in Britain lies in well-organised practices which are imbued with the culture of excellence in patient care, and which can give practical expression to this by having the capability of being able to describe in detail what their objectives for care are, what range and quality of services they provide, and at what cost. It is this culture of quality and excellence which will build confidence amongst both professionals and patients alike. Achieving this is the outstanding challenge for general practice in the next decade.

Further reading

Making Sense of Audit. Edited by Donald and Sally Irvine. Radcliffe Medical Press, Oxford, 1991.

Medical Audit in General Practice. Edited by Marshall Marinker. British Medical Journal, London, 1990.

The Practice Audit Plan: A Handbook of Medical Audit by R. Baker and P. Presley. RCGP, London, 1990.

Audit and Development in Primary Care by Charlotte Humphrey and Jane Hughes. Medical Audit Series 5. King's Fund Centre, London, 1992.

Managing for Quality in General Practice by Donald Irvine. Medical Audit Series 2. King's Fund Centre, London, 1990.

References

Baker, R. (1988a) *Practice Assessment and Quality of Care.* Occasional paper 39. London: Royal College of General Practitioners.

— (1988b) 'The accuracy of a practice based immunisation register'. *The Practitioner* 232, 681–683.

— (1990) 'Development of a questionnaire to assess patients' satisfaction with consultations in general practice'. *British Journal of General Practice* 40, 487–490.

British Medical Association (1965) *Charter for the Family Doctor Service.* London: British Medical Association.

Collings, J.S. (1950) 'General practice in England today'. *Lancet* 1, 555–585.

Creighton, P.A. and Evans, A.M. (1992) 'Audit of practice-based cervical smear programme: completion of the cycle'. *British Medical Journal* 304, 963–966.

Crombie, D.L. and Fleming, D.M. (1988) *Practice Activity Analysis.* Occasional paper 41. London: Royal College of General Practitioners.

Department of Health (1990) *Medical Audit in the Family Practitioner Services.* Health circular (FP)(90)8. London: HMSO.

Derry, J., Lawrence, M., Griew, K. *et al.* (1991) 'Auditing methods: the method of Oxfordshire medical audit advisory groups'. *British Medical Journal* 303, 1247–1249.

Donabedian, A. (1966) 'Evaluating the quality of medical care'. *Millbank Memorial Fund Quarterly* 4, 166–206.

Fleming, D.M. and Lawrence, M.S. (1981) 'An evaluation of recorded information about preventive measures in 38 practices'. *Journal of the Royal College of General Practitioners* 32, 98–102.

Freeman, J. and Byrne, P.J. (1976) *The Assessment of Post-graduate Training and General Practice. Research into Higher Education Monographs (second edition).* Guildford: Society for Research into Higher Education Limited.

General Medical Council (1992a) *Proposals for New Performance Procedures: A Consultation Paper.* London: GMC.

— (1992b) *Professional Conduct and Discipline: Fitness to Practice.* London: GMC.

General Medical Services Committee (1992) *Your Choices for the Future: A Survey of GP Opinion.* London: BMA.

Gray, D.P. (1991) 'Re-accrediting general practice'. *British Medical Journal* 305, 488–489.

Grol, R. (1992) 'Implementing guidelines in general practice care'. *Quality in Health Care* 1, 184–191.

Grol, R., Mesker, P. and Schevellis, F. (1988) *Peer Review in General Practice: Methods, Standards, Protocols.* Nizmegen: University Department of General Practice.

Hart, J.T. and Humphreys, C. (1987) 'Be your own coroner: an audit of 500 consecutive deaths in general practice'. *British Medical Journal* 294, 871–874.

Hart, J.T., Thomas, C. *et al* (1991) 'Twenty-five years of case finding and audit in a socially deprived community'. *British Medical Journal* 302, 1509–1513.

Horder, J. (ed.) (1992) *The Writings of John Hunt.* London: Royal College of General Practitioners.

Humphrey, C. and Hughes, J. (1992) *Audit and Development in Primary Care.* Medical Audit Series 5. London: King's Fund Centre.

Irvine, D.H. (1983) 'Quality: our outstanding problem'. *Journal of the Royal College of General Practitioners* 33, 521–523.

— (1990) *Managing for Quality in General Practice.* Medical Audit Series 2. London:

King's Fund Centre.
— (1993) 'General practice in the 1990s: a personal view on future developments'. *British Journal of General Practice* 43, 121–125.
Irvine, D.H. and Irvine, S. (eds) (1991) *Making Sense of Audit*. Oxford: Radcliffe Press.
Irvine, D.H., Russell, I.T., Hutchinson, A. *et al.* (1986) 'Performance review in general practice: education, development and evaluation research in the Northern Region', in Pendleton, D., Schofield, T.C.P. and Marinker, M. (ed) *In Pursuit of Quality*. London: RCGP.
Irvine, S. (1992) *The Manager in Practice: Balancing Dreams & Discipline*. London: RCGP.
Joint Committee on Postgraduate Training for General Practice (1992) *Accreditation of Regions and Schemes for Vocational Training in General Practice: General Guidance*. London: JCPTGP.
Kitson, A., Hyndman, S., Harvey, G. and Yerrell, P. (1990) *Quality Patient Care. The Dynamic Standard Setting System*. London: Royal College of Nursing.
Merrison, A. (Chair) (1979) *Report on Royal Commission on the NHS*. London: HMSO.
Newcastle upon Tyne Medical Audit Advisory Group (1990) *Learning by Doing: Chairman's Report on a Pilot Study*. Newcastle: Newcastle FHSA.
North of England Study of Standards and Performance in General Practice (1992a) 'Medical audit in general practice. 1. Effects on doctors' clinical behaviour for common childhood conditions'. *British Medical Journal* 304, 1480–1484.
— (1992b). 'Medical audit in general practice. 2. Effects on health of patients with common childhood conditions'. *British Medical Journal* 304, 1484–1488.
Royal College of General Practitioners (1972) '*The future general practitioner: learning and teaching*'. London: British Medical Journal.
— (1978a) 'Practice activity analysis 5: referrals to specialists'. *Journal of the Royal College of General Practitioners* 28, 251–252.
— (1978b) 'Practice activity analysis 6: visiting profiles'. *Journal of the Royal College of General Practitioners* 28, 316–318.
— (1983) 'Council policy on quality in general practice'. *Journal of the Royal College of General Practitioners* 33, 523–524.
— (1985) *Quality in General Practice*. Policy statement 2. London: RCGP.
— (1985) *What Sort of Doctor?* Report from general practice 23. London: RCGP.
— (1990) *An Educational Strategy for the 1990's*. Occasional paper 49. London: RCGP.
— (1990) *Fellowship by Assessment*. Occasional paper 50. London: RCGP.
Russell, I.T. and Grimshaw, J. (1992) 'The effectiveness of referral guidelines: a review of methods and findings of published evaluations', in Roland, M. and Coulter, A. (eds) *Hospital Referrals*. Oxford: Oxford University Press.
Secretary of State for Health (1991) *The Patient's Charter: Raising the Standard*. London: HMSO.
Secretaries of State for Health and Social Services, Wales, Northern Ireland and Scotland (1986) *Primary Health Care: An Agenda for Discussion* (Cmnd 9771). London: HMSO.
Secretary of State for Health and Welsh Office (1989) *General Practice in the National Health Service: The 1990 Contract*. London: HMSO.
Secretaries of State for Health, Wales, Northern Ireland and Scotland (1989) *Working for Patients (Cmnd 555)*. London: HMSO.
Standing Committee on Postgraduate Medical Education (SCOPME) (1989) *Medical Audit: The Educational Implications*. London: SCOPME.

Chapter 12

Putting Complaints Procedures into Effect

*Brian McClay**

Introduction

There has been a growing awareness, during the 1980s, that service users, their carers, their relatives and their advocates have views – and of course grievances – which can contribute to the development and planning of the services which they are receiving or which they hope to receive. The Government's White Paper 'The Citizen's Charter' (Prime Minister 1991) provided a framework to set standards in public services which would best meet the wishes of their users. A basic tenet of the Charter is that all public services, including those provided by local authorities, should have clear and well publicised complaints procedures. This means that when things go wrong there must be a simple way of putting things right. People must know how to complain. They must know to whom they should complain. They must have confidence that they can raise their concerns and that their complaints will be dealt with. Finally, where it is appropriate they should be able to obtain redress.

Local authority social services and social work departments have been statutorily required to have formal complaints procedures in place since April 1991. Prior to that date, there was a multiplicity of complaints schemes at local authority level, with officers who had some responsibility of complaints being located within departments in some authorities or at a corporate level, usually in the Chief Executive's office, in others.

---

* The author writes in a personal capacity.

Purpose of the legislation

Both the Children Act 1989, which applies primarily to England and Wales, and the National Health Service and Community Care Act 1990, contain new obligations with regard to representations from the public about the services provided by the local authority. 'Representations' includes complaints and may also relate to matters which do not directly affect the person who has made them. The local authority is required to establish formal complaints procedures to consider any representations which are made to it with regard to the discharge of its social services functions or about any failure to discharge these functions.

With regard to community care, the requirements in England and Wales are contained in the directions made under section 7B of the Local Authority Social Services Act 1970 inserted by Section 50 of the National Health Service and Community Care Act 1990, and for Scotland under Section 5B of the Social Work Scotland Act 1968 inserted by Section 52 of the National Health Service and Community Care Act 1990. Complaints procedures and arrangements for their publicity, including information for service users and staff, were required to be in place in local authorities by 1st April 1991.

In England and Wales, with regard to children's services, the Representations Procedure (Children) Regulations 1991 set the minimum standard provision that local authorities should establish to meet the requirements of sections of the Children Act 1989 and a complaints procedure was required to be in place by 14th October 1991. In Scotland, all client groups and service users are covered under the community care legislation.

The main features of complaints procedures

1. The procedure

The legislation gives complainants the right to make a formal complaint if they are dissatisfied. In many cases the matter may be resolved as a result of local investigation or action at the point of service delivery, and this is encouraged by Government guidance (described later). This may involve exhaustive, informal attempts to resolve the matter. However, complainants (in Scotland, 'complainers') have the right of access to the formal procedure at any time they choose and can make a formal complaint at an early stage in the process, particularly if they have little confidence in the informal mechanisms. Once this formal procedure has been invoked, there are two stages. At the **investigative stage** the local authority must appoint an officer, from within the authority, who will examine the circumstances of the complaint and provide a report which will form the basis of the authority's response to the complainant. Under the community care legislation, both in England and Wales and in Scotland, there is no requirement to involve an independent person at this stage. However, in England and Wales under the Children Act 1989 the regulations state that an independent person who will be actively involved in the consideration of the complaint must be appointed by the local authority.

If the complaint has not been resolved satisfactorily at the previous stage and the complainant is unhappy about either the outcome or the way in which the complaint has been dealt with, the procedure moves to the **review stage**. Here the authority is required to convene a panel of three people to consider the complaint and to review the decision that has been made. At least one member of the panel must be an independent person, defined so as to exclude, for example, members and officers of the local authority. Once the panel has made its recommendations, the local authority is required to involve the independent person in discussions about the action to be taken in response to the complaint, having given due regard to the findings of the panel. An independent person must be appointed at the review stage under both Acts.

2. Prescribed timescales

The intention in both Acts is that complaints should be dealt with speedily and with a minimum of delay. Once the formal procedure has been invoked, the local authority is required to consider the complaint and make a response to the complainant within 28 days of the receipt of the complaint. Under the 1989 Act there is no scope for any leeway in this, but under the 1990 Act, if it is not possible to meet the 28 day deadline, then the authority must give an explanation of the position to the complainant within the first 28 days and make a full response within three months of the receipt of the complaint.

Once the response has been made the complainant can ask, within 28 days of its receipt, for the response to be reviewed by a panel. This panel must meet within 28 days of the authority's receipt of the complainant's request for such a review. The panel must reach its recommendations and record the reasons for its actions within 24 hours of the completion of its deliberations and ensure that the recommendations are sent to the authority and to the complainant. The authority is then required to make a decision on its response to the panel's recommendations and to notify the complainant of the action it intends to take in the light of those recommendations. It must do so within 28 days of the date of the panel's recommendations.

3. *The management of complaints*

Each local authority is required to designate an officer to assist in the co-ordination of all aspects of the consideration of complaints. This officer takes responsibility for the day-to-day operation and management of the complaints system. The tasks of this officer usually include receiving and investigating complaints (or supervising the receipt and investigation of complaints); managing the system for running and processing complaints (e.g. recording formal complaints and ensuring that prescribed timescales are met) and giving advice on the response by the social services or social work department to individual complainants or complainers.

The local authority may also give responsibility for the overall organisation and effectiveness of its procedures to a senior officer of the department whose tasks are likely to include establishing, resourcing and monitoring the procedure; ensuring that arrangements are made for training and publicity; and collecting data about complaints and distributing this data to managers and members.

Government guidance on implementation

In November 1990, the Department of Health issued policy guidance on the requirements of the National Health Service and Community Care Act 1990 in England and Wales (DOH 1990). Chapter 6 of this is devoted to complaints procedures, spelling out the objectives and the essential requirements and describing what the relevant authorities have to do to implement the procedures.

In April 1991, the Department of Health issued policy guidance for England and Wales in relation to the Children Act 1989 (DOH 1991). Chapter 10 elaborates the requirement to provide a representations procedure for complaints about children's services. The style is very similar to the community care policy guidance, and helpfully it points out the differences in the requirements under each piece of legislation.

In July 1991, the Social Services Inspectorate of the Department of Health issued practice guidance to help local authorities to establish and run efficient complaints procedures under both community care and children's legislation (SSI 1991). It describes in more detail than in the two previous policy guidance documents how local authorities should implement the procedure.

In February 1991, in Scotland, the Secretary of State issued a circular which drew the attention of local authorities to the provisions of the National Health Service and Community Care Act 1990 relating to complaints procedures (Scottish Office 1991). The Social Work Services Inspectorate has also issued practice guidance on how authorities should implement the policy in Scotland (SWSI 1991).

Interpreting the legislation

The policy guidance and practice guidance documents are helpful in clarifying the intentions of the legislation, underlining mandatory and discretionary aspects.

One complaints system, or two?

In England and Wales some authorities have decided to have two systems, one for adults and one for children's services. Others have decided to have just one system. When service provision is organised along distinct client group lines it is perhaps easier to have separate complaints procedures for adults and children. However, it is less confusing for staff and for the public to have a single comprehensive complaints procedure which covers all client groups, which is the case in Scotland.

Authorities in England and Wales with one set of procedures have tended to build them around the Children Act 1989 requirements as they are more stringent. That means, incidentally, that adult complaints under the community care legislation would have to have an independent person involved at the investigating stage, so, arguably, a more rigorous investigation of complaints would take place than is actually required under the National Health Service and Community Care Act 1990.

Location of complaints function

Local authorities have considerable discretion about where, in the social services or social work department, the complaints function should be located. Traditionally, they have responded to new legislation by creating a structure which meets the particular needs of their own locality. This, allied with the considerable discretion already referred to, has resulted in a variety of structures, procedures and emphases within the procedures. For example, some authorities have decided to locate the complaints officer within the registration and inspection unit, arguing that the 'arms length' aspect is important if users are to feel that complaints will be dealt with impartially. That is an attractive argument and there are common elements to both functions which centre around the quality of service being provided. But there are differences.

Inspection units are concerned with the quality of care being provided in private and residential homes as well as with local authority establishments. Complaints procedures are concerned with arrangements for dealing with complaints about how local authorities discharge (or fail to discharge) their social services functions. There is the danger, because there is usually one complaints officer and there are a number of inspection officers, that the complaints function could be submerged within the inspection function.

On the other hand, the complaints function can be situated within the span of control under the senior officer with overall responsibility for complaints. Often, the senior officer has a planning or research role. There are, however, a small number of authorities where the senior officer's role is taken by the Director. One advantage of having the Director so closely associated with the complaints function is that it serves to underline the commitment that is placed on dealing with complaints within those authorities.

However, it can be useful to have the Director remain outside the complaints function so that the Director can respond to the complaint after the review panel stage without being compromised by involvement in earlier stages of the complaint which could arise via the responsible senior officer role. Directors, however, with or without that responsibility can still become involved in dealing with users before complaints can become apparent.

'Independent Person'

Although complainants under the legislation covering children's services in England and Wales have the right to have an independent person involved in the consideration of their complaint, the local authority also has scope to attempt to resolve the problems without the necessity of having to involve an independent person. The membership of the review panel/committee must include at least one independent person. The other two members can be whomsoever the authority considers to be suitable and could be either other independent persons or councillors.

Monitoring the procedures

Authorities are required to monitor the operation and effectiveness of their complaints procedures and to provide their Social Services or Social Work Committees with regular information about the numbers and types of complaints received, the time taken to deal with them and their outcome. At the very least this should provide a basis for authorities to disseminate this information to line managers so that the lessons that can be learned from individual complaints can be used to inform practice, for example to monitor the quality and consistency of the authority's response to complaints, to identify gaps in the provision of services and to highlight where staff training is required to change attitudes.

Considerable care, though, should be taken in interpreting the information. A greater number of complaints in one area does not necessarily mean that there are more causes for complaint in that area. It could also mean that the prevailing ethos within that area is such that service users can more easily make complaints than in another area where very few complaints have been received. A further factor which can make it difficult to compare information in different areas is that in many authorities the number of complaints which are handled without being recorded in a central monitoring system is simply an unknown quantity.

Evaluation of the procedures

Authorities are at different stages in implementing their complaints procedures and it is difficult to establish a coherent picture of the impact that they are making. However, the Social Work Services Inspectorate (SWSI) in Scotland and the Social Services Inspectorate (SSI) in England have carried out monitoring exercises which provide a good deal of information about how complaints procedures have been implemented.

In Scotland, the SWSI has published two reports. The first (SWSI 1992) focused on how the procedures had been introduced in the first 12 months, on training, the recording of complaints and the extent of the use of procedures. The second (SWSI 1993) describes the further progress made and focuses on the volume of complaints, measures of satisfaction with the procedures, how quickly complaints are dealt with and the appointment of independent persons to review panels.

A summary of the main findings shows the rate at which complaints are being received is increasing, probably due to increased publicity about procedures. A high proportion (almost 63%) of complainers are apparently satisfied with the outcome of their complaints. However, the views of the complainers themselves had not been sought, which might have provided a different perspective. In some authorities there are indications that some complaints have resulted in changes to social work practice. Almost two-thirds of all complaints were investigated within the statutory 28 day period. Many of those which were not investigated within this period were complex, so the failure to comply with the timescales may not have been due solely to the efficiency of the department. Very few review hearings were held and none of them met within the 28 days required. The independent persons had a wide range of experience and expertise. A number of them were professional social work staff from neighbouring authorities and while they are independent, it may be that from the complaints perspective, they are not seen as being truly independent. There are indications from the limited number of reviews held so far that uncertainties exist about the functions of review committees and the role of the complaints officer in relation to the review committee.

Two reports have been published recently by the SSI. The first (SSI 1993a) was based on a questionnaire circulated to 108 authorities in England. It focused on the giving of information about complaints procedures, training, the recruitment of independent persons for both the investigative and the review panel stages, monitoring systems, and the use and dissemination of information from complaints. The survey period was the first 15 months after the implementation of the community care legislation in April 1991. It found that all of the authorities emphasised the importance of informal problem solving, many had made arrangements for advocacy services and most intended to use information obtained from the monitoring of complaints to improve services. Keeping to timescales was a real problem for many authorities and, finally, staff who have been appointed to act as investigating officers would benefit from some training in that role.

The second report (SSI 1993b) was based on an in-depth study of five social services departments selected from different regions in England. This report evaluates the performance of the departments in relation to a series of standards set by the SSI. The standards covered all aspects of complaints procedures. Evidence was collected to assess performance against each standard by looking at documents, reports, policies and procedures, by interviews with staff, with representatives of the voluntary sector, with independent persons and by meeting with residents. A postal questionnaire was also used to elicit the opinions of complainants in each of the departments in the study.

A summary of the main findings in each of these categories shows that managers and staff had responded well to the concept that it is acceptable for service users to complain. Staff operating complaints procedures have been able to observe the traditional social value of maintaining confidentiality, while departments have been successful in recruiting, training and using independent persons and in setting up review panels.

Local authorities have, however, made limited progress in meeting some standards in other areas. The quality of the information leaflets about complaints which have been produced for service users has been good but the distribution of such leaflets has not been comprehensive. The distribution of documents about complaints procedures to staff has been good, but it has not been matched by consultation with service users and staff in some departments. Most departments had done well in setting up the new complaints procedures' systems and also in resourcing and managing them, although this had been limited by the failure to provide adequate follow-up training.

The departments have made relatively poor progress in meeting the standards in certain areas. There has been a lack of consistency in the recording and collating of complaints and in ensuring that complaints were made known to complaints officers in order to facilitate monitoring. The evaluation of complaints and the outcomes of investigations have not always been used to influence either policies or practices. There were difficulties in appointing investigating officers who were able to give sufficient attention to their task so that the investigation was concluded within the required timescales. New demands are being placed on investigating officers who may have to investigate the actions of their peers or who may have to investigate a complaint in an area of different professional expertise. Departments were poor at making the complaints procedures easily accessible to users and carers and in particular to children in foster homes, foster carers and to users receiving home care. In addition, the lack of privacy in residential homes meant that service users were seldom able to complain properly. Finally, all departments experienced the most difficulty in being able to resolve complaints quickly. Formal investigations were often taking longer than three months and the timescale of 28 days was considered to be almost impossible to meet.

Emerging issues and conclusions

Four current issues are discussed in this concluding part of the chapter –
adhering to timetables; formal procedures; implementing recommendations; and informing service users and getting their views.

Adhering to prescribed timescales

While responses in 28 days are required, complaints which have reached
the stage where the formal procedures have been invoked are often
complex, and investigating officers are finding that staff may need to be
interviewed at length and more than once. There are practical constraints,
like staff leave, staff sickness, arranging dates for interviews, recording
accurate accounts of interviews, writing reports, typing and checking
reports and, finally, wording the response, all of which can be extremely
time-consuming. One consequence of this could be pressure to extend the
timescales. That may enable better quality investigations to be carried out
but it must be weighed against the impact on service users of having to
wait longer to have their complaints addressed.

In many authorities, however, attempts are being made to comply with
both the spirit and the letter of the law by facilitating investigations so
that the timescales are met. This can require a considerable cultural shift
in the way that complaints are handled. Investigating officers are having
to rearrange their working day so that the investigation of a complaint,
for a short period, may take up all of their time and other work for that
period will have to be picked up by a colleague. This seems to work better
in authorities where staff do not have to be convinced that users have a
right to complain.

When to invoke the formal procedures

The monitoring exercises in both England and Scotland indirectly touched
on this issue. There are indications that, while some authorities have been
quick to invoke the formal procedures, the majority of authorities are
attempting to 'problem solve' complaints at the point of service delivery
and do what they can to satisfy complainants without using the formal
procedures. It is a matter of judgement at which point the problem solving
process moves into the investigative stage. Attempts to 'problem solve'
can drift and become confused with issues around service delivery to the
detriment of the complainant. Investigations which are entirely 'within
house' can, of course, be carried out as scrupulously as a formal 'independent' investigation. However, experience so far would suggest that

the input of the independent person can add an important dimension to the investigation by taking a fresh look at policies and how they have been carried out. Investigating officers from within an authority, even though they are trying to be objective, sometimes can be too close to distinguish where there have been deficiencies in practice.

Another factor which has begun to surface and which may gain momentum is that complainants welcome the independent input because they feel that it gives a guarantee that someone outwith the authority to which they are directing their complaint is involved in the investigation or, at the review stage, is on the panel. The involvement of an independent person at the investigative stage of a formal complaint by, or on behalf of, a child does go some way towards ensuring that the child's viewpoint is being considered. Nevertheless, from the complainant's perspective, formal investigations are still weighted very much in favour of the local authority in that its investigating officer is responsible for co-ordinating a report to the authority which must then notify the complainant of the proposed action. Further, in many authorities, once the review stage has been reached, it is likely that two out of the three representatives on the panel would be councillors of the authority against whom the complaints have been made. Some complainants, perhaps understandably, may have reservations about accepting that an employee of an authority can be impartial when the complaint has been made against that authority.

Ensuring that recommendations are implemented

After due consideration of the complaint, an authority has to decide what action to take. In many cases an apology is appropriate. This may seem to be a rather hollow response but is sometimes all that complainants want. It is a recognition that they have a genuine grievance, the effect of which cannot be undone, and that the authority has accepted responsibility for what has happened.

The action to be taken may include a recommendation that a monetary payment should be made to the complainant by way of compensation. This is a recognition by the authority of the upset and distress which has been caused to the complainant and is a tangible form of redress.

On a wider perspective, there may well be recommendations for policy and/or practice changes which are intended to be of benefit to other users of the service. This can be quite a common response. The failure to take action in the past cannot be undone, but it can identify where improvements need to be made so that the chances of the cause for complaint being repeated are minimised. It is crucial that the implications of this for relevant service staff are made clear so that policy can be amended and practice improved. Staff need to be reminded that the failure to implement recommendations can itself become a cause for complaint and, quite properly, would be highlighted as maladministration should the local government ombudsman become involved in further consideration of the complaint. Operational staff have to accept that it is their responsibility to carry out the recommendations. The authority must be seen to accept and implement changes which need to be made. Complaints officers have a responsibility, as part of the monitoring process, to check that such recommendations have been carried out.

Informing service users and getting their views

One purpose of a good complaints procedure is to provide a framework within which service users know how they can complain and to whom they can complain should things go wrong. The procedures must be accessible, available and capable of enabling users to feel that their complaints will be treated seriously, will be attended to promptly and will receive a considered response. It is vital that publicity about the complaints process reaches all users and potential users. Authorities need to think about how to reach, for example, people with visual handicaps, with hearing difficulties, with learning difficulties and people whose first language is not English. Explanatory leaflets may have to be augmented by using videos, cassette tapes and the various ethnic minority media. If these things happen, then the public should feel encouraged that, when they complain, their concerns will be listened to and dealt with.

Since 1991, authorities have been preoccupied with establishing procedures and putting them into place. Not a great deal is known as yet about how effective the new procedures are, although the response to the postal questionnaire eliciting the views of complainants participating in the in-depth study of social services departments in England (SSI 1993b) indicates that the majority of complainants are dissatisfied with both the length of time taken to respond to their complaint and with the outcome of their complaint. It is important to obtain the views of users, and some authorities have conducted simple surveys to find out from complainants what they think of the complaints procedure that they have used, how easy it was for them to complain and if they were satisfied with the response.

Procedures are there for the benefit of users and the findings from such local surveys together with the findings from more sophisticated projects will provide valuable information to enable authorities to revise their procedures so that the public can see that they are trying, genuinely, to put complaints procedures into effect.

References

Department of Health (1990) *Community Care in the Next Decade and Beyond: Policy Guidance.* London: HMSO.

Department of Health (1991) *The Children Act 1989 Guidance and Regulations. Volume 3: Family Placements.* London: HMSO.

Prime Minister (1991) *Citizen's Charter. Raising the Standard.* Cm 1599. London: HMSO.

Scottish Office (1991) *Community Care in Scotland. Complaints Procedures.* Edinburgh: Scottish Office.

Social Services Inspectorate (1991) *The Right to Complain. Practice Guidance on Complaints Procedures in Social Services Departments.* London: HMSO.

Social Services Inspectorate (1993a) *Progress on the Right to Complain: Monitoring Social Services Departments Complaints Procedures 1992/93.* London: DOH.

Social Services Inspectorate (1993b) *The Inspection of the Complaints Procedures in Local Authority Social Services Departments.* London: HMSO.

Social Work Services Inspectorate (1991) *Community Care in Scotland. A Right to Complain... Practice Guidance Complaints Procedures in Social Work Departments.* Edinburgh: Scottish Office.

Social Work Services Inspectorate (1992) *Community Care in Scotland. The Introduction of Local Authority Complaints Procedures.* Edinburgh: Scottish Office.

Social Work Services Inspectorate (1993) *Local Authority Complaints Procedures 18 Months On.* Edinburgh: Scottish Office.

Chapter 13

Performance Review and the Voluntary Sector

*Anne Connor**

Introduction

In the same way as performance review is of increasing importance – and the cause of some anxiety – to statutory social work and health care agencies, it is also becoming more of an issue among voluntary organisations. They are reassessing the roles the voluntary sector may fulfil in the light of community care implementation and other recent developments – which have, for example, brought an increased emphasis on contracts for service provision and a different role in planning processes – and the consequences these will have for the organisation, the statutory authorities and the service users. At first glance it may seem that the development of performance review affects voluntary organisations in just the same way as it does large statutory agencies or, indeed, profit-making companies, but the motivation behind these developments in the voluntary sector and the issues that arise in consequence merit separate consideration.

This chapter considers the major aspects of that motivation and the consequences associated with performance review – both externally-driven assessment and review from within the organisation – for voluntary organisations. Its focus is on performance review as a planned and specific activity, although it is recognised that this can – and should – be an integral element of on-going management. It outlines the most common present arrangements and some of the approaches which are emerg-

---

* The author writes in a personal capacity.

ing in an attempt to tackle the disadvantages for voluntary organisations associated with the traditional methods of performance review.

Background and context: The role and characteristics of voluntary organisations

Before going on to look at current and new arrangements for performance review within the voluntary sector, it is important to remember what it is we are examining. The term 'voluntary sector' covers a very wide range of types of organisations and areas of activity. There is no agreed definition of a voluntary organisation of 'the voluntary sector' – see, for example, the recent review by Knight (1993). Although the inclusion of larger, national organisations such as Barnardo's or the RSPCA is clear, the position of the many local activities organised on a group basis – such as mother and toddler groups – is less certain. Most commentators include such small groups as voluntary organisations, but the people concerned may not share this view.

It follows that there is no precise information about the size of the voluntary sector. The best recent estimates were obtained for the Efficiency Scrutiny of Government Funding of the Voluntary Sector, which is discussed below. The report noted that in 1988 there were some 160,000 registered charities in England and Wales, and it is estimated that the total number of voluntary organisations in the UK is well over 300,000 (Home Office 1990).

Voluntary organisations fulfil one or more of five broad types of functions:

- providing services to people or undertaking other activities for a wider benefit

- being a focus or channel for self-help or shared help among people who have a common experience, problem or interest

- campaigning to change the circumstances which cause a social problem, for example, by raising awareness among other people or in persuading other organisations to change their practices

- raising money so that someone else can do or change something

- supporting the work of other people or organisations, for example by providing support services to or co-ordinating between voluntary organisations fulfilling other roles.

Even among those voluntary organisations providing direct social care services there is a wide diversity. They vary in terms of size, complexity, balance of input from volunteers and salaried workers, and access to specialised resources. Some organisations are entirely self-financing, some entirely dependent upon grant support or contracts from public sector funders, while most draw on a range of income sources (Connor 1993a, Knight 1993).

Motives for performance review

Essentially, there are three basic reasons why anyone should review their own or another person's performance: to learn from the experience in order to improve the performance; to be able to tell other people about the experience or achievement; and to demonstrate accountability.

For voluntary organisations, improving the performance by **delivering better quality of services or better reflecting users' needs** should be a *sine qua non*. For most voluntary organisations the very reason for their existence is to provide something where no alternative is available or which is better than the alternatives. Another aspect of delivering the best possible service is to make better use of the available resources. This, however, has tended to be seen by staff and volunteers in voluntary organisations in a negative light, where voluntary organisations have been encouraged by funders, trustees or managers to manage on a smaller or static budget, or to use volunteers rather than paid staff. Correspondingly less attention is paid to ensuring such positive aspects as ensuring staff's/volunteers' skills and time are used to best effect and that the physical resources are maximised irrespective of the income sources.

For voluntary organisations providing social care, recent legislative and other changes have placed increasing emphasis on the need to ensure a high quality of services. For example, for elderly people and other client groups, community care implementation has brought an emphasis on the place of voluntary organisations' direct care services within packages of care. The most significant change is to the financial and legal relationship between the voluntary organisation and local statutory bodies through the move from grants – given as a general contribution to support an identified range of activities – to contracts which specify forms and levels of services to particular standards and how these will be demonstrated (Flynn and Hurley 1993). Grants-in-aid are themselves increasingly quasi-contractual in specifying what is expected.

Other developments are a greater involvement in strategic planning as consultees undertaking assessments where there is an agency role, and acting as advocates for users. The latter input often brings with it the need to record and review both the level and type, and the outcome of services given to individual people. Similarly, more explicit and often higher standards of records are also required, whether as a consequence of legislation such as the Children Act 1989; new funding or contracting arrangements (for example for social work services for offenders in Scotland); and the guidelines and statements of good practice which apply to many other specific aspects of social care services. In a similar way, organisations providing support to other voluntary organisations or campaigning need to listen to other people if they are to maximise their effectiveness.

Letting other people know about the organisation's activities, the circumstances of users and of the impact that activities can have is recognised as central to those voluntary organisations undertaking a campaigning or educative role. The voluntary sector is the source of much innovation, which it claims as a strength and justification for its role. Good, reliable review of performance of such new activities – followed by effective dissemination of the findings – is itself an important, but often overlooked, phase of developing new ways of delivering services or adapting existing models to new situations.

The main reason, however, why most voluntary organisations' performance is reviewed is financial: **accountability to funders or buyers** for grants and other payments. This is a major source of funds to the voluntary sector in the UK – for example, direct central government funding was almost £2.7bn per annum in 1990 (CAF 1992). (This does not take account of charities' additional income from the Inland Revenue in respect of covenanted donations.) One of the most marked changes in voluntary sector funding from the public sector in recent years has been a shift from grants for core functions or for entire 'projects', to contracts between the statutory authority and voluntary organisations for specific services (Connor 1993a, Edwards 1992, Flynn and Hurley 1993). For example, between 1985 and 1990 the level of central government grants to voluntary organisations decreased from £1,375m to £996m, although the total level of funding increased as a result of fees and charges (CAF 1992). The extent of the shift to contracts between local authorities and health authorities and voluntary organisations operating at a local level is expected to be of an even greater order.

This change has had implications for the type of information sought, with increased emphasis on outputs, rather than the more traditional focus on quantity of inputs or the arguably more desirable concern with quality of outcomes, and on the achievement of targets set out in the agreement – dates for certain events, volume or levels of service, completion of tasks. Although such targets were relevant when negotiated, there is a risk that they could no longer reflect quality of service and appropriateness to the needs of the individual users concerned. Contracts may also have implications for the type of activities which voluntary organisations can undertake:

> 'The move to greater reliance on contracting as a source of funding rather than traditional grant aid may squeeze out vital voluntary sector activities such as advocacy, co-operation, development, education, innovation and representation.' (SCVO 1991)

Knight has also noted the potential implications for such activities and for the continuance of particular types of organisations such as smaller, less formally structured groups, campaigning organisations and those concerned with 'minority' issues (Knight 1993).

Experience of contracting so far is mixed, with some examples of arrangements working well and others fulfilling the voluntary sector's concerns (Edwards 1992). The level of concern remains high; however, Knight reported that 'among all the topics raised by people in the interviews [managers and activists in national and local voluntary organisations throughout the UK] the contract culture caused the greatest anxiety'.

Implications for type of performance review

Within these three main reasons – performance management, dissemination and accountability – for undertaking performance review there are more specific incentives, again reflecting the circumstances and relationships underpinning the voluntary sector. These reasons form one of the key distinctions about performance review: whether it is initiated externally to the voluntary organisation, or internally. Most reviews are initiated by funders or other external sources, although the extent to which voluntary organisations are themselves initiating specific reviews is increasing. Another development is the extent to which performance review is a routine, integral part of good management by the organisation or external body, rather than only being used as an occasional exercise: both forms of performance review have their place.

Until a few years ago, reasons for internally and externally driven performance review were as set out below.

Reasons for Externally-Driven Performance Review	Reasons for Internally-Driven Performance Review
• financial stewardship • maximising efficiency • maximising effectiveness (e.g. value of service for users) • identifying capacity to change	• demonstrating value of type of service or organisation • staff development • getting users' views • testing the continuing relevance of aims and methods of achieving them.

Figure 13.1: Reasons for performance review in voluntary organisations

Reason	External Agency's Perspective	Voluntary Organisation's Perspective
Identify capacity to change.	Better able to achieve their interests.	Better also to adapt to changing circumstances, to take on new developments.
Listen to users.	Feedback required. Useful for wider planning.	User empowerment. Effectiveness of specific services.
Establish benefits of approach.	Learn from experience from wider planning purposes.	Make case for continued funding. Campaigning aspects – persuade others to take on methods or philosophy.

Figure 13.2: Examples of motives underlying externally- and internally-driven performance review

Today to a large extent the same factors are likely to motivate both externally- and internally-driven performance review. Voluntary organisations' managers are taking on the task of maximising the levels and impact of activity they undertake with resources that are under pressure. At the same time, funders/buyers and those responsible for strategic planning are seeking to promote reliable user feedback and to establish the contribution of different types of of service for general or strategic planning. The convergence is not complete, however; some reasons still have quite different meanings when viewed from the internal and external perspectives – as in the examples in Figure 13.2 – and some factors, such as staff development, will very rarely, if ever, be a motive for externally-driven performance review.

Efficiency scrutiny of government funding of the voluntary sector

In 1989 a Cabinet Office Efficiency Scrutiny was carried out of the type and impact of Government funding to voluntary organisations. A substantial report was published, entitled 'Profiting from Partnership' (Home Office 1990).

One of the main recommendations of the scrutiny was that a much greater emphasis should be placed on monitoring and evaluation of and by (in the form of self-evaluation) voluntary organisations. The report criticised many government departments' practice of focusing on financial accountability but failing to address the achievements of voluntary organisations, in terms of either their efficiency or effectiveness, and noted a widespread failure to take account of the views or outcomes for the ultimate customers of the voluntary organisations. One consequence of this has been that all government-funded schemes were reviewed by September 1993, with forms and guidelines redesigned to place more emphasis on clear aims and measurable objectives; advice and guidance on monitoring and evaluation arrangements; and clear requirements for annual reports.

Another important recommendation was that greater attention should be paid by funders to their own reviews of funding **programmes**, rather than solely concentrating on the individual projects (para. 3.3). Since funding to voluntary organisations is usually intended as a means of securing a policy objective, the success of the funded enterprises in achieving the policy objectives ought to be assessed (see chapters by Henkel, Mitchell and Tolan for this wider perspective). In this, the review echoed the recommendations which have been made for more consistent policy evaluation of all major initiatives (Cabinet Office 1988, Connor 1993a).

Although the Efficiency Scrutiny applied only to government funding schemes, many of the ideas underpinning this have been taken up by other funders, albeit sometimes for different reasons. In many local authorities, all voluntary organisations receiving funding through the Social Work or Social Services Department are likely to have to deal with clearer but tighter requirements for reviewing their performance and reporting back on achievements as a consequence of the contracts or revised grant arrangements prompted by the new community care arrangements in 'Caring for People' and the standards and practice guidance in associated documents (Secretaries of State for Health, Social Security, Scotland and Wales 1989). Trusts and corporate funders, on the other hand, are mostly looking for a different type of feedback – typically, less intensive reviews focussing on outcomes for users and others, and on the capacity of the organisations' management systems to sustain the intended results in the longer-term. In both situations, however, the principle underpinning the desire for better review of recipient organisations' performance is good management practice.

Links with wider policy initiatives

In addition to performance review and feedback about individual voluntary organisations, where the focus is on that organisation's performance standards, it must be remembered that funders/buyers and policy makers in both central government and local statutory bodies may also need information about the performance of voluntary organisations for other reasons. (A similar use of information from community care assessments is noted by Brace.) One area of particular importance is the link into wider service planning and programme evaluation. This aspect was noted above in the context of the Efficiency Scrutiny of government-funded schemes, but the interaction of project and wider review is, if anything, more acute in community care planning. Service managers will be faced with longer-term strategic decisions, such as the future balance between residential and domiciliary care, or whether the benefits to users are commensurate with the resources required to provide the activities. Some evidence to assist managers may be available from research studies and other general reviews of these types of services – and indeed from the types of information discussed in other chapters of this book. In areas where services run by voluntary organisations form a significant part of local community care provision, however, the routine review of performance by these organi-

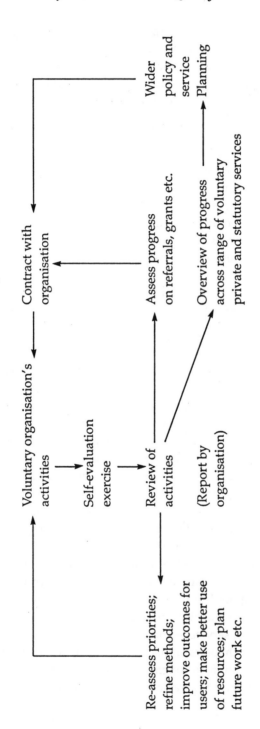

Figure 13.3 Planning and decision-making cycles of voluntary projects, funders and policy makers

Notes:

1. Other factors are, of course, involved in the decision-making by voluntary organisations and statutory agencies.
2. Social Work Departments, Health Boards and other statutory agencies may also be involved in the project's own re-assessment, eg through membership of management committee

sations will inevitably form a major part of any such service and policy planning.

Perhaps inevitably, this wider service or funding review will be tacked on to systems established to deal with review at project level. If such demands have been planned in from the outset it is possible that all the various requirements will be met. Otherwise, it is likely to be more of a gamble. Figure 13.3 shows the interaction of, on the one hand, these various interests and, on the other, the uses made of the central base of information from the review of the organisation's performance and achievements.

Taken overall, the requirements of any system for reviewing the performance of a voluntary organisation are that it should take account of:

(1) the voluntary organisation's need for information for its own management, for dissemination and for discharge of accountability

(2) the different types of information needed by voluntary organisations, their funders and referrers, and the different emphasis and importance placed on the same information by these interests; and

(3) information needed at different organisational levels within local authorities or other agencies in their capacity as funders and/or planners.

Types of performance review for voluntary organisations

It is not surprising that many different approaches have been developed to fulfil the multiplicity of demands and reasons for performance review of voluntary organisations. The main models are:

- routine monitoring of the contract or grant through regular (usually annual) financial and statistical returns
- ongoing supervision of the voluntary organisation by the funder ('keeping in touch')
- professional adviser's or consultant's assessment for the funder
- third party evaluation commissioned by the funder
- evaluation commissioned jointly by the funder and voluntary organisation
- monitoring and evaluation by the voluntary organisation
- funder's evaluation programmes.

Figure 13.4 summarises the main purposes of each type of performance review, along with the way in which it is typically used, the advantages, and the limitations. The models of performance review are described more fully in other publications with a more practical focus (Connor 1993b and 1994, Flynn and Hurley 1993).

				Model			
	A	B	C	D	E	F	G
Focus:							
specific aspects	√	-	*	*	*	*	*
overview	-	√	*	*	*	*	*
finances	√	√	√	*	*	*	*
outputs/scale	√	-	-	√	√	√	√
management structures	-	√	√	-	*	*	√
Enables voluntary organisation to:							
identify weaknesses	-	√	√	√	*	√	*
identify strengths	-	√	√	√	*	√	*
identify solutions	-	√	√	-	*	√	*
help implement solutions	-	*	*	-	-	√	-
learn skills	-	*	-	-	-	√	-
Enables funder to:							
adjust grant	√	√	√	√	√	-	-
assess project		√	√	√	*	-	-
assess programme	-	-	-	-	-	-	√

A: Routine monitoring through annual reports
B: Keeping in touch
C: Consultant's or Adviser's assessment
D: Evaluation for funder
E: Jointly commissioned evaluation
F: Self-evaluation by voluntary organisation
G: Funder's evaluation programme

√: Usually a feature
*: Varies – as contractor chooses
-: Rarely a feature

Figure 13.4 Typical application of approaches to performance review

Some situations – relationships between funder or contractor and voluntary organisation, the different types of voluntary organisations identified at the start of this chapter – are likely to be better served by certain approaches than by others. For example, reviewing the performance of an organisation through on-going contact such as having an assessor present at committee meetings (model B) has been much more common among trusts than among public sector funders and especially statutory authorities which are contracting only for specific services. However, this approach is now being used more frequently when there are no alternative providers and the contractor's concern is to ensure the continuation of a voluntary organisation capable of delivering a good quality, efficient service (Flynn and Hurley 1993).

The approaches also vary in the ease with which they can deal with inherent difficulties. The most frequently noted and/or most persistent difficulties arising in relation to performance review of voluntary organisations are:

- **multiple sources of funding** for the organisation or even for particular activities – for example, where a service is part-funded by two bodies with different review arrangements or criteria for success, or partly through a specific contract and partly through a core grant for the accommodation and management-related costs

- the extent to which the performance review method is used – or can be used – to identify the **quality of service provided**

- similarly, the extent to which the method can address situations other than delivering services to individual users, especially its **applicability to co-ordination or campaigning activities**

- the extent to which the model can address all relevant aspects of the voluntary organisation's performance, or tends to have **partial or distorted coverage**

- **demands on the voluntary organisation**, especially smaller and newer organisations, as a consequence of the recording and reporting arrangements

- **cost to the funder** – some methods of performance review are more expensive than others, especially in fees to external consultants or when other specialist experience or skills are needed

- **appropriateness of standards applied in the review** – for example, when the standards of a large public sector body are applied out of context to committee procedures and other aspects of management of a small, loosely-structured self-help group, or when the funder's performance review method ignores or under-estimates the costs and benefits of a high level of volunteer involvement

- the links between the performance review and the actions then taken by the voluntary organisation or funder are often complex, but some models of performance review are less likely than others to lead to **slow or partial implementation of the results.**

Issue	*Problems typically encountered or expected when model used*					
	A	B	C	D	E	F
Meeting demands of Multiple funders	*					
Able to identify quality of activities	*			*		
Applicable to campaigning or co-ordinating organisations	*					*
Partial or distorted coverage			*			
Appropriateness of standards		*	*	*		
Demands on voluntary organisations (esp. smaller)	*		*			*
Cost			*		*	
Slow or poor implementation of results	*		*	*		

A: Routine monitoring through annual reports
B: Keeping in touch
C: Consultant's or Adviser's assessment
D: Evaluation for funder
E: Jointly commissioned evaluation
F: Self-evaluation by voluntary organisation
G: Funder's evaluation programme

Figure 13.5: Potential limits of performance review models

As might be expected, experience of performance review in and of voluntary organisations is mixed. This is partly a matter of the inherent design of performance review models – some models are not well suited to certain purposes or situations, which is why other models have been developed. It is also partly a matter of experience – as models are applied and developed, the potential to maximise strengths and minimise or offset limitations is better understood. Figure 13.5 notes the situations where difficulties can be expected in the application of a model to a specific voluntary organisation or project, either because the model is not well-suited or because it is relatively under-developed.

It is to be hoped that as experience grows and is shared, still further refinements will be made. Already experience is showing ways in which even these difficulties can be successfully addressed. Common factors are:

- clarity of aims, objectives and targets for the activity covered by the grant or contract;
- clarity of the purposes of the performance review
- initial agreement between the funder and each recipient organisation of indicators of successful performance
- flexibility in the format and timing of performance review and especially of submission of reports to the funder or contractor
- good on-going communication between the funder/contractor and organisation.

Evaluation of funding programmes

As has been noted, many programmes of support to voluntary organisations are a means of fulfilling other aims, such as a policy of a government department or to publicise and kick-start an under-developed area of service provision. In a similar way some of the larger trusts set medium to long term priorities where the intention is to develop an area of voluntary sector activity over five years or so. Often the intention is that the whole will be more than the sum of the parts as a result of publicity, dissemination activities and the demonstration value of the supported projects. In these situations each project or grant to a voluntary organisation should be contributing to this overall programme and it therefore makes sense to evaluate not only the achievements of the individual projects but the overall impact and achievements of the programme.

Another reason for evaluating funding programmes is to learn from the experience: what types of projects or support are more effective? For example, is it better to support the full cost of a few projects or partly to support a greater number? Are some types of organisations more prone to running into difficulties than others?

Reviews of the performance of funding programmes are rarely made by any type of funder. Some voluntary organisations have noted it as ironic that although funders expect the recipients to tighten their monitoring and evaluation procedures for good management and accountability, this is a model approach which funders rarely follow themselves. This view was endorsed by the Efficiency Scrutiny, which recommended that for every grant scheme the relevant department should have criteria against which the scheme will be evaluated and arrangements for evaluating the scheme as a whole.

Many of the problems and issues which arise in relation to evaluation of funding programmes are more acute examples of the problems besetting evaluation of voluntary sector projects or the work of individual voluntary organisations. Particular factors associated with appropriateness or success include:

- **appropriateness of aims**: the underlying policy aims which the programme is intended to further may themselves be expressed in vague terms (for example, 'the relief of poverty', 'benefit older people'). Similarly, the links between the aim and the activities supported may be a matter of trust or dependent on wider policy evaluation – for example, grants given to youth clubs as a means of preventing inner city violence.

- **appropriateness of evaluation criteria**: these may also be unclear, or inappropriate, or determined by factors outwith funders' or the organisations' control. A funder may give very little thought to the criteria against which a funding programme of several million pounds per annum will be assessed, or concentrate on financial or scale of activity performance indicators ('proportion of applications funded', 'average award of 75% of funds sought') rather than indicators which identify the effectiveness and outcomes of the programme.

- **timescales**: the impact of a funding programme will generally only become apparent in the longer-term, especially if the intention is to have a demonstration or pump-priming impact, and this may go beyond the funded life of the component activities.

- **the voluntary organisations' incentive to co-operate** may be limited: although evaluation of a funding programme is quite clearly of benefit to the funder, and perhaps to the wider community, it is rarely of benefit to the voluntary organisations directly involved.

Implications for performance review of services provided by voluntary organisations

Putting the users' needs first, being aware of unmet need and the limitations of existing services, demonstrating the value of their activities to other bodies and being aware of the outcomes of services are essential aspects of quality assurance and other aspects of performance review. Similarly, making the best use of often scarce resources and being accountable to funders – whether the general public or grant-making bodies – are concepts which voluntary organisations recognise as valid. Reviews of these factors have been made by virtually all voluntary organisations, but often more gradually and less formally than the term 'performance review' as traditionally used would imply.

In this respect, many of the ideas identified by Peters and Waterman and other management writers which underpin the current emphasis on performance review are not as alien to the experience and philosophy of the voluntary sector as they might at first appear (Peters and Waterman 1984). Drucker's writings refer mainly to the not-for-profit sector in the United States of America, which has important differences from that existing in the United Kingdom, but he has shown how organisations have incorporated good innovative management practices – including performance review – into their work without sacrificing their principles (Drucker 1990).

New performance review methods are now emerging to complement or replace methods originally developed in traditional commercial settings. One example is social auditing (Zadek and Evans 1993), which brings together business effectiveness and social values by identifying the ethical and social, as well as the financial, dimensions in assessing the overall 'profit and loss' of an organisation. These approaches have been developed for community businesses and similar commercial ventures, but also have a relevance for more conventional voluntary organisations.

It still has to be recognised, however, that the values and assumptions in ideas and material focusing on profit-making ventures and much of the language used are threatening to voluntary organisations and can be inconsistent with their aims. Performance reviews based on these different premises can themselves be damaging if this discrepancy is not taken into account, the necessary adjustments made to the approach and the appropriate criteria applied. Such adjustments are not always made and voluntary organisations may have good reason to be apprehensive at the prospect of performance review.

It has to be recognised that the challenges and impact of performance review, even when appropriate, can be far from easy. This new way of thinking has proved to be a challenge to many companies, government departments and local authorities who thought they were doing a good enough job until called on to review performance against such factors as meeting users' needs, ability to tackle new ventures, quality of service delivered rather than volume of work done and fundamental review of whether they should be doing these activities at all ('doing the right thing as well as doing it right').

It should come as no surprise that some voluntary organisations are found to be getting stuck in delivering services no longer as appropriate as when they first began, or using staff, volunteers and other resources in ways that do not make best use of their potential contribution. Yet the way in which such an assessment is received is often of a different order for a voluntary organisation. It can be more than usually damaging to the individuals concerned: being told you are doing a poor or unnecessary job when you are paid for it is bad enough, but when you have given freely of your time and efforts as a volunteer or committee member the rejection can be doubly hard. The consequences of a review that highlights disappointing performance in key areas may also be more severe for a voluntary organisation than an equivalent statutory body. A local authority might decide to reduce or not renew a contract or allocation of grant to a voluntary organisation where levels of service were lower than expected, but would not expect to see the same order of cut on its budget or staffing if its performance was below target – indeed, it may itself have no equivalent target.

With the changing role of voluntary organisations, managers on committees and in senior posts are having to change the way they use and respond to performance review. They also have to take steps to maximise benefits and minimise disadvantages for those putting the organisation's activities into effect and for the users and other people with whom the organisation works. At the same time, funders will have to consider more carefully their place in the new partnership and the implications for performance review: what information they require of voluntary organisations, how this is obtained, the impact performance review can have on the organisations, and their own response to the information they receive. For both groups of people involved, a greater awareness of the range of possible approaches to performance review and their inherent strengths and limitations will be an important factor in how these new relationships are established.

References

Cabinet Office (1988) *Policy Evaluation, A Guide for Managers*. London: HMSO.

Charities Aid Foundation (CAF) (1992) *Charity Trends, 1992* (15th edition). Tonbridge: Charities Aid Foundation.

Connor, A. (1993a) *Report on Evaluation by Voluntary Organisations*. Edinburgh: HMSO.

Connor, A. (1993b) *Monitoring and Evaluation Made Easy – A Handbook for Voluntary Organisations*. Edinburgh: HMSO.

Connor, A. (1994) *Funders and Evaluation*. London: Charities Evaluation Services.

Drucker, P. (1990) *Managing the Non-Profit Organisation*. London: Butterworth-Heinneman.

Edwards, K. (1992) *Contracts in Practice*. London: National Council of Voluntary Organisations/Directory of Social Change.

Flynn, N. and Hurley, D. (1993) *The Market for Care*. London: Public Sector Management, London School of Economics and Political Science.

Home Office (1990) *Profiting from Partnership*. London: HMSO.

Knight, B. (1993) *Voluntary Action in the 1990s*. London: Home Office.

Peters, T.J. and Waterman, R.A. (1984) *In Search of Excellence*. London: Harper and Row.

Secretaries of State for Health, Social Security, Wales and Scotland (1989) *Caring for People, Community Care in the Next Decade and Beyond*. Cm 849. London: HMSO.

SCVO (Scottish Council of Voluntary Organisations) (1991) *Community Care Contracting – A Voluntary Sector Code of Practice*. Edinburgh: Scottish Council of Voluntary Organisations.

Zadek, S. and Evans, R. (1993) *Auditing the Market – A Practical Approach to Social Auditing*. London: Traidcraft, Gateshead and New Economics Foundation.

Part 4

Performance Revisited

Chapter 14

Performance and Quality in Public Services

Anna Coote

Introduction

'Quality' means different things to different people. These differences can be controversial – especially when applied to public services. In this chapter I explore four distinctive approaches to quality which are currently in use: traditional, scientific, managerial and consumerist. I summarise their strengths and limitations, and then outline briefly another approach which combines the best of these.

The traditional approach

This is the most familiar usage, the one most readily understood outside the world of 'quality' specialists. The traditional and still widespread assumption is that a quality product or service is superior to others, and probably more expensive. It speaks of high standards of production, delivery and presentation associated with expensive restaurants, French perfume, Rolls Royce cars. It is about 'no expense being spared' and delivering 'the best that money can buy'. It suggests luxury and perfection. It has class connotations: 'the Quality' is how working class people used to refer to upper class people – at least in some Victorian novels. In the market place, this kind of quality confers status on the customer. If you buy a quality product you signal to others that you are someone special or superior, or richer than others.

With public services which are delivered free, on the basis of need, this meaning has no direct relevance. However, it has an important influence – because no matter how the word 'quality' is used, this is the meaning that sticks to it. Even when measures are introduced more to camouflage a deterioration of services than to promote an improvement in them, if those measures are referred to as 'quality' initiatives it will make them sound as though there is a striving for perfection. So this meaning has a public relations function, because of its association, through the traditional usage of the word, with 'no expense being spared' or 'every effort being made' to ensure the best possible product or service.

The scientific approach

According to this approach to quality, experts define and prescribe standards of acceptability. It is associated with scientific management – a set of ideas developed during the first quarter of this century, about how to manage organisations. This has continued, until recently, to exert a strong influence over many parts of the public and private sectors. It grew out of the era of mass production ('Fordism') and assembly line working methods, in which skills were fragmented and jobs broken down into repetitive tasks ('Taylorism').

The scientific approach is about measuring 'fitness for purpose'. The British Standards Institution refers to assessing 'the totality of features and characteristics of a product or service that bear upon its ability to satisfy a given need' (BSI 1987). Features and characteristics have to be specified to set standards and then performance is monitored to assess conformance to standards. The idea is that goods and services that fail to come up to scratch are rejected; the producers or providers may be punished by loss of contract or job, or by incurring a financial or other penalty.

This approach challenges the notion of professional autonomy in decision-making, for instance the 'clinical freedom' of doctors to decide about treatment. It can improve information about outcomes; about what is expected and what is delivered, and establish shared standards of practice. These may be regarded as positive factors. On the negative side, the scientific approach tends to promote measures of quality which are unilateral and brook no dissent: they are laid down by experts, have an aura of scientific authenticity and are not generally negotiable. Moreover, this approach is paternalistic. The experts are in control. They decide what is a 'given need'; they decide what is 'satisfaction'. They may or may not be guided by a public service ethic. They may or may not tailor standards to suit their own predilections. The 'scientific' and quality assurance approaches are preoccupied with specification of inputs, not outputs or outcomes, which are usually all that matter to the user.

The managerial or 'excellence' approach

According to this approach, quality is about satisfying the customer. Customer satisfaction is central to the management philosophy which is currently fashionable and fast becoming dominant in the commercial world, and is also a force behind the restructuring of public services. It was developed in the US between the wars, and taken up enthusiastically by Japanese manufacturers and by innovative British retailers such as Sainsbury and Marks & Spencer. The key text is Peters and Waterman's *In Search of Excellence*, published in 1982. This argued that customer-orientation was the key to commercial success and made the pursuit of quality in this sense a managerial holy grail. While the scientific approach can be said to be Fordist, this is post-Fordist.

The managerial approach promises managers a strategy for survival of their organisation in rapidly-changing competitive environments. While more traditional strategies advocate the accumulation of tangible and intangible assets as a hedge against hard times, the 'excellence' strategy is to 'get it right first time, on time and to cost'. Getting it right is about giving the customers what they want.

In place of control by bureaucratic procedures which prescribe how things are to be done, there are strategies which focus on results and aim at controlling output. Management by status is replaced by management by leadership. The issuing of mission statements is becoming a familiar feature of the 'excellence' landscape – to express an organisation's philosophy and goals, to motivate the workforce and impress customers. Total Quality Management (TQM) is the strategy which most thoroughly expresses the managerial approach to quality. According to this approach, everyone is responsible for output, not just the person at the top: the whole workforce is involved. Customer satisfaction is the key to success. All workers have a stake in the success of the organisation and therefore are committed to satisfying the customer. However, it must be stressed that TQM is only as good as the sum of measures invoked in its name – and these can vary almost infinitely.

In pursuit of 'excellence', vertical organisation may give way to horizontal structures, which help to spread responsibility. Large organisations may be broken down into smaller, semi-autonomous units, to get close to the customers, in order to improve understanding of how they will be satisfied, and to respond more effectively to their demands. Control by ownership is replaced by control by contract – both inside and outside the organisation's boundaries. The aim is to be able to respond more flexibly to changing customer demand.

An obvious strength of the managerial approach is that it encourages an organisation to focus on what the customer/user wants instead of what the expert thinks is best. It can help break down hide-bound bureaucratic structures, increase flexibility and transparency of decisions, and make for more responsive services.

However, there is one fundamental aspect of this approach to quality which does not transfer easily from the commercial to the public sector. Where services are free and allocated on the basis of need (as in the public sector) and where resources are limited, there is no straightforward causal link between customer satisfaction and organisational success. Indeed, if customer satisfaction leads to increased demand, rather than adding to the success of the providing organisation by boosting business and profits it can merely add to its troubles, because all the extra demand must be met with the same, finite resources.

The managerial approach promotes the idea of competition between alternative providers (to see who can satisfy the customer best). In the public sector, however, competition is not always appropriate, and where providers fail to satisfy their customers, it may sometimes be a more effective use of public funds to help them improve their service, rather than simply to force them to close down.

This approach transfers power from professionals towards managers (and is thus very popular with managers). There has been a vast influx into the public sector, especially the Health Service, of managers whose job it is to manage, not to provide. A wide range of decisions has passed into the domain of managerial discretion. Management as a 'science' is supposed to be value free and above politics but in fact it can be highly political, especially when it operates in the public sector. Unlike doctors and other professional groups, managers have no self-imposed code of ethics or practice. Nor are they directly accountable to the public. This points to a need for a new management discipline, and a new structuring of managerial discretion, which is geared towards the goals and values of the public sector.

Furthermore, the managerial approach, by focusing on the customer, side-steps an issue of central importance in the public sector. The customers (in the sense of service users) are not the only ones who matter. The interests of the general public must be taken into account. Some services have more than one customer. Take schools, for example: whose interests are paramount? The children who are currently at the school or their parents, or local employers, or the community at large? And what about tomorrow's parents and pupils? Surely all of these are important. And where community care is concerned, carers and service users have different and sometimes conflicting requirements. Today's able-bodied taxpayers may be tomorrow's customers: each group has a valid interest in how services are developed.

The consumerist approach

While the excellence approach emphasises the desire of producers to satisfy customers, the consumerist approach emphasises the desire of customers to be satisfied. It casts customers in an active role and seeks to increase their power.

An important dimension of this approach is the encouragement of customer choice through enhanced competition. The idea is that customers reject shoddy goods and shop elsewhere, so that providers either mend their ways or go out of business. How readily providers respond depends on the selling power of the provider and the purchasing power of the customer. A monopoly supplier can afford to worry less about satisfying customers. A monopoly buyer has considerable clout.

In the commercial sector, consumers may be individual buyers or large and powerful purchasers (an example would be a large motor company such as Ford or Nissan: when they buy components from suppliers they are extremely powerful in their position as customer). An equivalent in the public sector is the new institutional consumer, such as a fund-holding GP, a health authority, or a local authority when it puts services out to tender. Individuals have far less muscle, but their consumer power can be increased in two ways. One way is by joining forces with other individuals in consumer groups and movements, such as the Consumers' Association or (in a more institutional mode) bodies like Oftel or Passenger Transport Authorities. Another way is through the development of enforceable consumers' rights.

The Citizens' Charter encapsulates the consumerist approach to quality. It is based on the premise that individuals can be 'empowered' by means of specified (though not enforceable) guarantees about the nature and content of services. It is committed to increasing competition and choice, so that individuals can exercise power by 'shopping around' for alternatives. And it endorses strong and clear procedures for complaint and redress if guarantees are not met. (One example is the guarantee in the Patient's Charter that patients will receive treatment within two years of being placed on a waiting list.)

The consumerist approach shares many of the strengths of the managerial approach to quality. It focuses on the user rather than on the provider and places great emphasis on the importance of the user's satisfaction with goods or services. In addition, it seeks to increase the power of individual users to express satisfaction or dissatisfaction, and to put pressure on providers. It would be hard to overstate the value of measures to empower ordinary citizens in a modern democracy.

The main weakness of the consumerist approach (and the Citizen's Charter) is that, like the managerial approach, it can relate to individuals only in their capacity as customers or service users. Yet members of the public have a far more complex relationship with public services. They are both customers, interested in what happens to them today at the point where they use a service, and citizens, interested in what happens to their families and their neighbours, today, tomorrow and in the years to come.

Consumerism relies on individual choice as a means of empowerment. But choice may be illusory or irrelevant in the public sector. Where some types of service are concerned, such as accident and emergency treatment, alternative providers cannot easily be found. Of course, such work is not open to bidding at present, but even if it were, it would be unlikely to be considered viable (let alone profitable) by potential bidders. In some cases, users may not want to 'take their custom elsewhere'. For example, a young man with a broken leg just wants to get his bones set; an elderly woman in a residential home may not want to pack her bags and go elsewhere, preferring to stay in familiar but improved surroundings.

Rights to complain or receive redress may amount to too little, too late. In extreme circumstances, if a doctor or a social worker gets something wrong, the results may be fatal – and in general this kind of problem is likely to have more serious consequences than imperfect goods purchased in a high street store. The consumerist approach does not embrace rights of appeal against decisions, or public participation in decision-making.

As far as consumer groups are concerned, those which deal with public services were mainly developed in the 1960s and 1970s, when service providers were different from the ones we know today. The groups were geared to challenge big bureaucracies and monopoly suppliers, not the fragmented, market-oriented structures of the 1990s. They have found it hard to adapt to new conditions and have had no help from the government to do so. No strong alternative models have yet emerged.

The new institutional consumers of the public sector, shaped by the reforms of the 1980s and early 1990s, are supposed to represent the individual consumer and act on their behalf. However, it is doubtful that they can ever be relied upon to do so, since they must also serve their own interests. A fund-holding GP, for example, may be influenced in her decision about which treatment to purchase for a patient not just by what the patient needs, but also by a desire to protect the financial viability of her practice.

It is also doubtful whether these fund-holding bodies can or should behave as consumers, shopping around among competing providers to find the best bargain. In some cases, it would be an unacceptable waste of public money to create a choice – for example, in a rural area where one hospital serves the whole population. In other cases, it is possible to generate competition for a contract, but this can be hard to sustain over tendering rounds. In many major aspects of health and social work services, the break-up of monopoly supply and the creation of competition is neither possible nor relevant to the pursuit of quality.

Where the choice of institutional purchasers can be maintained, it may be no guarantee of quality from the user's point of view. This will depend on the criteria for choosing between competitors. If choice is driven chiefly by a desire to contain costs then quality will probably suffer. Where resources are scarce, there is bound to be a tension between the desire to contain costs on the one hand, and the desire to improve services. How that problem is resolved depends on who takes part in decision-making, whose interests have priority, how quality is defined and how resources are allocated.

A 'democratic' approach to quality

In this final section of the paper, I shall outline an alternative approach to the pursuit of quality in public services. This acknowledges the difference between commerce and welfare. It recognises that the public has a complex set of relationships with welfare services – as citizens, customers and providers. It is concerned with planning and delivery. It draws upon other approaches to quality and adapts them accordingly. The traditional approach (conveying prestige and positional advantage) is clearly inappropriate. The remaining three all have something to offer.

First, it embodies the goal of **fitness for purpose**, derived from the scientific approach. This approach to quality starts from the premise that the primary purpose of a modern welfare system, for which services must be 'fit', is **equity**. This does not mean giving everyone the same, but giving everyone an **equal chance in life**: an opportunity to participate in society, enjoy its fruits and fulfil their own potential. If this is the purpose, then we must take account of the fact that people do not start out as equals. Some have disadvantages, which may be avoidable or unavoidable. It is part of the purpose of a welfare system to eliminate avoidable disadvantages and compensate for those which cannot be overcome. It is also necessary to recognise that individuals have diverse and varying needs and that people want and need more control over their own lives.

The goal of equity (or equal life chances) thus points to two further goals: **responsiveness**, derived from the managerial approach, and **empowerment**, derived from the consumerist approach. The first goal may conflict with those of responsiveness and empowerment: as far as possible, these must be reconciled. The process of defining and assuring quality is, in effect, the means by which that reconciliation can be negotiated.

Strategies for making the public more powerful

1. *Openness*

An open system is one which makes relevant information easily accessible to the public, sustains transparent decision-making, is open to information from the public, and is susceptible to ideas for change which come from the public.

Individuals have different information requirements as customers and citizens. As customers, people need to know what services are available and how to apply for them; the bases on which decisions are taken about their own treatment and care; information which will help them participate in those decisions; how to complain about unsatisfactory services and how to appeal. As citizens, people need to know how welfare services are planned and delivered, how money is spent; who makes the relevant decisions, and where and when they are made; information about outcomes, for example: how different forms of treatment and care affect patients and clients; what patterns can be detected; what are the costs and benefits; criteria for rationing and targeting; and how members of the public can influence decision-making.

People need easy access to this information, in a form they can readily understand, in their own first language. Individuals may need someone to help them process the information and make appropriate use of it, especially where it involves technical knowledge. It is also important that everyone knows where to go to get this information.

2. *Rights for customers and citizens*

The case for a new framework of rights in health and social services is developed elsewhere by the Institute for Public Policy Research (Coote 1992). Rights cannot be seen as any kind of panacea, but it can be argued that they are essential if power is to be shifted towards the citizen/user, and as such they are an important part of a democratic approach to the pursuit of quality.

Rights are not worth having unless the public understands they can be claimed and enforced – although this should not inevitably lead to a system overrun by lawyers. Particularly relevant to this discussion are proposals for **procedural** rights, which promote the fair treatment of individuals, by ensuring that they have access to information, advice and advocacy, as well as to a range of rights governing decision-making procedures (Galligan 1992). Where resources are scarce, procedural rights may be easier to enforce than substantive rights (i.e., rights to stated benefits or services).

An important new dimension to the idea of welfare rights can be found in recent local experiments with **service agreements**. Briefly, these are the product of negotiation between local authorities and local communities – about what services should be provided and to what specifications. They incorporate a guarantee that services should be provided as agreed, and specify channels of complaint and modes of redress for individual users, should things go wrong. Pioneering work by the London Borough of Islington suggests that different approaches to the development of such agreements are required, depending on whether the service is universal (such as refuse collection), elective (such as swimming pools and libraries) or needs-based (such as community care). Where universal services are concerned, negotiations have taken place between council representatives and neighbourhood forums – open meetings which take place in the Borough's neighbourhood centres. Where elective services are concerned, there have been further consultations with user groups to develop appropriate agreements. With a needs-based service such as community care, consultations with groups of carers and users' representatives have helped to develop a framework in which individual agreements are drawn up (Thomson 1992).

3. *Public participation in decision-making*

A democratic approach to the pursuit of quality depends on members of the public participating actively in decisions about what constitutes a quality service, and whether such services are actually being delivered.

Individuals can participate collectively as citizens and individually as customers. The impediments to public participation are manifold: for example, the time and place at which meetings are held, the language in which they are conducted, and the difficulty of balancing paid employment with the demands of unpaid work. In effect, these impediments have become a way of controlling and measuring participation in the democratic process. Where sufficient numbers do not turn up regularly, the process is dismissed as 'unrepresentative' and therefore worthless. Individual 'representatives' of the public who sit on decision-making bodies are often ill-informed, isolated and without any firm sense of purpose in being there; they may be overwhelmed by impenetrable documentation, or thrown into confusion when committee papers arrive late. There may be no effective channels for reporting back to the people they are supposed to represent. Often, people in this position burn out quickly and drop out – or else the job falls to those who are rendered unsuitable by their relish for unrepresentative committee work.

Many individuals do not want to participate, because they have been led to believe through long experience that their voice will not be heard. In order to take a more active role, people need to believe that it will bear some positive results; they must feel they have the power to make a difference. They must also feel they will not be tyrannised by a few who are 'expert' at public participation.

What all this points to is the need for a strong infrastructure supporting different forms of public participation. Relevant information should be made accessible – not simply available to people who come in search of it, but taken to people who would not otherwise know it existed. Individuals should have clear rights to participate at different stages of decision-making. There should be proper support for representatives and effective channels for them to communicate with the public they are representing, as well adequate space and resources to hold public meetings and publicise them widely. Furthermore, strategies should be developed to ensure that the views and experience of those who cannot participate are taken fully into account. Data about decisions that are taken and how they affect the public should be collected and publicised on a regular basis. But perhaps the greatest spur to public participation is likely to be provided by clear signs from public authorities that they want to negotiate with the public, and that they will listen and be guided by its views.

In general, communication between individuals and public authorities can be aided by **intermediate bodies** – for example, user and community groups. These can be a source of information, advice and advocacy, a catalyst for individual involvement, a forum for discussion and decision-making, and a means of representation. Public policy can be aimed at supporting these intermediary bodies, recognising the vital part they can play. However, intermediate bodies should not themselves escape the quality process: they too must be open, responsive and subject to audit.

4. Choice

Choice has a useful but limited part to play in the pursuit of quality. The scope for collective choice can be enhanced through service agreements and generally by opening up decision-making to public participation. The scope for individual choice can be widened too. It depends on alternatives being available and on people having access to the information necessary to make choices which will benefit them. Where choices – large or small – can be provided without undermining the common goals of a welfare system, they should be supported and sustained.

Strategies for building a responsive system

Most people would favour the idea of a welfare system which responds to individual needs. However, a system whose primary goal is to give everyone an equal chance in life, and whose resources are limited, cannot hope to respond equally to all individuals' needs. Some are more urgent than others; some have been unjustly overlooked in the past. If these differences are to be accommodated, some individuals must get more and others less. Responsiveness involves deploying information about needs and resources, and negotiating with the public about how resources are allocated. That process of negotiation should take place within a framework of nationally agreed goals, and attempt to develop agreements with local communities about how those goals are reached.

1. Involving the workforce

A key factor in the pursuit of quality in welfare is the motivation of the workforce – especially those in direct contact with the public. Resources are scarce and, as we have noted, productivity is not linked to profitability in welfare as it is in commerce: financial incentives cannot be regarded as a major way of motivating staff. Even in the commercial world it is now widely recognised that success depends on gaining the commitment of all workers at all levels to the pursuit of an organisation's goals. It is also understood that commitment is not bought by money alone, but by training, security and involvement in developing products.

However, a sense of commitment cannot survive the continuous punishment of low wages and poor working conditions, without prospect of improvement. A combination of factors is needed to harness the commitment of public sector workers and maximise the contribution they can make. These factors would include training and career development, flexible working arrangements and employment protection measures – especially for those with family commitments. They would also include involvement in planning and organising services by employees at all levels: 'front-line' workers who are closest to the public often know more about how to meet needs than managers, and professionals and other more senior personnel. For this to happen there would need to be substantial changes in the rules governing competitive tendering. Employees of the welfare services are citizens and customers too. You cannot build a system which aims to give everyone an equal chance in life on a disadvantaged and exploited workforce.

2. Changing management and professional cultures

The concept of **public service orientation** represents an attempt to translate the 'excellence' approach into the language of the public sector. In their pioneering work for the Local Government Training Board, Michael Clarke and John Stewart have argued that it is possible to develop a rigorous and distinctive form of management that does not simply reproduce the patterns of commercial management, but is geared to the special requirements and conditions of public service, and able to manage for equity as well as for efficiency (Clarke and Stewart 1990). John Stewart has suggested that there is scope for extending these ideas to begin to change the ethos of the 'caring' professions to one marked by outward focus, continuing development and strong communication.

Strategies for ensuring 'fitness for purpose'

All the strategies listed so far should help to ensure that welfare services are fit for their purpose – which is to give everyone an equal chance in life. Last but not least, it is important to stress the value of systematic auditing, built into the system, based on specifications negotiated with the public and using methods of review which take full account of users' needs and experience.

Note

This paper is based on Pfeffer, N. and Coote, A. (1992) *Is Quality Good for You? A Critical Review of Quality Assurance in Welfare Services*. London: Institute for Public Policy Research.

References

British Standards Institution (1987) BS 4778:4.1.1. London: BSI.

Clarke, M. and Stewart, J. (1990) *Developing Effective Public Service Management*. Local Government Training Board.

Coote, A. (ed.) (1992) *The Welfare of Citizens*. London: Institute for Public Policy Research/Rivers Oram Press.

Galligan, D. (1992) 'Procedural rights in social welfare', in Coote, A., *ibid*, 55–68.

Peters, T.J. and Waterman, R.H. (1982) *In Search of Excellence*. New York: Harper and Row.

Thomson, W. (1992) 'Realising rights through local service contracts', in Coote, A., *op. cit.*, 129–151.

Chapter 15

Reflections on the Politics of Quality

Ann James

Introduction

The public could be forgiven for thinking that the aim of quality is to improve service to users. Much of the talk among professionals, managers and elected representatives in the caring services appears to reinforce this view. Maybe this is what the aim should be. Maybe this is what it could be. But reflecting on how quality has been employed in public service organisations in the 1970s, 1980s and early 1990s would suggest that implementing quality has done little to improve services to users in practice. Indeed, a study carried out for the Department of Health and Social Services Inspectorate in 1991 acknowledged that, at what was an early stage in formal development of quality in their departments, Social Services Departments were using it primarily as a means of financial restraint, secondly as a demonstration of policy achievement, and only thirdly as a mechanism to enhance service to users (James 1992a).

Dissonance between what professionals, managers and elected representatives say they do and how organisations behave in practice is always interesting. When that dissonance is between what those professionals, managers and elected representatives intend to do, even persuade themselves they actually are doing, and what they see happening, they become variously confused, angry, disappointed, frozen, sometimes distressed. The result is that quality, or the particular tool in use (for example, Quality Assurance, Total Quality Management), gets tarnished, even blamed, for the rather more serious malaise of powerlessness. This results from not acting 'authentically', for acting authentically requires people to act in accordance with their own values and their agreed professional standards. It requires individuals to match up what they say with what they do and to address the shortfall in between. It is when people do not act authentically that quality, along with a series of other mechanisms, is perceived as useless, when the real uselessness felt is about oneself and one's capacity to deliver.

This chapter explores the dissonance between what quality is described as being about and what it appears in practice to be about in public service. The central thesis of the chapter is that quality, like performance review, has become attached to a specific political agenda, namely that of the New Right, and in this attachment has adopted a certain social construction. This social construction is managerialist in character and the managerialism it represents is that of the Thatcher era.

The intention of this chapter is to begin to separate quality from the political 'noise' it has collected around it. The purpose of this exercise is not to promote the mirage of a value free tool or technique, nor to criticise the very real need, intention and achievement in improving the management of public service. It is simply to help to free professionals, managers and elected representatives to use the power they could have to redefine quality – and indeed management – in ways which allow them to act authentically and which take the views of users more seriously.

The ideas presented here draw on several sources. The first is the literature on quality in the private sector (reproduced as a literature search (James 1992a)) and, increasingly, in the public sector. This is essential to an understanding of the place of quality in social care and similar settings. The second is an on-going dialogue between the author and others arising out of statements made in previous publications (such as James 1992a and b). Third, they draw on the vast international literature on post-Fordist (i.e., post-industrial) organisations and management, spawned from the 1970s onwards, and developed in relation to changes in the UK public service sector by the author elsewhere and at length (James 1994). Most especially, they draw on observations derived as a consultant within the health and social service sectors. In some respects they have interesting links with contributions elsewhere in this volume, particularly those by Coote and Henkel. These ideas are put forward not as firm conclusions, but are designed to invite readers to continue to reflect for themselves on the interplay between politics, managerialism and quality.

Typology of quality

Acknowledging the dissonance between what quality is and how it is described has to begin with acknowledging the gap between the very fragmented and diverse ways in which quality has been formally defined in the public service and those definitions in everyday use.

Characteristics	Quality control	Quality assurance	Total quality management
Works through	Standards	Systems	People
Purpose	Uniformity to standards	Efficiency of systems	Improve outcomes for users
Responsibility	Inspectorate or Qe unit	Each division or each unit	Everyone but led by manager
View of quality	Absence of defect	Preventive	Opportunity
Primary concern	Detection of error	Co-ordination	Impact
Popular forms of expression	Inspection	Quality assurance systems	Total quality management Continuous quality improvement Quality improvement process Quality improvement teams/ quality circles

Source: Published with amendment from, James 1992a

Figure 15.1 Approaches to quality

The matrix from 'Committed to Quality' (James 1992a), reproduced here in amended form as Figure 15.1, looks and is simple. It identifies three different kinds of activity going on under the umbrella term of quality. There is **Quality Control**, which identifies error and corrects it, and uses mechanisms such as inspection. **Quality Assurance** can be identified as a specific form of activity. It involves predicting potential pressure points and acting to facilitate flow. However, the term is also popularly used as an umbrella term for all approaches to quality. Third, there is **Total Quality Management**. This is a quite different level of concept which focuses not on operational tasks but on the culture of the organisation and how it is represented in the attitudes of people to their jobs and therefore about the attention they pay to how they do those jobs.

The matrix offers a framework for thinking about quality and a firmer language from which we can move on to a dialogue about quality. What it does not do, and what it needs to do, is match up that framework and language with assumptions and language about quality in our everyday lives.

Talk about quality in everyday life often means something rather different from the meanings in the matrix. First, the word 'quality' can be used to mean 'high quality'; we talk for example about 'quality clothing' or 'quality fittings' (Coote makes this same point). Second, quality is understood as a relative and subjective term; in other words, what one person means by quality may not be what another means – and both meanings can be acceptable. Third, we seem to employ, quite naturally, a number of criteria in our definition. To take an example from an everyday situation, Esther Rantzen in her TV series 'That's Life' sought to compare the quality of roses on Valentines' Day by considering characteristics such as size, colour, length of stem and long-lasting properties. Finally, we have little difficulty in everyday life in putting together these three different and even competing notions of quality. So, for instance, Esther's list of criteria (or performance indicators) can be attached to what can be over-whelming subjective judgements: judgements related to who sent the roses and therefore about their implied significance to the receiver.

Regrettably, this commonsense view of quality seems to get lost when the debate moves into the realm of management. Back in the workplace, we tend to de-skill ourselves and attribute expertise to others. Practitioners, managers and elected representatives, we fail to acknowledge the joint contribution of subjective and objective criteria. Indeed much of the professional debate around the meaning of quality has centred around a rather arid dualism of subjectivity versus objectivity. Put crudely, either quality seems to be about everything, or it is about checklists. In reality, of course, it is about both. In Pirsig's words, it is about 'Zen and the Art of Motorcycle Maintenance' (Pirsig 1976), about life philosophy and about day-to-day practicalities. Most of all it is about the space between the two. It is about understanding who sent the roses and why (the meaning), and about the roses themselves meeting expected criteria (the checklist). Only when the two come together, and the conclusions are put into practical effect, is quality achieved. Or as a hospital porter put it, 'For me quality is avoiding the bumps in the car park'.

Quality, management and politics

How quality gets defined in public service is important because this has a bearing on how quality is perceived and implemented. But how quality gets into the public domain or into the public consciousness at all also has an impact on its implementation.

Identifying this route requires some reflection on the development towards a market in public services since the mid 1970s and in particular on the inadequacy of the management and professional arrangements in place at the time to construct and deliver effectively that development. That is not to criticise in any way the very serious and sometimes profound attempts by the people concerned to do so. Rather, it is to see the 1980s and early 1990s – and probably the late 1990s too – as a series of attempts to find ways of managing that transition within a set of theories based on what worked in the past but were largely inappropriate for managing in a very different environment.

Whether we see Margaret Thatcher as the architect of that transition or one jobbing builder in a much bigger transformation that included the disintegration of nations and nation states across the Western world is not at issue here (James 1994). What is common, however, at global and at local levels, is the protracted, difficult and arguably abortive search for managerial solutions. For while transformation may be necessary for the creation of new ways of working, all too often its value is apparent only in hindsight. Instead of letting the transition run its course to transformation, people shut it down because the experience of transition, the coping with ambiguity, can be so painful. They grasp at activities which are perceived as solutions. All too often, those perceived solutions have more to do with the desire to act, and to be seen to be acting, than with addressing the process of transformation itself.

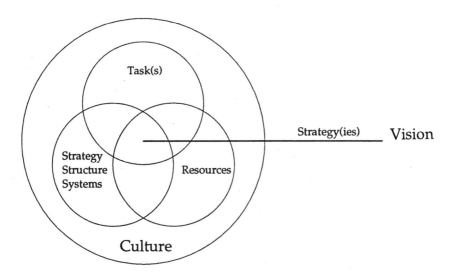

Figure 15.2 Management and Organisations

In the late 1970s and early 1980s, a distinctive approach to management began to surface widely in the UK. Figure 15.2 is a model which utilises the nomenclature of 1980s managerialism to identify what needs to happen within the organisation for it to relate effectively to its environment. The organisation needs to be clear about its key tasks – or what it is being asked to do, why and when and possibly how. It needs to be able to identify, mobilise and monitor its resources; these include staffing, capital and physical resources. In order to deliver on task, it has to have systems, strategies and structures in place within the organisation. Finally, how it operates, its style or its culture, needs to be consistent with these other factors. The organisation relates to its environment by means of strategies which are consistent with its mission and vision.

What is significant about the model and the nomenclature is the way that, in the absence of a comprehensive managerial theory, models like it became received wisdom and became not only descriptive, but also prescriptive of organisational behaviour. So Figure 15.3 catalogues the series of managerial 'solutions' canvassed since the 1970s to issues which were increasingly construed as management problems.

Management by:

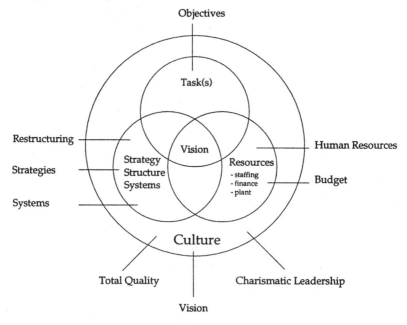

Figure 15.3 The managerial solutions

One of the first 'solutions' to be picked up was 'management by objectives', even though it had been developed a quarter of a century earlier (Drucker 1954). 'Management by objectives' concentrated on clarifying task, separating and prioritising objectives and identifying targets for achievement of tasks. So, for example, large public sector businesses, such as the Post Office, were split up into smaller business units according to core tasks, arguably in preparation for privatisation. In a similar way, in the NHS, objectives were relentlessly converted into annual targets and mapped against business plans in an ever increasing attempt to rationalise the non-rational processes of change.

Certainly 'management by objectives', which intervened to clarify task, was an improvement on 'management by accident' which arguably preceded it (Osbourne and Gaebler 1992). But as Peters and Waterman pointed out (Peters and Waterman 1984) the success of 'management of objectives', as promoted in the business schools, may have had more to do with operating in a buoyant economy, when what was planned could actually be implemented, than with the quality of theory itself.

If it was not possible to achieve the desired changes or level of control by management by task (and arguably the whole of the public sector changes of the 1980s was an attempt to clarify task), another perceived 'solution' was to manage through controlling resources. Cash-limited budgets and decentralised budgets might be another way of persuading people to focus on preferred activities. But at the same time this approach alienated professionals and confused managers, who often fell into equating doing the business with paying for the business. Human resource management, another 'solution', was equally difficult, requiring the development of a whole series of new and comparative techniques for multi-professional and multi-skilled settings, including competence assessment and appraisal, amongst many others.

If managing through task or resource constraint did not deliver the intent, another way might be to manage through structure, through strategies and through systems. The whole of the NHS and much of the educational system were restructured and strategies and systems put in place to direct, encourage and require certain kinds of preferred behaviours and not others from staff in these settings.

If none of these 'solutions' worked, then the last resort was to fall back on managing through controlling 'hearts and minds', for that in essence has been the evangelical message of Peters and Waterman and their contemporaries. Organisations, it was claimed, could be managed effectively through mission statements, through vision and through values.

It is within this context of a 'holy grail' search for a managerial solution that certain kinds of intermediate mechanisms started being borrowed from other – notably private sector – settings and applied to public service. At the heart of the transition and what required resolution was the core issue of how the centre – central government or another central source of authority – governs, manages or relates in other ways to a rapidly changing situation at the local level (see Figure 15.4).

How could local accountability can be promoted for services which are to be developed in a mixed economy under centralised control? Those elements of the public sector already privatised suggest that the organisations involved remain highly political in nature and continue to be regarded as in the public domain. Privatisation depends upon the removal of existing bureaucratic rules and accountabilities to work at all, and this removal can itself have unforeseen consequences for public accountability

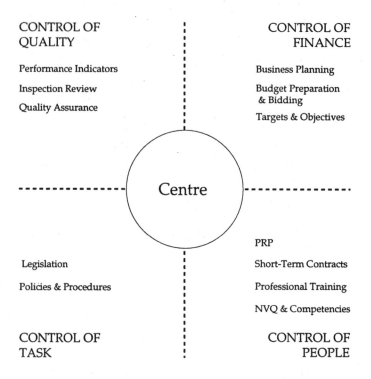

Figure 15.4 Mechanisms of potential control for the centre

as privatisation rolls out. The creation of new checks and balances takes time.

Meanwhile, the creation of 'quasi-markets' (Le Grand 1990) – opting out of schools, creation of self-governing hospital trusts, introduction of Probation Boards in England and Wales, market testing of prisons, reform of magistrates courts, even Producer's Choice at the BBC – has also required change in the nature of the accountabilities between the authority located at the centre and that located at the local level. Before 1979, the central-local relationship was arrived at through bureaucratic and professional collaboration and alliance. Of course there were arguments – but they were confined within that alliance. Professionals might disagree with bureaucrats, doctors might disagree with health service managers, but mainly they respected each other's differences (and self-perceived superiorities). However, once both were required to practice in quasi-markets, with the managerial supremacy required of the new setting, then traditional tensions could no longer be held in check.

In addition, the required outcomes for central-local relationships were often challenged by devolved management arrangements. Delegated budgets and staffing arrangements required central authorities to act as back-seat drivers in a process driven at the local level. The breakdown in professional-bureaucratic alliances (for example, on GP contracts) combined with devolved management arrangements in a new and unpredictable quasi-market setting to require different and demonstrable mechanisms of accountability between central and local authorities. So, contrary to professional expectation, strikes in England and Wales on teachers' pay arguably hastened, rather than prevented, the demise of collective and national pay agreements and promoted an enhanced, professional challenge in the form of the National Curriculum. The accountability mechanisms which emerged were arguably of four major kinds: control of staff; control of task; control of finance and control of quality.

Figure 15.4 illustrates the way in which private sector mechanisms are used to add to the range of approaches already available, often – it seemed – not with any predetermined strategy but spewed out, possibly in response to mounting fear by the centre about rapid changes at local levels. So, for example, if the centre could no longer control staff through the very simple and single model of ensuring they were professionally qualified (and rising numbers of non-professional and multi-professional staff suggested it could not), then maybe appraisal, or short-term contracts, or performance related pay or competence based training (NVQs) would work instead. Other indirect controls were about prioritising certain tasks, through the use of, for example, legislation, policies and procedures. Still others were about resource constraint and used mechanisms such as business planning and budget delegation.

Quality has been used as just such a mechanism. Quality control, manifested in inspection and contractual conditions, has been a way of ensuring recognition of agreed standards within a mixed economy. So, for example, the Registered Homes Act required local authorities to inspect independent homes for elderly people. Quality assurance, operating as it did by focusing on the restriction of flow at pressure points in organisational processes, worked both within organisations (for example in restricting hospital waiting lists) and across multi-agency settings (for example across health and social care agencies by focusing on hospital discharge and bedlocking). Above all, the 'Total Quality' philosophy was a way of ensuring that the core values of the host organisation were transferred into the emerging culture of the market place. Equal opportunity clauses, for example, could be made a condition of service agreements with independent contractors, such that the quality of the mixed economy system as a whole could be reinforced.

In other words, quality becomes the safety net at the centre and the price paid at the locality for enhanced local diversity and accountability. Only by guaranteeing quality could local experiment and local innovation be managed within a centralised system of accountability.

Reconstructing quality

There remain a number of challenges to managing the development of the mixed economy in public service. Certainly our tools are inadequate in their scope or application for the job and others need to be developed. Quality is one of them. All too often quality has been caught up in inter- and intra-organisational rivalries for power and status, not least among professionals.

This is apparent in the rise and fall of quality initiatives in the public and private sectors. The experience of a single organisation such as the NHS confirms that how quality initiatives are established and by whom has significance for their success. Where quality initiatives are given high status and reinforced from the top of the organisations, then embracing quality can be a way of collecting power. Where they are of low status they can reinforce existing marginalisation of certain groups. Occasionally they can be a way of shifting power from certain groups to others and to users (Shearer 1991). Quality can be a way of capturing power and status in organisations that are currently chaotic.

Managing quality can be shorthand for developing the skills required to manage in the mixed economy. It remains to be seen whether those who acquire these skills keep them to themselves or share them across their organisations. What is emerging in the 1990s is ambivalence between a statement of intent that 'quality is everybody's business' and a language used currently not to enhance dialogue but to enhance exclusivity. The over-dependence on the quality 'expert' is a direct result of such exclusivity, for if quality is having the intended impact, then, like effective anti-racist practice, it is fully integrated into everyday life.

Sadly, one of the responses of professional practice to the mixed economy has been to see quality as a challenge to what some professionals regard as core values. Each profession considers itself to hold the premium on values often described through contrast to the practices and perceived values of other groups; or as a social worker put it, 'quality is something I have and you don't'. 'Total quality', like the concept of 'core values' before it, can be captured by professional groups and used to hang on to what they perceive of as essential ways of working. For the professional ethic, even when renamed as core values or total quality, is still potentially a way in which professionals can seek to capture the moral high ground.

In practice, of course, by taking the moral high ground professionals simply give power away. For in a health and welfare market place – even a social market – it is not a profession's capacity to define values for oneself and one's profession that generates power, but the capacity to exchange, to reciprocate, to interface, and to trade with other players in the market. It is not that values are not important: it is simply that they are not to be traded. Indeed the whole point of values is that they are not negotiable. So while hospital waiting lists may be a matter for public debate, arguably the professional ethic of doctors is not. Or is it? Because values are non-negotiable, conflicts of values have to be converted into conflicts of interests to be resolved. Not to convert them ultimately weakens professional values as well as professional interests. So the professional ethic of teachers was eventually called into question through their reluctance to negotiate over the National Curriculum. In the same way, the special relationship of doctors to patients was perhaps called into question by bickering over the GP contract. For it cheapens professional values to use them as trump cards in a game based on exchange. By failing to pay attention to the generation of exchange mechanisms appropriate to the market, professionals run the risk of marginalising themselves and, ultimately and ironically, marginalising their values. So the teachers' strike of the 1970s, the social work strikes of the 1980s and, in health, the Royal Colleges' position statements throughout the period have come to represent not professional strength, but weakness in a new environment. Quality, language and the lack of professional heritage can assist here. Quality can be a substitute for core values when core values are being challenged.

Quality has the potential to be part of a shared language, a language able to focus on the common professional concern for the user. At the simplest level quality can be a channel of dialogue across professional and organisational boundaries which can be potentially neutral in that the concept is relatively new to public service. What is important about quality is that it does not devalue one professional or organisational language in favour of another, and it is a concept that is generally understood. It can, therefore, provide an inter-professional and an inter-agency language.

More than this, quality can provide an intermediate language between managers, professional practitioners, and politicians: a kind of Esperanto which is artificial and restricted but which nonetheless provides another code for communication. By ignoring the language of quality – or any other new and foreign language – professionals reduce their ability to communicate and, inadvertently, marginalise themselves and thereby give power away to those who are able to speak in other tongues.

This explains why ideas based on 'total quality' have found much more resonance with professionals than have 'quality control' and 'quality assurance', which smack of administrative or managerial dominances. Some of the 'noise' around quality for professionals is not about quality at all, but about fear of dominance either by a set of principles to which they cannot subscribe or by a set of people whose approach they regard as inferior to their own. That is not to say, of course, that professionals are not seriously concerned about quality (which they call 'best practice'). It is simply to acknowledge an additional process going on here.

Finally, quality can be one of a series of ways on managing the transition from the old organisation to the new. In a world where we have learned that organisations need vision to survive, loss of vision is catastrophic. Whether or not one agreed with Margaret Thatcher, her direction was clear, although the subsequent fragmentation of the Cabinet under John Major might suggest to some that her direction was a result less of vision than of an autocracy. Perhaps vision was itself simply the brainchild of management gurus Peters and Waterman (1984), a response to a crying need. Perhaps it was an illusion, in reality only a term applied by or to leaders who had their own charisma. Either way, after Margaret Thatcher's premiership came a period of uncertainty and lack of direction. What is emerging from that period is that the real challenge lies in leading without vision and without clear direction, but rather learning by reflection on success and failure.

Quality is one of those tools which operate at the middle level. It operates somewhere between a *weltanschauung* (or world view) and the detail of everyday life. More than this, it works by linking the two (*Zen and the Art of Motorcycle Maintenance*). Vision is not a prerequisite for quality, although it helps to have vision. Rather, quality is an intermediate goal which is acceptable across the various divides – between agencies, between departments, between professionals and between sectors. As such it can be a good stand-in until vision comes along.

In conclusion

This chapter began by considering dissonance: dissonance between 'expert' and everyday notions of quality; dissonance between subjective and objective definitions of quality; and dissonance between what quality is described as and what it seems to be about in public service practice.

At one level dissonance is healthy and this volume is itself tribute to an ongoing conversation about the meaning and value of quality. At another level what we find is less dissonance than quality hijacked to resolve issues well beyond possible resolution by means of specific management tools and mechanisms. For the design and delivery of services to be driven not by professionals but by users is nothing short of transformational. Certainly, if transformation is to be planned for at all it must be grounded in indicators of progress. But those indicators are not themselves identical with the progress: bringing down hospital waiting lists is unlikely of itself to deliver better health. In the pain of transition to a new way of working and a better outcome for users, and with it the urgent search for an end to the associated disruption and for realisation of the change, all too often means are constructed as ends. So, community care has increasingly come to mean only the implementation of the NHS and Community Care Act.

It is this mismatch between ends and means, and at the same level our recognition of the tension, which tells us we are not acting authentically and which in turn produces feelings of powerlessness. If it is no longer possible to separate the social construction of quality from the political agenda of the market in public welfare, then we must use quality as a means to influence that agenda. Quality may not – yet – have much to do with users of service. But it could have if we chose to make it so.

References

Drucker, P.F. (1954) *The Practice of Management.* New York: Harper + Bros.

James, A. (1992a) *Committed to Quality: Quality Assurance in Social Services Departments.* London: HMSO.

James, A. (1992b) 'Quality and its social construction by manager in care service organisations', in Kelly, A. and Warr, B. *Quality Counts: Achieving Quality in Social Care Services.* Whiting & Birch/Social Care Association, London.

James, A. (1994) *Managing to Care: Public Service and the Market.* London: Longman.

Le Grand, J. (1990) *Quasi-Markets and Social Policy.* University of Bristol, SAUS.

Osbourne, D. and Gaebler, T. (1992) *Reinventing Government: How the Entrepreneurial Spirit is Transforming the Public Sector.* Reading, MA: Addison-Wesley.

Peters, T.S. and Waterman, R.H. (1984) *In Search of Excellence: Lesson from America's Best-Run Companies.* New York: Harper & Row.

Pirsig, R. (1976) *Zen and the Art of Motorcycle Maintenance.* London: Corgi.

Shearer, A. (1991) *Who Calls the Shots?* London: King's Fund Centre.

Chapter 16

What Does The Citizen's Charter Mean?

*Stewart Black**

Background and aims

The Citizen's Charter, announced in July 1991, is an important Government initiative in relation to the performance and quality of public services. It has an impressive scope, applying to the entire public sector and beyond – central government; local government; the National Health Service; the criminal justice system; and nationalised industries, including privatised utilities. It relates to activities which account for almost 40 per cent of the Gross Domestic Product (*Economist*, 1 February 1992).

The initiative is closely associated with John Major. He described the aim of the White Paper shortly before its publication, in the context of a speech in which he set out his personal philosophy, as being to 'give the customer more clout and the manager more responsibility' (*Scotsman*, 28 June 1991).

The Charter (Prime Minister 1991) has four main aims:

- improving the quality of public services
- increasing choice for consumers
- setting standards for services
- improving value for money.

It rests on a 'consumer' view of quality, the significance of which is discussed later. The Charter contains over 80 proposals intended to raise the standard of public services – including privatisation; competition

---

* The author writes in a personal capacity.

through contracting out; performance pay for certain public employees; publication by the agencies involved of information about service availability and standards for this; new requirements for these bodies to publish information as to their standards of performance; and financial compensation for users who have had poor service.

The Conservative Charter initiative is well known, but it was not the only one. The Labour and Liberal Democrat parties also published charter proposals – indeed all three appeared in the same month, July 1991 (Labour Party 1991; Liberal Democratic Party 1991). A useful review of these is provided by Miller and Peroni in which they contrast 'social democratic' and 'right-liberal' models which offer collective entitlements and market freedoms respectively (Miller and Peroni 1992).

Neither the term nor the concept of the Charter is new. The term 'Citizen's Charter' was first coined by a Labour politician, Herbert Morrison, as long ago as 1921 (Seely and Yeadell 1992). The Conservative government itself created a 'Charter' for local authority tenants in 1980, and another for taxpayers in 1986.

Following the Charter White Paper, a series of 'mini-charters' has been published. By December 1993 there were 38 of these. Consistent with the initiative's orientation to the 'citizen', these were originally conceived of as being 'for' different user groups rather than simply relating to agencies or their services – for example those for parents, patients and passengers. These documents have an unusual status: they clarify and identify the standards which users can expect, yet they have 'no legal effect' (Barron and Scott 1992).

In November 1992, Mr Waldegrave, the Cabinet Minister responsible for implementing the initiative, indicated that while further charters were planned, the Government's future emphasis would be on the strengthening of existing charters rather than the creation of new ones. At the same time, other activities to complement the charters were announced or re-launched: an emphasis on the value of user surveys (see chapter by Connor and Black); a complaints task force; the launch of the 'Charter Mark' awards scheme; and the Charterline telephone information initiative.

A Government-commissioned survey (Citizen's Charter Unit Office 1993) has been the chief test to date of popular knowledge of and reaction to the Citizen's Charter. The 3097 adults involved were asked for their views on 28 public services covered by the Charter, and three private services for comparison. Social work services were not included.

Almost two years after its launch – and after intensive expenditure, associated with the publication and distribution of the Citizen's Charter and related documents excluding the original white paper and first report on the charter, amounting to £14.370m (Hansard Written Answer, Col. 787, 2 February 1994) – 71 per cent had heard of the Charter. The recognition rate for individual charters was appreciably lower, ranging from 1 per cent to 40 per cent, although those who were aware of mini-charters felt these would help improve standards. There was modest support for the publication of performance information and strong support for independent inspection (Charter Unit Office 1993). On the fundamental test of whether respondents, as users, felt that public services had improved since the initiative, this was felt to be the case for only 6 of the 28 public services (Owen 1993).

Local Government Act, 1992, and service standards

For local government services, including social work services, it is the Local Government Act, 1992, which has given effect to the Citizen's Charter White Paper. However this does not directly 'translate' the Charter into a set of legislative requirements. Perhaps the most surprising aspect of this is not what the Act says but what it does not, for, contrary to the expectation created by the Charter, there is no reference in the Act to 'quality', one of the four aims of the Charter. This key concept, which is clearly at the very heart of the Charter initiative, is addressed only implicitly.

In local government, the best-known effect of the Act is the new responsibilities it has created for the reporting of performance. The Audit Commission in England and Wales and the Accounts Commission in Scotland – statutorily independent bodies – have been given a duty to direct local authorities, with effect from April 1993, to gather information to permit performance to be assessed. As required, in late 1992, each Commission published its first Direction specifying the information to be collected and published (Audit Commission 1992, Accounts Commission 1992). Social work, as one of the major local government services, is included in each Commission's Direction, although, as is also the case for the other council services involved, there are differences in the nature of the performance information specified by each Commission. Each Direction also embraces other services such as housing, education and police.

The process is an annual one, and a second Direction for 1994/95 was published by each Commission in late 1993.

Each local authority in Britain is required to publish information on its own performance in 1993–94 by December 1994 in its local press, while the two Commissions will subsequently publish national data for all local authorities. The process is then repeated annually, to permit comparisons between different authorities in the same reporting period and also comparisons of the same authority's performance over time, with the scope for refined and additional information being included in subsequent Directions.

The data required to be published are often termed 'performance indicators', although the information actually specified in the Commissions' Directions are often more modest than a common sense understanding of this term might suggest. Many report information on volume of activity as distinct from specific measures of departmental or corporate performance. Consistent with the view of the Charter Unit (Arnold-Foster 1992), the Directions do not impose an external standard on authorities, but rather seek publication of authorities' own standards, where these exist, and performance against them. In fact, few local authority services – including social work services – have such locally-specified targets. The publication of information is clearly part of a wider change in the nature of accountability in public services.

The Citizen's Charter and 'consumerism'

As several commentators have observed, the Charter initiative rests on a 'consumerist' view of quality, where – almost despite the title of the initiative – the emphasis is less on the 'citizen' than on the 'user' as consumer (Barron and Scott 1992, Stewart and Walsh 1992, Miller and Peroni 1992, Sanderson 1992 – and the chapter by Coote). Indeed, it has been suggested that the Charter initiative is overwhelmingly consumerist in orientation: 'The Government's various charters are generally concerned neither with rights nor with a recognisable concept of citizenship, but with consumer protection' (Bennington and Taylor 1992). For these reasons, standards in service performance are of particular importance. It should be acknowledged that targets for these are not always – or even mainly – set by Government, but by those elected, appointed or employed to do so.

Significance of Citizen's Charter for social work services

It is noticeable that no mini-charter has been published for users of social work services, nor was one proposed when the progress of the first year of the Charter was reviewed and future plans announced (PM and Chancellor of Duchy of Lancaster 1992). (This is not to suggest that of social work services users may not benefit from other charters, such as those for health, education or the criminal justice system.)

Consequently, implementation of Charter principles for social care is more reliant on the original Charter and, in particular, on other sources such as general legislation and the development of national inspection. These merit closer consideration.

The Charter White Paper twice discusses social work services. These references give emphasis to user information; individual care plans; national standards; independent inspection; independent representation and complaints; and standards in residential care (Prime Minister 1991, p.21) and, second, to a new role for the Government's own Social Services Inspectorate in England and Wales (p.41). (See also the chapter by Mitchell and Tolan.) However, most of these had previously been enacted or announced (see below) and, while consistent with it, did not originate in the Charter initiative. Meanwhile, despite the prominent recognition of the needs of carers in the White Paper 'Caring for People' (Secretaries of State 1989), the precursor of the NHS and Community Care Act, 1990, surprisingly, the Charter does not develop this concern. Consequently, it has been suggested of the Charter initiative that 'in relation to social services very little is on offer' (Taylor 1991).

For social work services, the Charter initiative therefore appears to rest substantially on the prior, if recent, provisions of the Children Act 1989, and NHS and Community Care Act 1990. While these two statutes have contrasting backgrounds and envisage different roles for social work (Hallett 1991), each contains in-built mechanisms intended to secure performance goals similar to those of the Charter. The 1989 Act (which applies primarily to England and Wales) gives emphasis to consistency and effectiveness, within public law, in relation to the basis for intervention and identification of children in need. The 1990 Act carries this further, notably in relation to new requirements for local authority inspection, complaints procedures, and user-centred assessment (see chapters by Mitchell & Tolan, McClay and Brace, respectively).

Reinforcing this has been the Government's own inspectorial efforts in relation to social work services, which have been strengthened throughout Britain. In England and Wales, the responsibilities of the Social Services Inspectorate, established in 1985, were already being strengthened as a result of these changes in legislation, and the changes in strategic planning and practice which had begun to result (see chapters by Henkel, and Mitchell and Tolan). In Scotland, a Social Work Services Inspectorate within the Scottish Office was constituted much later, in April 1992, but this also has origins which pre-date the Charter initiative. The inspection programmes of each Inspectorate can be expected to assist development of the Charter.

A charter in relation to one aspect of social work services has been proposed. A 'community care charter' was called for in July 1993 by the House of Commons Health Committee to 'provide an indication of the level and quality of service which citizens are entitled to expect' (Health Committee 1993). Interestingly, this proposal appears to have been inspired less by an intention to hold local authorities to account, as might have been expected, than to do so in relation to the Health Secretary and the Department of Health, whose responsibilities, the Committee concluded, had become much more extensive since the Committee's previous report only four months earlier. In particular, the Committee identified that the Government itself had substantial statutory responsibilities for community care.

The Government's written response (Secretary of State for Health 1993) did not answer this last point directly. In relation to the proposal for a community care charter, the Government argued, in effect, that many of the benefits of such a Charter were already in place – for example, community care implementation was based on user choice and information; Government monitoring and evaluation was established; and the government expected local authorities and others to review their own performance. Its answer therefore implied that the Charter proposed by the Health Committee was unnecessary.

What The Charter has meant for users of social work services

It is evident that the Charter's achievement – for users of social work services at least – is less than the 'revolution' hoped for by the Prime Minister (PM and Chancellor of Duchy of Lancaster 1992). This is not, however, simply a matter of the arrow falling short of the target, but, to extend the metaphor, also one of the means of aiming at the target and indeed the choice of target. There appear to be at least four aspects to this:

- the identification of 'citizen' and 'consumer' interests as synonymous
- the appropriateness of the consumer model in the case of at least some of the public services involved
- the value of the benefits conferred
- the assumptions underlying selection of these benefits.

'Citizen' or 'consumer'?

The initiative is titled a 'citizen's' rather than a 'citizens'' charter. The location of the apostrophe in the title does not appear to be accidental. The significance of this appears to be twofold. First, it gives emphasis to individual rather than collective well-being. Second, and more important, consistent with this is the view of citizenship it embodies – one based not on political and social rights but on those arising from the individual's role as consumer in relation to public services seen as a market. Detailed further discussion of the differences between 'citizen' and 'consumer' interests is beyond the scope of this chapter but see Miller and Peroni (1992) and the chapter by Coote. This distinction, not made within the Citizen's Charter, has provoked considerable discussion and indeed has provided the greatest single focus for debate on the Charter initiative as a whole. The general criticism made is that the Charter promotes a narrow, individualistic concept of well-being: the particular criticism is that this may be inappropriate in relation to human welfare services.

The appropriateness of the 'consumer' model

This leads to a related second criticism: the appropriateness of the 'consumer' model to certain of the public services, since the Charter does not recognise the extent to which users may be involved in the production of their own services. The boundary between 'producer' and 'user' is not necessarily absolute.

In interpersonal services such as education and health, successful service delivery depends, at least in part, on the co-operation or participation of the 'user'. Social work services not only provide further examples of this in relation to virtually every user group, but also, possibly uniquely amongst public services, examples of 'users' or 'citizens' who do not want a 'service' – for example, old people or people recovering from mental illness who do not wish community care; children and their families who are resistant to the imposition of care orders; and offenders who do not wish to be supervised.

This analysis suggests that not only the practical benefits but also the philosophical assumptions underpinning the Charter initiative may be at least ill-fitting if not inappropriate in the case of the more personal public services. The Charter, however, does not acknowledge, far less attempt to resolve, these conundrums. This is not to imply that the initiative is wholly unwanted by all the users of such services, nor that it fails to offer them actual benefits, but it does suggest that not all public services should be treated in the same way, on a uni-dimensional consumer model, as the Charter presently does.

The actual benefits conferred, and how these are likely to be valued
A third set of criticisms relates to the actual value of the benefits the Charter confers. Most immediately, as has been widely observed, the benefits which have been offered to citizens as a result of the Charter have been limited, and indeed have often been characterised as trivial; for example, requiring public agency staff to wear name badges. Meanwhile, compensation schemes under the Charter (e.g. for passengers and benefits claimants), under which an estimated £9.383m has been paid out (Hansard Written Answer, Col. 940, 21 January 1994), are simply unavailable for users of social care services.

Other innovations have emblematic qualities. In social work services, the proposal for the involvement of lay people in inspections – in this case made by Government rather than service-producing agencies – is not the result of demand for this from users of those services. Nevertheless, this has become a central principle of the Government's proposals for the development of inspection, as is evident from its discussion of the Charter initiative itself (Prime Minister and Chancellor of Duchy of Lancaster 1992) as well as its proposals for inspection by both central and local government (for example, Scottish Office 1993).

Another benefit offered by the Charter – the publication of information – is justified in large measure in terms of the need for users to be better informed, particularly as to the availability and performance of services. To the extent that this ensures that information not previously available (or available in a particular form) enters the public domain, clearly of itself this is, in principle, a benefit to users.

This should also offer benefits in practice, but the limitations should be recognised. First, having such performance information available may in fact be of little importance to citizens. Many may not be users of the services, and even if they pay for them through taxation they may nevertheless have little interest. Second, identification of priority areas in which performance data are collected and published, without also confirming that these areas are also of interest or concern to users, may have perverse effects. For example, information on important issues such as the speed of assessment or time for service provision, says little about other important issues such as the range of services available – and vice versa. Clearly, many types of information may be of interest, yet in practice not all will be available, and all have collection and publication costs, including the perhaps unrecognised cost of focusing the attention of providers on boosting performance in one target area while another languishes. Provision of additional information, while likely to be beneficial for users on balance, is not therefore an unambiguous improvement.

Third, the use-value of service information, as 'market' information, may be negligible. A key principle of the consumerist approach is that users must have information to make informed choices about services, including choice of provider. Yet in the case of many social work services this type of choice is not available. Although promotion of alternatives has been an explicit policy objective of the Government since the White Paper 'Caring for People' (Secretaries of State 1989), clearly this is not a reality for many services and in many localities, and to this extent consumers cannot use Charter information to 'shop around'. Moreover, the model where the consumer's ultimate sanction is to take her or his 'custom' elsewhere may simply be inappropriate as the 'unwilling users' examples identified earlier indicate – another shortcoming of the consumer model in this context. Meanwhile, users who are willing consumers are at least as likely to want better services from an existing provider as a change of provider.

These qualifications are not to suggest that users will not benefit by the Charter's innovations but these have not been identified as a priority by social work service users themselves, nor has the Charter initiative involved confirmation of whether they are in fact regarded as a priority by users. This leads to the fourth, and perhaps the most important limitation of the Charter.

Rights

Essentially, the initiative is vulnerable to the criticism that it creates procedural rather than substantive rights. The Charter does not create fresh rights to services themselves. It is analogous to the 'rights' conferred by the NHS and Community Care Act, 1990: the citizen has the (procedural) right to be assessed, but not the (substantive) right to receive a service as a result of that assessment. The Charter White Paper 'promises no new entitlements to welfare provision' (Barron and Scott 1992).

It has been suggested that what is required is the more radical objective of empowerment of people and their communities (Hambleton and Cumella 1992). In the field of social work services, supporters of user advocacy see the Charter as ineffectual without accompanying civil rights, for example for disabled people (Sutton 1992).

Summary of Charter benefits

The conclusion which should perhaps be drawn from the discussion above is that the Citizen's Charter is vulnerable to the criticism of making a fuss about offering users modest benefits and devices which they may not consider important while at the same time failing to act on issues which are seen by them as of high priority. Bluntly, users are much more likely to want rights of access to services than information, compensation and the like.

In its first report on the Charter (Prime Minister and Chancellor of Duchy of Lancaster 1992), no successes are claimed by the Government in relation to social work services. It does not comment on, far less offer any evaluation of, these local authority services. A single paragraph describes the arrangements recently initiated to 'reform' inspection in England and Wales, with similar initiatives intended in Scotland and Northern Ireland. Additional tabular information is provided on other aspects of the regulatory process (which varies slightly across Britain) – independence of each inspectorate from the services inspected; possible involvement of lay people; and publication of inspectorate reports. These processes were acknowledged to be incomplete in late 1992, at the time of reporting (ibid).

It is interesting to note that social work agencies have a particular advantage over other public agencies in their capacity to be responsive to the actual preferences of users or would-be users. This is by virtue of their increasingly needs-led approach in identifying through assessment processes the preferences of users (and carers) as distinct from the services available or provided. This process, moreover, is intended to inform strategic service planning, and local authorities are now obliged to consult on their community care plans and to publish these. Additional possibilities (not peculiar to social work services) include user representatives on service planning groups; user 'panels'; and analysis of complaints data. Local authorities can consolidate the service standards which users can expect. Thomson discusses how this might be achieved by use of service contracts (Thomson 1992a,b). While these processes are not yet fully in place, and of course are all within the context of limited resources, nevertheless social work agencies have particular scope here. One particularly important and potentially fruitful area – getting and using user views – is discussed in detail in the chapter by Connor and Black.

Summary and conclusions

The concept of a Charter initiative, as acknowledged above, was one around which there was not only a surprising degree of consensus but also simultaneous activity on the part of all three major political parties in bringing forward proposals. Moreover, at local level, a number of councils have independently developed charters for their own areas. The common focus of all has been a concern to improve the 'responsiveness' (Weale 1985) of public services. They have also been inspired by differing political philosophies. The generic principles underlying charters for public services do not therefore lie solely in one part of the political spectrum, and the four explicit aims of the Government's Charter are not controversial.

Nevertheless, the Citizen's Charter has not yet managed to command widespread support, nor to be regarded by users as effective in raising public service standards in practice. While there may be several reasons for this, two in particular emerge. First, no substantive new entitlements have been created by the Charter. Second, and closely related to this, the pre-condition for the initiative, that it be introduced at zero additional cost, appears at odds with the spirit of the Charter. Colloquially, it gives the message 'you can have more information, and more compensation for poor service, but not the investment identified as required to improve services'.

Despite this, the Citizen's Charter has become an established part of the landscape of public services. Moreover, in his Foreword to the first report on its progress, Mr Major describes it as a 'ten year programme of radical reform' (Prime Minister and Chancellor of Duchy of Lancaster 1992). It has features attractive to any Government, not necessarily Conservative, in relation to its own management of the public sector. The Permanent Secretary at the Office of Public Service and Science, where ministerial responsibility lies, has suggested that the Charter's 'underlying themes will still survive, even if there were a new government' (*Municipal Journal*, 26 November 1993).

The general analysis above tends to understate the significance of the Citizen's Charter for social work in particular. Because the Local Government Act, 1992, requires local authorities to publish information to permit comparisons of performance over time, the inclusion of social work services in the Directions of the Audit and Accounts Commissions ensures that these services will continue to be a focus of the Charter. Moreover, in the context of the range of services provided by local government services, social work appears to distinguish itself in being one of the few areas of local government service which is experiencing a growth in responsibility and resources rather than contraction, albeit, the Government intends, accompanied by a shift in balance from direct service delivery to 'enabling'. This suggests that the scrutiny begun by the Charter may become increasingly important for social work, despite it having had such low prominence within the initiative in its first two years of life. Related to this, the work programmes of the Government's Social Work Inspectorates can be expected to become increasingly important.

It is now possible to tie together the strands above. A principal objective of Government policy in the public sector is to create a series of 'quasi-markets' (LeGrand and Bartlett 1993) or 'social markets' (Davies 1992). Creating markets in turn creates a new need for regulation. The Citizen's Charter helps provide this. It simultaneously establishes the regulatory pressure needed to keep managers on their toes by increasing one particular type of accountability – market accountability – while at the same time offering service users consumer protection in circumstances where they would be expected to be disadvantaged. This protection is procedural, taking the form of quasi-market rights, rather than substantive in the form of social or political entitlement, since the regulatory intention is to support the market power of users, not to increase entitlement.

References

Accounts Commission (1992) *Citizen's Charter: 1992 Direction*. Edinburgh: Accounts Commission.

Arnold-Foster, J. (1992) 'Is The Citizen's Charter made to measure?' *Local Government Chronicle*, 26 June.

Audit Commission (1992) *Citizen's Charter Indictors: Charting a Course.* London: Audit Commission.

Barron, A. and Scott, C. (1992) 'The Citizen's Charter programme'. *Modern Law Reform* 55 (4), July.

Bennington, J. and Taylor, M. (1992) 'The renewal of quality in the political process', in Sanderson, I. (ed) *Management of Quality in Local Government.* Harlow: Longman.

Citizen's Charter Unit (1993) *Citizen's Charter Customer Survey: Research Report.* London: Cabinet Office, Office of Public Service and Science.

Davies, H. (1992) 'Public Services and Public Perceptions'. *Financial Times,* 4 September.

Hallett, C. (1991) 'The Children Act 1989 and community care: Comparisons and contrasts'. *Policy and Politics* 19 (4).

Hambleton, P. and Cumella, M. (1992) 'Breaking the cycle of alienation'. *Local Government Chronicle,* 14 August.

Health Committee (1993) *Sixth Report. Session 1992–93. Community Care: The Way Forward.* London: HMSO.

Labour Party (1991) *Citizen's Charter: Labour's Better Deal For Consumers and Citizens.* London: Labour Party.

LeGrand, J. and Bartlett, W. (1993) *Quasi-Markets and Social Policy.* Basingstoke: Macmillan.

Liberal Democratic Party (1991) *Citizen's Britain: Liberal Democratic Policies for a People's Charter.* London: Liberal Democratic Party.

Miller, S. and Peroni, F. (1992) 'Social politics and the Citizen's Charter', in Manning, N. and Page, R. (eds) *Social Policy Review.* London: Social Policy Association.

Owen, D. (1993) 'Citizen's Charter appears to be bringing little improvement: Public services rapped'. *Financial Times,* 26 August.

Prime Minister (1991) *The Citizen's Charter: Raising the Standard.* Cm. 1599. London: HMSO.

Prime Minister and Chancellor of Duchy of Lancaster (1992) *The Citizen's Charter: First Report 1992.* London: HMSO.

Sanderson, I. (1992) 'Defining quality in local government' and 'Quality strategy: A planning and performance review', in Sanderson, I. (ed) *Management of Quality in Local Government.* Harlow: Longman.

Scottish Office (1993) *Inspecting Social Work Services in Scotland.* Edinburgh: Scottish Office.

Secretaries of State for Health, Social Security, Wales and Scotland (1989) *Caring for People.* Cm. 849. London: HMSO.

Secretary of State for Health (1993) *Government Response to the Sixth Report from the Health Committee Session 1992–93. Community Care: The Way Forward.* Cm. 2334. Department of Health. London: HMSO.

Seeley, A. and Yeadell, A. (1992) *The Citizen's Charter. Reference Sheet 92/8.* London: House of Commons Library Research Division.

Stewart, J. and Walsh, K. (1992) 'Change in the management of public services'. *Public Administration* 70, winter.

Sutton, D. (1992) 'Unequal balance'. *Community Care,* 25 June.

Taylor, D. (1991) 'A big idea for the nineties? The rise of the Citizens' Charters'. *Critical Social Policy*, issue 33, winter.

Thomson, W. (1992a) 'Realising rights through local service contacts', in Coote, A. (ed) *The Welfare of Citizens*. London: Institute for Public Policy Research.

Thomson, W. (1992b) 'Local experience of managing quality', in Sanderson, I. (ed) *Management of Quality in Local Government*. Harlow: Longman.

Weale, A. (1985) 'Why are we waiting: The problem of responsiveness in the public social services', in Klein, R. and O'Higgins, M. *The Future of Welfare*. Oxford: Martin Robertson.

Chapter 17

Getting and Using User Views for Performance Review

*Anne Connor and Stewart Black**

Introduction

Many of the key policy initiatives highlighted in the other chapters in this book – such as community care implementation and the Citizen's Charter, as well as more local initiatives – have at their heart the recognition of the importance of users' views as providing a form of performance review through the commentary users can offer service-providing bodies. Many observers and participants consider that these have, or should have, primacy. In practice, however, such feedback may barely be registered in any sense.

Two examples show the importance which has been attached to users' views. In its review of the first year of the Citizen's Charter, the Government anticipates increasing use of 'customer' research. It is stated as a Charter principle that 'it is good Charter practice to ask people what they think of the services they use and what they see as the priorities for improvement' (Prime Minister and Chancellor of Duchy of Lancaster 1992). Second, the National Consumer Council has launched a long term programme of surveys

> 'to find out what people think of services... the aim is to see whether people's attitudes change over time and, if so, how'. (NCC 1991)

While likely to command widespread assent, these initiatives underplay the difficulties for service providers in establishing what users and others

---

* The authors write in a personal capacity.

actually want. Moreover, the link between discovering these views and putting them into effect in service delivery is not straightforward. Finally, providers may not even be convinced of the value of collecting – far less acting upon – information from users.

This chapter therefore explores

- the attitude of service providers (including purchasers) towards users of and payers for services
- the methods producers have used to take account of these views
- the value which users in particular are likely to place on these methods
- how information on user views can be used, and mis-used; and
- and the contribution user views can make to performance review.

We wish to make five initial points. First, this chapter does not discuss the need which users and the public have for information about services (e.g. availability), an important but separate issue examined elsewhere (e.g. Berry 1990, Walsh 1991). However, we would note that some observers consider this a pre-requisite for informed user feedback (NCC 1983, Shearer 1991).

Second, a linked point is that this chapter does not address the issue of user involvement or empowerment per se (e.g. Beresford and Croft 1993), although – as we argue below – this is consistent with seeking the views of users.

Third, the basis on which people receive services has to be recognised. As argued in the chapter on the Citizen's Charter, in this respect users of social care services may differ from the users of other public services – and both differ from those buying services from private sector providers. Moreover, in the public sector, the market place logic of 'giving customers what they want' has less relevance. The consumer model does not always fit social care services (e.g. Coote and Pfeffer 1991, Lupton *et al.* 1991). It is therefore necessary to check whether a method developed in one sector to identify user views is in fact appropriate in another.

Fourth, in any given situation there may be no single 'user' – for example in the case of an elderly person and her carer; pupil and parent – and all need a 'voice'. Fifth, the immediate user may not be the only voice: there may be a range of 'stakeholders' or 'local shareholders' (Gyford 1991) – actual, would-be and potential users; taxpayers; the general public – who may have a view on service delivery and may wish to express this.

Different approaches

Before considering how user feedback can be obtained and used, it is important to recognise the attitudes the service provider – and its personnel – brings to this issue.

It is possible to use models to represent the different attitudes exhibited by public service organisations to the publics they serve. These models are necessarily generalised, but have some illustrative value. They are tabulated in Figure 17.1 below.

Attention to user feedback is not new. As long ago as the early 1960s, commentators noted both the importance of users' views in any consideration of social work service provision and the rarity of attempts to establish such an input. Interestingly, the Seebohm Report of 1968, which formed the basis of organisation of modern social work services, was criticised for its lack of regard for users' views (Sinfield, quoted Mayer and Timms 1970).

In The Client Speaks, Mayer and Timms (1970) made the case for seeking and listening to clients' views and demonstrated that widely-held methodological concerns – the value of 'subjective' data; collection difficulties – were not justified. However, they also set limits on the weight given to user feedback. They saw clients' views as secondary to professional judgement, and focused on potential improvements to the effectiveness of casework rather than on users' views about the type of service provided or how this was organised. They also saw researchers as the sole channel for user feedback.

In many respects this study, influential at the time, anticipated – or established – approaches which were common in the following years. A literature search reveals many instances over the last 25 years or so where user views have been sought. However, in practice these have had important shortcomings: a focus on issues more of interest to practitioners than users; sporadic use of such feedback; and little or no linking of this to performance review.

Fifteen years on, the ideas proposed by Mayer and Timms and the subsequent development of clients' views as a contribution to social policy research were examined by Fisher and colleagues (Fisher 1983). They advocated that greater value should be given to clients' views and

Attitude type	*Principal characteristics*
bureaucratic	The most restrictive for users. Public has only two roles in service delivery – taxpayer and/or passive recipient. This model is wholly producer-driven, based on statutory duties.
administrative	Permits expression of grievance and offers remedies likely to be based on 'maladminist-ration' model (infingement by the service provider of its own rule-bound behaviour) rather than appropriateness or quality of the service to users.
participative	Provider attempts – either on its own initiative or because of some external requirement – to ascertain popular (not necessarily user) views on particular initiatives. Traditionally used for physical planning initiatives, for example.
access	Provider undertakes range of improvements, e.g. 'friendliness' to users; wider information on service availability; possible de-centralised and/or 'one stop' delivery points; elements of a complaints procedure.
consumer	Information on service standards as well as service availability; user views actively sought; aspects of service delivery are re-designed to suit the user first (e.g. out-of-hours service); some user-oriented performance standards; use of surveys; full complaints procedure; like 'access' model, based on customer relations, not user rights; sympathetic to user empowerment.
empowering	Learns and accommodates views of stakeholders as integral part of service delivery; systematic user-based performance standards; promotes user empowerment; sympathetic to staff empowerment; some user/carer membership of strategic planning bodies; systematic use of unmet needs data; comments procedures.
radical	User choice – user views may prevail over those of professionals at 'case' level; some user control over care budgets; routine involvement in all strategic planning; contractual specifications reflect standards agreed with users.

Figure 17.1: Models of provider attitude to users

considered how the contribution of this feedback to planning and decision-making by social work practitioners and managers could be enhanced. They still regarded social policy researchers as the channel for
obtaining and presenting these views, however, and argued that client
studies would not achieve their potential impact until the barriers between researchers and their target audience were broken down.

The scale and range of user surveys picked up dramatically in the
1980s, for example in community care planning. A typical example is
provided by Hull and Spiers (1989) who describe consultation with users
of mental health services in Cambridgeshire, where group discussions
and interviews with individual users were used to identify issues which
the new arrangements were to address and where the tone of the reported
accounts is descriptive rather than evaluative.

Users' views have, however, played an integral part in service planning in some situations – most notably self-help groups and other organisations run by members/users, as the chapter by Whittaker illustrates.
Until recently, it was the role of users in shaping the direction and form
of the agency's activities that marked out these services – whether run by
voluntary organisations or a specific project within the statutory services
– from other social care services.

Since the early 1990s, the principle of 'users' voice' (not the same as
'users' choice': see Figure 17.1 above) in the services they receive has had
statutory force – in particular, from the Disabled Persons Act 1986, the
NHS and Community Care Act 1990 and the Children Act 1989. These
create an explicit expectation, reinforced by guidance, that at case level
local authorities will routinely seek the preferences of users (and where
appropriate those of carers and guardians) in relation to their own care,
and local authorities will attempt to act on these. Similarly, at strategic
planning level there must be wide consultation and publication of intel-
ligible plans. The 1990 Act also creates analogous responsibilities for
health authorities and health boards.

More recently, users may be seen as 'experts' (e.g. Steele 1992). This
sharply contrasts with the model offered by Mayer and Timms. Nevertheless, such empowerment does not necessarily lead to a reversal so much
as a re-balancing of the power relationship between user and provider.

Feedback and Consequences

Associated with each of the 'attitudes' set out in Figure 17.1 are a number of methods through which the views of users, and to a lesser extent those of other parties, are sought. Figure 17.2 below attempts to capture these and comments on how they may be used. The relationship between the provider and the user (Col.1) is related to different methods of obtaining user involvement in service delivery (Col.2), and finally to the consequences for users of giving feedback (Col.3).

Relationship	How Feedback is Identified	Consequences of Feedback for Users
bureaucratic	• no opportunity to contribute	• none: passive receipt of services
administrative	• comment after event	• may feel better
	• formal complaints procedure	• repetition of poor performance may be prevented
		• entitlement to action on complaints or comments
		• redress in relation to specified standards
participative	• general attitude surveys	• may feel they have had an influence
	• consultation as part of planning process	
access	• research by provider	• long-term improvement in services
	• suggestion boxes	• better able to make specific complaints
		• better able to get access to services
		• possibly more likely to have complaints actioned

consumer	• user surveys	•. more convenient services
	• lay involvement in strategic planning bodies	• better choice of services
		• standards followed up by managers reflect users' concerns
	• lay involvement in inspection	
	• user panels or focus groups	
	• recording of user/ carer views in assessments	
empowering	• incorporated into service delivery	• service development reflects users' ideas and views
	• user advisory groups	
	• discussion groups	
radical	• user-provider management groups	• user/carer views prevail in assessments
		• users have control over some resources

Figure 17.2: What organisational attitude means for users

We wish to make three points. First, the figure sets out a hierarchy. The benefits to users are typically incremental, building on the benefits from previous models. Second, Figure 17.2 notes the consequences for users which represent the minimum provider response to the feedback. Service providers may vary in their responsiveness, and this is in part explained by the provider's 'attitude' to getting and using user information (see Figure 17.1). Third, whereas some of the models at Figure 17.2 lead to a direct improvement for these individual users (who have given the feedback), other models – such as the participative model – will result more in a general improvement of services from which individual users may perhaps benefit.

Sources of information

Having described the different attitudes of providers to user involvement and the different methods used, we now consider the sources of information arising from these methods and how they may be used by providers. We identify six sources which are discussed below – surveys; operational information; user groups; public consultation; lay involvement in strategic planning; and lay involvement in setting or monitoring quality standards.

1. Surveys

The form of user feedback which perhaps comes to mind most readily is surveys. It is not unusual for the term 'survey' to be used without qualification, yet clarity is necessary because there are different types of survey which perform different tasks. **General surveys** relate to collection of public attitudes and opinions (and need not relate to users at all). **User surveys** are confined to actual (or would-be) recipients who are asked about their experience of services and views of what should be provided.

Surveys are often carried out by an 'independent' person or agency, such as a researcher or a consultant, or by a unit within the providing organisation which is separate from the direct service provision. By its nature, the survey is research-based – that is, it involves non-routine collection of data. This is in contrast to the information systems of the organisation, and indeed is often undertaken as a conscious attempt to supplement these – see below. The significance of independent data collection and analysis is that it can more easily be claimed to give authority to any conclusions reached. Nevertheless, providers can and do carry out surveys of their own services. This is often, in the case of local authorities, undertaken by staff separate from those undertaking service provision – not solely for reasons of 'independence' but also because of the skills (e.g. research) involved.

The scope of such surveys can range from contact with a single service – for example, home care – to an entire organisation such as the Social Work Department, the NHS, or even 'public services'. The level of detail will also vary, generally becoming more superficial as the level of specificity lessens, given the practical parameters set by factors such as time, costs and data analysis. Larger scale surveys will inevitably yield quantitative rather than qualitative findings. In-depth studies can be targeted on specific groups of users, however, and yield a very different type of information.

2. Operational information

Users also make their views known in the course of their day-to-day or periodic contact with services. Information is generated at a number of points, such as referral, assessment and subsequent assessments or re-reviews. Some feedback may find its way into referrals or case information systems. Complaints and comments data are another source of operational information.

Two sets of information can be identified. First, there is 'formal' information which is gathered by front-line workers – not just personal details but also the user's own views of his or her needs, the services which may be or have been offered, and the services preferred. It is unlikely that such information has been gathered systematically in the past, but its value in operational terms is increasingly critical. Its systematic use, including information on unmet needs (i.e., needs which are not fully met or only partly met), has become central to guidance on assessment and care management in community care, where it is explicitly recognised as having not only operational but strategic planning significance.

Second, there is 'informal' commentary which need not be, and usually is not, gathered and used to inform practice. This can be in the form of specific statements about the services in less obvious ways – for example, the everyday exchanges between users and providers, sometimes in throw-away comments (Jones *et al.* 1987, Connor 1993).

What is important and interesting about operational information is its under-development. Inter-personal services provide an opportunity to gather immediate information, from the mouths of actual or possible users, at the time of contact with front-line staff at the time of assessment, service provision or review, and at no additional contact cost to the provider. Moreover, this affords a routine yet natural opportunity of learning not only user preferences (as in the general survey model) but also the reasons for and circumstances of this (as in the panel model) – and, moreover, for all users and carers, not just a sample.

This is not to suggest that the gathering of this information is without cost, since good practice suggests this would be required at 'case' level with essential statistical and other details also fed into organisational planning systems, such as those for operational and strategic management, and for external reporting. It is probable that some professional staff (e.g. those conducting assessments) will not collect such information – and this would have to be systematised through organisational information strategies rather than left to individual initiative. In some organisations, data entry to computerised systems is made by administrative staff, to free professional time. Accordingly, each group would have a responsibility.

Against these processing costs must be set the opportunity cost of **not** having such information; the new requirements to collect at least some of this for community care and some children's services; its significant advantages over more general types of survey information in terms of range, depth and cost; and the risk of misconception as well as financial cost when survey models are used as a substitute for information which could or should be obtained from operational sources (Pollitt 1988, Connor 1993). In short, good operational and strategic management alike depend on the availability of user satisfaction information, as part of performance review information.

3. User groups

'**User panels**' or '**focus groups**', which bring together by invitation – usually from the service provider – a range of users to provide structured discussion and appraisal of services. These differ again in that they reveal not only user preferences but more of the underlying reasons for these. These may be 'one-off' or more continuously convened bodies. They will rely on structured discussion, and also, uniquely, on interaction of viewpoint between users (Cooper 1980, chapter by Barnes and Wistow).

4. Public consultation

This approach is associated with strategic planning and is described at Figure 17.1 above as 'participative' in orientation. Its use has traditionally been voluntary, arising from an initiative on the part of the service-providing agency – often, but not always, a statutory body.

The basis for public consultation has recently been refined considerably by the NHS and Community Care Act, 1990, which requires social work and social services authorities not only to consult but to do so widely and on the basis of a written plan in relation to the entire range of community care services. This has immediately and dramatically widened the extent as well as the basis of such consultation. Nevertheless, local authorities have considerable scope as to how they discharge this duty. Some have prepared a series of documents; organised exhaustive local meetings; and provided substantial factual information.

5. Lay involvement in strategic planning bodies

Lay involvement in the planning process may be one way of drawing on and incorporating users' views (e.g. Osborne 1991, Shearer 1991). Early experience has, however, highlighted negative aspects. Examples are leaving those involved in the planning of committee processes isolated at meetings, with no back-up support; providers selecting people who are more articulate and confident and who hold 'sound' (or safe) views, and so may not be representative of all users; and 'user representatives' having few opportunities and no resources to consult other users (Murray 1991).

Nevertheless, there are examples of user involvement in planning being positive and constructive both for the individuals concerned and the wider agency and its users. Murray (1991) has described how users of HIV care in Hammersmith have influenced service development. There is now routine involvement at an early stage in all new planning.

6. Lay involvement in setting quality standards

There are two possible aspects to this – the initial contribution to defining standards, and subsequent inspection.

There is a small number of examples where users have been asked to have active involvement in identifying the factors which contribute to quality and the relative importance each should be given. This involvement is more substantive than 'being surveyed'. There are examples where users' views have been used in two positive ways – their routine incorporation in setting standards for particular services, and in identifying quality standards which can be picked up in inspection (e.g. Kerruish and Reardon 1992, Murray 1991).

Lay involvement in inspection has been given prominence by the Government in the early 1990s, consistent with the Citizen's Charter initiative, in relation to the inspection work of the Social Services Inspectorate in England and Wales, and the Social Work Service Inspectorate in Scotland (Scottish Office 1993). It is noticeable that there is not always clarity as to whether the 'lay' representatives are actual (past or present) users, members of bodies which represent users, or simply 'non-social work professionals'. Nor is it clear whether their involvement is in a personal and individual, or a representative capacity.

While such involvement has desirable aspects, there are risks in both approaches, particularly the involvement of non-social work professionals. The risks include tokenism, lack of balance, and complacency based on an assumption that the users' view is 'covered' by lay involvement in committees.

Use and misuse of these methods

Here we summarise the chief characteristics of the two main methods, that is, those which are most useful in producing large-scale user views information – **surveys** and **operational information**. We identify three sets of characteristics of each: inherent strengths; inherent limitations; and factors affecting the use (and misuse) of each method. We would emphasise that these and other methods have limitations, for example in relation to the nature and range of data they produce and ease of analysis.

SURVEYS

Strengths:

- provide supplementary information not otherwise available, including information from non-users
- provide 'broadbrush' preferences of respondents
- may provide a reliability check for other data
- if sufficiently large scale, provide useful data through quasi-consultative methods
- can produce results quickly, if resources are available for analysis.

Limitations:

- may report satisfaction levels without these being in relation to other user experience – where there is no 'benchmark'. Users may say they are 'satisfied' without having anything with which to compare their current experience. While this is not to suggest users are dissatisfied, the survey response may easily mask the scope for improvement (Fisher 1983 Judge 1993)
- as 'one-off' data collection, the validity of the survey data may decline over time as user attitudes change
- possibly damaging to the user/provider relationships, especially when a close relationship has been built up between the user and the direct service providers (Connor 1993)
- data may relate to a sample only (e.g. because of resources available; difficulty in tracing 'population'.

Factors affecting use:

- Experience suggests that commissioners of surveys tend not to involve users in planning or in taking the results forward – for example in how their views are reported. However, there are some examples of users being involved (Kerruish and Reardon 1992; chapters by Barnes and Wistow, and Whittaker). Also, certain groups of people may be particularly marginalised, for example elderly people and those from ethnic minorities (Atkin 1991; Walker 1991).

- Major surveys may appear to respondents – and may in fact be – a token attempt to gather user views, intended more for symbolic and public relations purposes than genuine understanding of users' wishes and needs. It is not unknown for user surveys to be undertaken because the service provider wishes to appear sympathetic to users, where this is instrumental in generating political goodwill rather than managerial information (e.g. Jones *et al.* 1987).

- There may be a danger of broad 'satisfaction' data being misinterpreted by senior managers or elected members who become complacent about the standards of service when such surveys show a high proportion of people being 'generally or very satisfied' and setting aside any information about problems in service provision which still need to be addressed, even if these affect only a minority of users.

- There is likely to be an expensive form of data collection, particularly when specialists have to be hired.

OPERATIONAL INFORMATION
Strengths:

- validity of information derived from everyday contact, rather than periodic surveys
- reliability: comments made in context
- comprehensiveness: data can be collected from all users and carers
- continuity: data are available on current and continuing basis permitting time-series analysis
- case level information can easily be used for wider purposes (e.g. performance review; strategic planning) (e.g. Connor 1993)
- response to issues raised by individual users is more direct (and possibly more likely)

- users may have an opportunity for greater influence over the agenda and topics raised.

Limitations:

- even when the case notes or reports of assessment meetings are made, these may focus on the service provider's views, responsibilities and action, and may not adequately reflect users' views which contributed to or commented on these plans
- more vulnerable to inconsistencies in recording and in interpretation
- users may not realise that their feedback is being used, and might otherwise give additional comments.

Factors affecting use:

- few organisations have actually arranged to collect such information as a matter of routine
- nevertheless, information recording should also be integrated with service delivery, for example as in the care management model of good practice (see chapter by Brace)
- different values may be given to, and use made of, the information obtained through formal and informal mechanisms. (Although the contact between the users and service providers may be formal in content – for example assessment reviews, planned regular meetings – the information gathered may be less formal)
- although front line workers may have detailed knowledge of users' views, particularly through day-to-day contact, the managers will inevitably be more distanced (Flynn 1990). Managers should be seeking information from the direct care providers, but much will depend on how this information is then presented to the managers
- users may not realise that their feedback is being used, and might otherwise give additional comments
- again, the tendency is often to concentrate on quantitative measures. The next step is how managers then interpret this information, which can distort the views and experience of the users still further
- information from day-to-day contact needs to be recorded, however, for it to be available for analysis of user preferences. This prevents knowledge from becoming simply anecdotal. It is also possible for day-to-day user feedback to be systematised and shared in a routine

way, leading to a rational analysis of preferences based on available resources (e.g. Connor 1993).

Application of user views

So far, this chapter has discussed different methods of obtaining user views, and the merits of these. But why is this information valuable? The value of user information is not in its collection but in interpretation and application in, literally, informing service management. Surprisingly, most commentators treat the value of user views as self-evident, rather than go on to suggest how service providers should use them. Three important applications are: using feedback to inform resource allocation decisions; to set standards; and to provide overall performance review.

Resource allocation: Both survey and operational data can help to inform resource allocation decisions. The former can gauge the relative popularity of, say, certain services or the balance between home and day care. The latter can, for example, provide information about unmet need. Both can – and should – inform strategic planning. Positive consequences of this include better targeted services and reduction of unwanted services.

Setting standards: Survey and operational data can suggest directly the standards users/carers expect to have or would wish to see. Both are central to consideration of performance and quality.

Overall performance review: Operational data in particular can routinely be used to check user views of the quality of care received, whether in absolute terms or in relation to explicit standards already operational. Both offer performance review, but in different and complementary ways.

One other application which is less common and more controversial is campaigning and raising public awareness. There are at least two reasons for this: the direct effect of user voices is very powerful and providers may fear the unpredictable effects of this. Second, there is concern about the possibility of users being exploited for campaigning purposes.

Nevertheless, these reservations can be overcome. Allard *et al.* (1992) give an example of a voluntary organisation providing services for children and families which used user feedback appropriately for wider campaigning and policy issues. Here, direct quotations from users, which identified the services they valued, were used to campaign for additional provision, and also to persuade other agencies (including local authorities) providing child care services to adapt and change.

Conditions for success

We suggest there are two principal conditions for success – getting the right method, and having a receptive organisational culture.

Selecting the method: The selection of method, not confined to the six alternatives discussed in this chapter, is dependent on a careful consideration of the circumstances: what type of information is needed; the sensitivity of the issue for the user; and how the information will be used (Booth 1983, Fisher 1983, Jones *et al.* 1987). It is also essential to remember the potential of the available methods of obtaining feedback: experience confirms the wisdom of 'going with the grain' in accepting limitations as well as exploiting the strengths noted above. There may also be merit in planning to use a combination of methods and sources to complement and reinforce each other – for example, a general attitude survey in conjunction with feedback from current users through operational information or a user panel.

Attention to responses from user surveys may be at the expense of information from ongoing contact and users' behaviour. There can be greater attraction in the apparent validity and independence of a quantitative survey carried out by an external consultant, even though the questions may be very superficial.

Culture change: As we have shown above, both empirical research and practical experience indicate that performance review which involves giving user feedback a place necessitates more than simply 'bolting' this onto the organisation (Parsloe and Stevenson 1993). It requires a cultural change towards being more 'user-centred' (and of course performance-minded).

The way front-line staff treat users may be a reflection of how they are treated themselves within their employing organisation. As Lauerman, a social services director, argues, 'the hallmark of a successful organisation is one in which the employees have a sense of purpose; the task is not over-whelming; and there is recognition of achievement' (Lauerman 1993). Lowell contrasts 'machine-bureaucratic' and 'customer-responsive' organisational cultures in the public sector (Lovell 1992). It is probable that the different organisational attitudes set out earlier in Figure 17.1 can be used to assess the extent to which a positive organisational culture has been fostered.

Conclusion: getting and using user views

The discussion up to this point has considered the attitude of service organisations to users, the methods they employ to gather user views, the characteristics of these methods, and how these may affect outcomes for users. In this final section, we draw together the broad conclusions arising from this analysis.

Some issues arise from how information is gathered and how it is then used:

- providers should not be distracted by spurious distinctions between 'subjective' and 'objective' information, rejecting the value of user views as too 'subjective' to be reliable (Pollitt 1988, Mayer and Timms 1970)
- similarly, providers should not be deterred by the negative attributes of users or carers – who may be viewed as 'ignorant, ill-informed, overly-demanding, volatile, apathetic, inconsistent, and so on' (Potter 1988)
- operational information and user surveys have distinct properties and should not be used carelessly as substitutes for each other in discovering 'what users think'
- operational information is often under-appreciated, under-developed and under-used
- surveys have their value, are increasingly promoted by central government consistent with 'consumerist' approaches to service delivery, and are increasingly favoured by service providers – but they have a number of drawbacks in terms of scope, depth, cost and potential for misuse
- the choice between methods (operational information, surveys, etc) should not be confused with the different value given to, and uses made of, 'customer' information
- providers should be aware of the danger of users' views being used as a form of monitoring – merely gathering information – rather than an evaluation leading to changes in those services.

Finally, it has to be remembered that getting users' views is only a means; the end is using them to improve the responsiveness, quality and management of services.

References

Allard, A. *et al.* (1992) *What the People Want.* London: The Children's Society.

Atkin, K. (1991) 'Community care in a multi-racial society: incorporating the user view'. *Policy and Politics* 19(3), 159–166.

Beresford, P. and Croft, S. (1993) *Citizen Involvement.* Basingstoke: Macmillan.

Berry, L. (1990) *Information for Users of Social Services Departments.* London: National Consumer Council/National Institute of Social Work.

Booth, T. (1983) *Residents' views, rights and institutional care', in Fisher, M. (ed) Speaking of Clients.* Sheffield: University of Sheffield Joint Unit for Social Services Research.

Connor, A. (1993) *Monitoring and Evaluation Made Easy: A Handbook for Voluntary Organisations.* Edinburgh: HMSO.

Cooper, J.D. (1980) *Social Work With Elderly People in Hospital.* Stoke-on-Trent: Beth Johnstone Foundation.

Coote, A. and Pfeffer, N. (1991) *Is Quality Good for You?* London: Institute for Public Policy Research.

Fisher, M. (ed) (1983) *Speaking of Clients.* Sheffield: University of Sheffield Joint Unit for Social Services Research.

Flynn, N. (1990) *Public Sector Management.* Hemel Hempstead: Harvester Wheatsheaf.

Gyford, J. (1991) *Citizens, Consumers and Councils.* Basingstoke: Macmillan.

Hull, S. and Spiers, R. (1989) *Consultation with Users of Mental Health Services.* Cambridgeshire County Council.

Jones, L. *et al.* (1987) *Consumer Feedback for the NHS – A Literature Review.* London: King Edward's Hospital Fund for London.

Judge, K. and Solomon, M. (1993) 'Public opinion and the National Health Service: patterns and perspectives in consumer satisfaction'. *Journal of Social Policy* 22, Part 3, 299–328.

Kerruish, A. and Reardon, C. (1992) 'Power sharing'. *Health Services Journal,* 23 April, 26–27.

Lauerman, M. (1993) 'A change is not an event'. *Local Government Policy Making* 20(1), July.

Lovell, R. (1992) 'Citizen's Charter: Cultural challenge'. *Public Administration* 70, Autumn, 395–404.

Lupton, D. *et al.* (1991) 'Caveat emptor or blissful ignorance? Patients and the consumerist echoes'. *Social Science and Medicine* 33(5) 559–568.

Mayer, J.E. and Timms, N. (1970) *The Client Speaks.* London: Routledge and Kegan Paul.

Murray, N. (1991) 'Their own boss'. *Social Work Today,* 17 October, 18–19.

National Consumer Council (1991) *Consumer Concerns 1991: A Consumer View of Public and Local Authority Services.* London: NCC.

National Consumer Council (1983) *Measuring the Performance of Local Authorities in England and Wales: Some Consumer Principles*. London: NCC.

Osborn, A. (1991) *Taking Part in Community Care Planning*. Edinburgh: Age Concern Scotland and Leeds: Nuffield Institute for Public Health Service Studies.

Parsloe, P. and Stevenson, O. (1993) *Community Care and Empowerment*. York: Joseph Rowntree Fund.

Pollitt, C. (1988) 'Bringing consumers into performance measurement: Concepts, consequences and constraints'. *Policy and Politics* 6(2).

Potter, J. (1988) 'Consumerism and the public sector: How well does the coat fit?' *Public Administration* 66, Summer.

Prime Minister and Chancellor of the Duchy of Lancaster (1992) *The Citizen's Charter: First Report 1992*. London: HMSO.

Scottish Office Social Work Services Group (1993) *Inspecting Social Work Services in Scotland*. Edinburgh: Scottish Office.

Shearer, A. (1991) Who Calls the Shots? London: King's Fund Centre.

Steele, K. (1992) 'Patients as experts: Consumer appraisal of health services'. *Public Money and Management*, October-December.

Walker, A. (1991) 'No gain without pain'. *Community Care*, 18 July, 14–16.

Walsh, K. (1991) 'Citizens and consumers: Marketing and public sector management'. *Public Money and Management*, Summer.

Chapter 18

Conclusions

Anne Connor and Stewart Black[*]

This chapter is not a simple summary by us of the chief points made by our contributors. It also develops fresh and perhaps searching questions about performance review and its relationship with quality – and suggests some answers.

We hope that, like the other chapters in the book, this final chapter will stimulate debate. This should not be difficult since many of the issues which are discussed in the book are topical, like performance review and the concern with quality themselves.

Part One: Management Practice

In summarising developments discussed in this first part of the book, four initial observations are appropriate.

The new emphasis on performance review and quality is not peculiar to social work services, nor to inter-personal services or even the public sector. Preoccupation with performance is a feature of the public, private and 'third' sectors alike. Although performance review takes different forms in each, there is value in being aware of ideas and practice being developed in other settings. Indeed, this was a major reason for the range of chapters commissioned for this book.

Second, the role of the Government in driving ahead this initiative is unmistakable. In contrast, in the personal social services, the role of the agencies and professions providing these public services, as several chapters in this book attest, has often been a passive one. Organisations have generally adapted to, and complied with, new requirements, rather than

---

[*]   The authors write in a personal capacity

taking the initiative in setting their own local standards for service delivery; reviewing performance in this, and developing appraisal mechanisms.

Third, the Government's new emphasis on performance has tended to be identified with the political party which has held power during the decade in which these changes have been introduced. The chapter by James reflects this perception and the associated concerns. However, the method and even some objectives of performance review (and even more so those in relation to quality) are not in fact peculiar to a particular political party or philosophy. The origin of thinking on the concept of the 'Citizen's Charter', as noted in the chapter by Black, provides an illustration of this. A quite different example is provided by Irvine in his historical account of quality initiatives in the NHS, which both pre-dates recent developments and has been professionally driven.

Our fourth preliminary observation is that performance and 'managerial' concerns should not be equated with a particular set of objectives or values. For example, in local government, councils of all political hues have established committees for performance review, often by that name, and have encouraged the development of officer fora with similar objectives of assessing corporate or departmental performance. At national level, the Labour and Liberal Democratic Parties have each proposed approaches to public services which incorporate mainstream managerial ideas of the type described by Henkel and by James.

Few contributors have been concerned with performance indicators (PIs) *per se*. A concern that is reflected in several chapters, although not addressed explicitly, is the 'ownership' of PIs. We distinguish performance initiatives which are externally and internally initiated. The former relate more to organisational accountability; the latter more to local management of operational effectiveness.

In local government services, the most comprehensive PIs are those required under the Local Government Act 1992 (see chapter by Black). Similarly, Mitchell and Tolan describe the development of PIs from existing material, where the intention is for the indicators to be objective and independent. Although no examples are offered in this book, in some cases, local agencies have developed their own PIs to assess their own performance (e.g. Black and McNeely 1994). However, as other writers have noted, even PIs which have been developed 'in-house' and are not intended to be threatening can be perceived by practioners as imposed and management-led (Burningham 1990, Barnes and Miller 1988, Pollitt 1990). This is no less true of PIs developed 'in-house'.

It has been recognised that when staff understand and agree the relevance of PIs, their value and reliability is enhanced for all those using the information. Data quality is higher and the effectiveness of services more likely to be addressed. It has also been noted that PIs are most useful when they inform and enhance professional judgements, enabling managers and staff to identify key – and often challenging – questions (Pollitt 1990). The consequences of staff not 'owning', and not working with, PIs can be far-reaching. Distortions can be caused by concentrating performance review on achieving inappropriate or partial goals while other weaknesses pass unnoticed, with damaging consequences for the service and its users.

However, a more damaging – and possibly more commonly occurring – situation is that in which managers have little or no performance information. Moreover, they may, by virtue of their training and work experience, have little appreciation of the need for and value of such information.

The tensions between managerial and professional pre-occupations are not necessarily between two distinct groups of people. Both Willoughby's and Payne's chapters note the situation of managers who are uncomfortable with their role when reviewing the performance of their staff. Performance review will inevitably pose challenges. Objective data – qualitative as well as quantitative – can run contrary to a manager's beliefs about how a service (or team, or individual) is functioning. Some managers use information to reassess the situation, using professional skills and experience to understand the causes of the unexpected pattern and then to take appropriate steps to build on strengths or remedy weaknesses. Others will see performance review as a threat to their professional judgement and reject such information – or at the other extreme become over-dependent. Such reactions need to be recognised and addressed. As several chapters in the latter two sections note, the successful implementation of performance review often involves a culture change throughout the organisation.

Part Two: User Perspectives

Putting the user 'at the centre of service delivery' has, arguably, been a trend in public services which has been even more prominent than 'managerial' performance review. This relatively recent development was the starting point for the analysis of the processes described in Part Two by Brace, Barnes and Wistow, Whittaker and Fitzpatrick and Taylor. The later chapters by Black, and Connor and Black develop this further by considering respectively the origins and operationalisation of this approach.

It is important to remember that 'user' here is a short-hand term. It embraces actual and would-be users of services, and their carers. More confusingly it can embrace both 'consumer' and social and political aspects of citizenship (see chapter by Black). This gives rise to more awkward questions, not only about the standards (of performance, or quality) which stakeholders can expect of public services, but also about the basis for such expectations.

Meanwhile, as the debate continues on the meaning of 'user' and its significance for public services, the four chapters which comprise Part Two report different initiatives to develop practice. In assessing the extent to which organisations are user-oriented, comparison might be made by the reader with Figures 1 and 2 in the chapter by Connor and Black.

There are two dominant themes within 'User Perspectives' – getting users involved, and getting user views. Chapters highlight the complex and varied links between involvement and feedback, whether for individuals (Brace) or groups drawing on their own experience to enhance the user perspective of services that will be used by them (Barnes and Wistow, Whittaker, Fitzpatrick and Taylor). All four chapters demonstrate that getting user views is difficult to do well.

Part Three: Implementation

Our contributors in the first two parts of the book have provided a series of perspectives on performance review from both 'managerial' and 'users' perspectives. Each suggests the requirements needed. In the third part of the book, contributors have examined how these requirements can and have been implemented in key aspects of personal public services.

Implementation has traditionally been regarded as the 'acid test' of practice in service provision. However painstaking the specification – for example in terms of policy goals, intended outputs and outcomes, and detail of strategy – this must be capable of successful implementation. Implementation is concerned centrally with action. It is here that 'performance', in a tangible sense, emerges. Traditionally, this is where intended changes flounder, and not just in the public sector.

For most users, the acid test of services and the manner of their delivery is acceptability (but see chapter by Black). As McClay explains, this is provided in part by complaints procedures. These are intended to offer minimum standards, not excellence. Meanwhile, Leckie and Irvine both show that quality initiatives (and by extension performance review) is patchy. Effort is needed to put these into effect and also to maintain momentum. We suggest that mechanisms for performance review and quality appraisal should not be discrete from other activities in the organisation. In particular

- operational or professional staff should be involved in assessing service effectiveness

- managerial staff – regardless of the degree of decentralisation – have important responsibilities for routine assessment of organisational effectiveness in relation to policy; and

- those with the responsibility for setting strategy (elected members in local government, 'board' members in health and the voluntary sector) must also be involved in strategic monitoring.

Connor's chapter illustrates the further difficulties in implementing performance review in the voluntary sector, where funders or purchasers are a fourth set of players. This is not to suggest there is no role for specialist performance review and quality appraisal staff. They will be essential for gathering, analysing and reporting performance data. Such staff are also likely to spend a greater proportion of their time on such activities than any other group. Nevertheless, the three (or four) groups above have a particular responsibility for assessing and taking necessary action – that is, for implementing performance review.

In applying performance review there are potential risks. Several chapters (Leckie; Barnes and Wistow) suggest that there are likely to be difficulties – for example, looking at information out of context (e.g. data for a single year rather than considering the trend); not completing the review cycle to carry through the results of performance review (see Irvine's 'bringing about appropriate change'); failing to use performance review to plan ahead (e.g. revising targets); and collecting only output and cost, but not outcome, data.

Hennessy suggests that the big objectives do not get looked at. We agree with him that they can and should be (Hennessy 1990). The chapters in the 'user perspectives' part of the book show how issues such as 'quality of life' can be addressed. The technical skills to overcome these problems already exist and are being refined. What is needed is the will – and resources – to make it happen.

A third risk is that staff – especially professional staff – may reject performance review out of hand without considering the longer term advantages it offers them to evaluate their own performance.

Most operational and other managers in social work are, of course, drawn from the professional ranks. It is therefore especially worrying when there is little 'performance-mindedness' at any level, as Payne suggests.

Part Four: Performance Revisited

The first three parts of the book confirm that there have been rapid developments in performance review and quality appraisal, and they trace the interaction of 'managerial', 'user' and 'implementation' issues. In the final part of the book these two aspects – developments and interactions – are reconsidered.

Major and common themes running through the book are:

- the need to be clear about the basis on which people receive public services (Black, Coote, James)
- methods of appraising performance need to help both users and providers (front-line staff and managers alike).

It is probable that because of developments in public sector management, they need also to permit open accountability.

The pursuit of quality in services is increasingly recognised as important (Coote, James, Leckie, Black): the contribution of performance review to this less so. The chapters in Part Four highlight in different ways that without the end result of enhanced services for users, the concept of 'quality' is meaningless.

Conclusions

Performance review needs to be kept in context. This means not getting carried away by the latest fad or transplanting approaches to problems without also making available the necessary resources or commitment; both these factors may have contributed to the dissatisfaction with a series of management approaches described by James. Rather, it is about understanding what techniques can offer and using them appropriately. It is also necessary to draw on a range of management-led and user-oriented approaches – as reflected in the structure of this book.

We have attempted to encourage a critical approach in examining the questions 'who is reviewing whose performance, on which authority, and for whom?'. Government, scrutineers, managers, providers, citizens, and users and other stakeholders all can have a role. Different chapters suggest what these roles are, and they might be developed.

It is clear that hitherto the Government is the major actor in this. It has the most obvious objectives in relation to performance review, and this helps its own management in the public sector. This has two aspects, we suggest: performance review assists the Government's management of the public sector, and also assists it in encouraging improved management within public agencies. Its initiatives – as described by Henkel, Mitchell and Tolan, Connor, James and Black – often rely on bringing to bear pressures, disciplines and constraints which are intended to create or synthesise those which exist (or are believed to exist) in the private sector but would otherwise be absent in public services. Examples of this include business planning, separation of purchaser and provider roles, increased external and internal financial accountability, and performance information.

'Performance' at this 'macro' level is essentially a managerial concept. The link with 'quality' is not straightforward or readily understood, as the chapter by James illustrates. This is clearly at the heart of the Citizen's Charter initiative, yet the White Paper itself (Prime Minister 1991) – save for a brief discussion of the British Standard Institution's BS5750 – offers no discussion of how this is itself to be achieved. In practice, we suggest, 'quality' has been viewed in terms of two perspectives. In managerial terms, it is seen as a matter of quality assurance. This approach, which is precisely that offered by BS5750, is preoccupied with specification of inputs and is process-oriented. It is neutral in relation to outputs and outcomes. The second perspective, which is more evident in Government thinking, here as elsewhere, is identification of 'quality' with user interests. Here, the user is envisaged as a consumer whose market rights require protection.

Last, although not discussed elsewhere in the book, there are two pre-requisites for performance review and quality assurance. These are routine information and targets or standards.

While it is self-evident that service providers (or enablers) need good information to review performance, the under-development of data-bases to do so is both widespread and well-known. Second, even if information is available about who received what, when, from whom, and at what cost, of itself this says nothing about how this has been achieved in relation to the intended standard of the service. Indeed, no standard may have been identified. Targets, which of course must be quantified if they are to be capable of measurement, thus permitting the provider to monitor its own performance, are even less frequently identified. It is one thing for a provider to say that all 'simple' assessments will be carried out 'as quickly as possible'; another to arrange to collect routine information to permit calculation of an average completion time from referral to notification of, say, five hours; and another to use this information to compare average time with a target completion time of, say, eight hours.

The science of 'performance review' may be relatively new, but the art of reviewing performance by drawing on experience to plan future improvements and developments is not new (Connor, Irvine).

It is also necessary to keep in mind the strength and limitations of performance review and quality assurance, both as methods in their own right and also in the ways they are applied. As many of the contributors have shown, performance review brings many advantages. But the experience is not always positive. This situation can arise where there is poor design (e.g., where an individual/team/organisation is held accountable for a 'performance' for which it is not wholly responsible; where performance review has been designed to meet a preconceived objective) or implementation (e.g., where performance judgements are formed without sufficient data).

Even when the technical aspects of performance review are well designed and conducted, there can still be difficulties with the introduction of performance review into an organisation. Typical problems are:

- highlighting existing problems, such as lack of certainty about the role and direction of an organisation or team

- making people feel anxious and de-skilled

- becoming associated with the introduction or implementation of unwelcome change.

It has to be recognised that performance review is about problem **finding**. It can contribute to problem **solving**, but does not of itself bring solutions. Performance review is not a substitute for the professional skills, expertise and managerial judgement to determine the action required. Experience shows it also needs an organisational culture which encourages honest appraisal and recognises the fears many people have about performance review and what it brings in its wake.

In conclusion, good performance review is attention to detail, for which everyone has responsibility.

References

Barnes, M. and Miller, N. (eds) (1988) 'Performance measurement in personal social services'. *Research Policy and Planning* 6(2).

Black, S. and McNeely, T. (eds) (1994) *Performance Indicators: How Do You Measure Up?* Seminar Paper No. 7. Dundee: Social Services Research Group – Scotland.

Burningham, D. (1990) 'Performance indicators and the management of professionals in local government', in Cave, M., Kogan, M. and Smith, R. (eds) *Output and Performance Measurement in Government: The State of the Art.* London: Jessica Kingsley Publishers.

Hennessey, P. (1990) 'The political and administrative background'. In Cave *et al. (op cit).*

Pollitt, C. (1990) 'Performance indicators, root and branch', in Cave *et al. (op cit).*

Prime Minister (1991) *Citizen's Charter: Raising the Standard.* Cm 1599. London: HMSO.

The Contributors

Anne Connor

Anne Connor worked as a researcher in the Social Work Services Group of the Scottish Office for 11 years, where her main responsibilities were the voluntary sector and community care. She initiated and undertook a major study of the potential application of self-evaluation by voluntary organisations. Her published research includes evaluations of innovative community care projects and of other government funding programmes, including support to homeless young people, and practical guides on developing community care services and on monitoring and evaluation. She is currently based in The Scottish Office Science and Technology Unit.

Stewart Black

Stewart Black is Convener of Social Services Research Group – Scotland, and Manager at the Accounts Commission. He has previously worked at the Convention of Scottish Local Authorities, in both local and central government, and in the university and voluntary sectors. He is author of a number of papers and articles on public sector services.

Mary Henkel

Mary Henkel is a Senior Lecturer in the Department of Government at Brunel University, where she teaches on a Masters programme for managers and policy makers in social care services. She has carried out substantial research on evaluation in the public sector and her recent publications include *Government, Evaluation and Change*, Jessica Kingsley Publishers 1991.

Stephen Mitchell Stephen Mitchell has academic qualifications in history, social administration and policy analysis. After leading research projects in community care services in two London social services departments, and spending four years as a Development Officer in Hammersmith and Fulham SSD, he joined the Social Services Inspectorate (SSI) of the Department of Health in 1986, leading the national inspection of home care services. As Assistant Chief Inspector (from 1989) he managed the Department of Health's policy programme on social services training, and the development of SSI's inspection and monitoring methods. In September 1993 he was seconded to the Public Health Laboratory Service as Head of Corporate Affairs.

Frank Tolan Frank Tolan has graduate and a postgraduate academic qualifications and a professional qualification in social work. In 1982, after working in local authority social services departments, he joined the academic staff of the School for Advanced Urban Studies (SAUS) at the University of Bristol where he was responsible for postgraduate studies and research work on local government and on health and social care. In 1990 he joined the Social Services Inspectorate where he has led work on improving the SSI's methodological approach to its work and on finance and statistics issues. Following secondment to the London Borough of Croydon to manage mental health services, he is now Assistant Chief Inspector in the SSI.

Susan Willoughby Susan Willoughby obtained a PhD in Psychology and worked for 14 years as a clinical psychologist and researcher in Ireland and the UK. This included developing and evaluating addiction services and pioneering the use of an innovative quality assurance procedure. She joined Charities Evaluation Services in 1992 and provides advice, training and constancy in evaluation to voluntary organisations throughout the south of England. She is an Honorary Research Fellow at the University of Southampton.

Malcolm Payne   Malcolm Payne is Professor of Applied Community Studies, the Manchester Metropolitan University. He previously worked in probation, social sciences departments and the national and local voluntary sector. He is the author of *Modern Social Work Theory*.

Sue Brace   Sue Brace is Planning and Coordination Manager (Older People) in Lothian Regional Council Social Work Department, where she has been involved in developing Lothian's community care assessment and care management arrangements. Her research work includes studies of the role of social workers with older people, and the interdisciplinary assessment of older people facing admission to long-stay care.

Marian Barnes   Marian Barnes is Senior Lecturer in the Department of Sociological Studies, University of Sheffield and was previously Principal Research Fellow at the Nuffield Institute for Health, University of Leeds. Her current research interests are focused on consumerism and citizenship amongst users of health and social services. Before moving to university-based research, she worked for seven years in research and development posts in social services departments. She has contributed to collaborative projects to develop performance measurement within social services and to monitor the implementation of the 1983 Mental Health Act. She is also a Mental Health Commissioner and has a particular interest in mental health services for women.

Gerald Wistow   Gerald Wistow is Professor of Health and Social Care and Head of the Community Care Division at the Nuffield Institute for Health, Leeds University. He is the co-author of ten books and numerous other publications on the health and personal social services. He chaired a Welsh Office working party on consumer involvement, and was a consultant to the Department of Health on community care planning. His current research includes an ESRC-funded study of user and citizen involvement in the fields of mental health and physical disability.

Andrea Whittaker   Andrea Whittaker is Project Manager, Building Inclusive Communities, which is part of the Community Care Group at the King's Fund Centre. Her work covers user participation and self-advocacy, particularly with people with learning difficulties. She has had a major involvement in the King's Fund Ordinary Life initiative and is now developing work related to community participation. She has been closely associated with the self-advocacy organisation People First since it began in 1984 and was its Adviser until October 1988, when People First set up its own independent office.

Bridie Fitzpatrick   Bridie Fitzpatrick (MSc) is employed as a research fellow in the Department of Social Policy, University of Glasgow. Initial research experience and training was obtained as a researcher to the Glasgow MONICA Project which is part of a WHO multinational collaborative study of cardiovascular disease.

Rex Taylor   Professor Rex Taylor (PhD) is Head of the Department of Social Policy and Social Work, University of Glasgow, and a previous member of the MRC Medical Sociology Unit. He is the author of five books and around 60 scientific papers on various aspects of social and health problems.

Tom Leckie Tom Leckie is a social worker by profession who specialises in mental health. After working in local authorities for several years, he joined the Social Work Services Group at Scottish Office in 1988. He is now an Inspector with the Social Work Services Inspectorate. He had a lead input to SWSG's discussion paper on quality assurance.

Donald Irvine Donald Irvine is a general practitioner at Ashington, Northumberland, and Regional Adviser in General Practice at the University of Newcastle upon Tyne. He is a Fellow of the Royal College of General Practitioners and has been a member of the Audit Commission since 1990. Dr. Irvine's publications include several books on quality in general practice and on audit, and chapters and papers on medical education. He received a knighthood in 1994.

Brian McClay Brian McClay graduated from Trinity College, Dublin with an Economics degree in 1963 and holds a Diploma in Social Studies and a Diploma in Applied Social Studies at Liverpool University. He has worked as an Assistant Area Children's Officer in Lancashire Children's Department, in Knowsley Social Services Department as a Research Officer, and the Policy and Information Section of the Directorate of Social Services, Bradford in 1976, working principally in child care. He has been Bradford's Complaints Officer since December 1991. He is a member of the Social Services Research Group, has been a member of its National Executive Committee since 1983 and is currently national Membership Secretary.

Anna Coote Anna Coote is the Hamlyn Fellow in Social Policy at the Institute for Public Policy Research, where she directs the Institute's social policy research. She is editor of *The Welfare of Citizens: Developing New Social Rights* (IPPR/Rivers Oram Press, 1992). Her other recent publications include *Is Quality Good for*

You? A critical review of quality assurance in welfare services (IPPR 1991); *The Family Way* (IPPR 1990); *Power and Prejudice* (Wiedenfield and Nicolson 1990) and *Sweet Freedom* (Basil Blackwell 1987). She has been Deputy Editor of the *New Statesman*, Editor of *Diverse Reports*, a current affairs series for Channel Four Television and in 1988/89 wrote and produced Next Left, a four-part documentary series for C4 TV on political ideas in Europe. In 1993 she returned full-time to IPPR to take up the newly-created Hamlyn Fellowship.

Ann James

Ann James joined the Kings Fund College in 1989, where she is Fellow in Human Service Organisations. She concentrates on interface work between the Health Service and other agencies and leads a major intiative developing female Chief Executives in the NHS. She graduated in theology and went on to become a qualified social worker and probation officer, and has wide-ranging post-graduate qualifications. She created the first social services management unit in the country at the University of Birmingham, where she holds an honorary Senior Lectureship. She has extensive consultancy and management development experience for central and local government and the voluntary sector. In 1993 she became the National Chair of Family Service Units.

Research Highlights in Social Work Series

No. 4 Social Work Departments as Organisations
Edited by Joyce Lishman
ISBN 1 85302 008 7 Paperback

No. 6 Working With Children
Edited by Joyce Lishman
ISBN 1 85302 007 9 Paperback

No. 8 Evaluation 2nd Edition
Edited by Joyce Lishman
ISBN 1 85302 006 0 Hardback

No. 9 Social Work in Rural and Urban Areas
Edited by Joyce Lishman
ISBN 0 9505999 8 0 Paperback

No. 11 Responding to Mental Illness
Edited by Gordon Horobin
ISBN 1 85091 005 7 Paperback

No. 12 The Family: Context or Client?
Edited by Gordon Horobin
ISBN 1 85091 026 X Paperback

No. 13 New Information Technology in Management and Practice
Edited by Gordon Horobin and Stuart Montgomery
ISBN 1 85091 022 7 Hardback

No 14 Why Day Care?
Edited by Gordon Horobin
ISBN 1 85302 000 1 Hardback

No. 15 Sex, Gender and Care Work
Edited by Gordon Horobin
ISBN 1 85302 001 X Hardback

No. 16 Living with Mental Handicap: Transitions in the Lives of People with Mental Handicap
Edited by Gordon Horobin
ISBN 1 85302 004 4 Hardback

No. 17 Child Care: Monitoring Practice
Edited by Isobel Freeman and Stuart Montgomery
ISBN 1 85392 005 2 Hardback

Jessica Kingsley Publishers
116 Pentonville Road, London N1 9JB

Jessica Kingsley Publishers
116 Pentonville Road, London N1 9JB